Walking the
Cathedral Cities
of Eastern England

Walking the Cathedral Cities of Eastern England

ROWLAND MEAD

TWENTY-EIGHT ORIGINAL WALKS
AND TOURS AROUND THE
CATHEDRALS AND CATHEDRAL CITIES
OF EASTERN ENGLAND

First published in 2000 by
New Holland Publishers (UK) Ltd
London • Cape Town • Sydney • Auckland

24 Nutford Place
London W1H 6DQ
United Kingdom

80 McKenzie Street
Cape Town 8001
South Africa

14 Aquatic Drive
Frenchs Forest, NSW 2086
Australia

218 Lake Road
Northcote
Auckland
New Zealand

ISBN 1 85974 339 0

Commissioning Editor: Charlotte Parry-Crooke
Editors: Paul Barnett, Rowena Curtis, Pete Duncan
Cartographer: William Smuts
Designer: Alan Marshall
Indexer: Janet Dudley

Reproduction by pica Colour Separation Overseas (Pte) Ltd, Singapore
Printed and bound in Singapore by Kyodo Printing Co (Singapore) Pte Ltd

Photographic Acknowledgements
All photographs by the author with the exception of the following:
Life File/Emma Lee plate 8; Life File/Andrew Ward plates 1, 2; Photobank/Adrian Baker
back cover, plates 21, 24, 25, 33, 34, 35; Photobank/Jeanetta Baker plate 6; Photobank/Peter
Baker front cover, plates 5, 9, 11, 12, 13, 29; Travel Ink/Ian Booth plate 31; Travel Ink/Leslie
Garland plate 19; Travel Ink/Dogan Kemanci plate 4; Travel Ink/Mike Nicholson plate 20;
Travel Ink/Tony Page plate 10; Travel Ink/Andrew Watson plate 23

Front cover: Durham Cathedral across the River Wear,
photographed by Peter Baker, Photobank

Contents

Acknowledgements   6

Introduction   7

English Cathedrals   8
  – An Introduction

Cathedral Architecture   14
  – Glossary of Terms

Key to Maps   16

Map of Eastern England   17

London: St Paul's   18
Tour of the Cathedral   19
Walking Tour from St Paul's   25
  Cathedral

London: Westminster   29
Tour of the Abbey   30
Walking Tour from   35
  Westminster Abbey

London: Southwark   40
Tour of the Cathedral   42
Walking Tour from Southwark   45
  Cathedral

Canterbury   51
Tour of the Cathedral   53
Walking Tour from   57
  Canterbury Cathedral

Rochester   65
Tour of the Cathedral   67
Walking Tour from   69
  Rochester Cathedral

St Albans   75
Tour of the Cathedral   76
Walking Tour from St Albans   79
  Cathedral

Bury St Edmunds   83
Tour of the Cathedral   85
Walking Tour from   87
  Bury St Edmunds Cathedral

Ely   91
Tour of the Cathedral   93
Walking Tour from Ely Cathedral 97

Norwich   102
Tour of the Cathedral   104
Walking Tour from Norwich   107
  Cathedral

Peterborough   114
Tour of the Cathedral   116
Walking Tour from   121
  Peterborough Cathedral

Southwell   126
Tour of the Minster   127
Walking Tour from   130
  Southwell Minster

Lincoln   133
Tour of the Cathedral   134
Walking Tour from Lincoln   140
  Cathedral

York   144
Tour of the Minster   145
Walking Tour from York Minster 150

Durham   156
Tour of the Cathedral   157
Walking Tour from Durham   161
  Cathedral

Further Information   166
Bibliography   173
Index   174

Acknowledgements

This book derived from an enthusiastically accepted early retirement and the wish to use the increased leisure time in a constructive way by visiting the ancient cathedrals of England. After I had studied several cathedrals in detail, it occurred to me there was a need for a book which provided information for a day out in a cathedral city, combining a tour of the cathedral, an agreeable lunch and a walk around the historic core of the city.

I set about writing the first regional guide and toted the idea around various publishers. No luck! Just when I was beginning to despair, the publishing firm of New Holland received my ideas with enthusiasm. I must therefore record my thanks to New Holland's former Publishing Director, Charlotte Parry-Crooke, and Publishing Manager, Tim Jollands, for their encouragement and advice. My principal contact at New Holland was initially Rowena Curtis, and one could not have wished for a more efficient and courteous colleague.

From the start of my research I determined to avoid contacting any cathedral authorities formally: I wanted to give a totally unbiased view. I did, however, speak to a vast number of cathedral staff and guides, who often revealed some gems of information normally omitted from official brochures. My thanks to all who unwittingly helped in this way.

The same comments apply to the staff of the cities' Tourist Information Offices. They were invariably cooperative and helpful, despite the fact that I often caught them at times when they were busy and harassed.

Last but not least, my thanks to my wife for her encouragement and valuable theological knowledge. She uncomplainingly tested out all the tours – in what often turned out to be vile weather. I could not have wished for a better companion with whom to visit our wonderful cathedral cities.

Rowland Mead
Leighton Buzzard

Introduction

For many people, English cathedrals have a special fascination. They are undoubtedly the supreme expression of English architecture. In terms of enclosed space they were, until Victorian times, the largest buildings in the country. They are also extremely varied, both individually and in comparison with each other, lacking as they do the strict symmetry of the Classical style. Furthermore, English cathedrals often have as near neighbours the remains of their associated abbeys, and are usually surrounded by their host city's historic core, full of engrossing domestic architecture, ancient defensive walls and other sites of interest.

Numerous books have been written about the English cathedral, some emphasizing the architectural aspects and others of a more spiritual context. Most city authorities have produced a 'town trail' describing a route through the centre. This volume aims to combine these aspects on a regional basis. Each section begins by looking at the historical background of the cathedral and city. This is followed a guided tour of the cathedral itself (with a plan for easy reference), concentrating on not just the architecture but also on relevant odd quirks and historical relics. Then there is a walking tour, beginning and ending at the cathedral, of the historic core of the city (again with a map). Options and alternative routes are supplied to suit the energy of the visitor and the time available. Possibilities for refreshment en route are suggested, with particular attention to historic pubs and old coaching inns, essential features of the English cathedral city.

This, the first of two regional guides, deals with fourteen cathedrals and their cities in Eastern England. A further volume covers the western part of the country.

English Cathedrals – An Introduction

A cathedral is a place of Christian worship that contains a *cathedra* – that is, a bishop's seat or throne. The *cathedra* was the bishop's symbol of authority; should the *cathedra* be moved, the cathedral building would have to be redesignated.

In medieval times, if a cathedral was attached to a monastery (a Norman innovation), the bishop had the further title of abbot, although the effective head of the monastery was its prior – an arrangement which often led to friction. Of the seventeen cathedrals in medieval England, eight were monastic, usually Benedictine (e.g., Canterbury, Ely and Winchester). Such cathedrals had a range of adjoining monastic buildings, usually on the south side, including a chapter house, dormitory, refectory, infirmary, hospital (or guest hall) and cloisters.

The other cathedrals were served by canons. There were two types of these: secular canons and canons regular, the latter working to fixed rules. The most important canons regular were the Augustinians, followers of the writings of St Augustine (d604); their liberal approach to life meant they had a much more workable relationship with the townspeople than did the monks.

The secular canons, on the other hand, were unhampered by rules and were generally free to live where they liked. They depended on a prebend or endowment (usually from a wealthy landowner), and were thus often known as prebendaries. This was the situation at Southwell, for example, many of the large houses around the cathedral being those provided for the prebendaries. The canons' function was to run the cathedral and its services, a role fulfilled by the dean and chapter today.

Newer Cathedrals

The cathedrals run by secular canons were collectively known after the Reformation as the Old Foundation. The five new sees created by Henry VIII – Oxford, Peterborough, Chester, Gloucester and Bristol – plus the surviving monastic cathedrals were the New Foundation. Confusingly, many of the secular cathedrals (e.g., Lincoln) have cloisters, although these were largely ornamental rather than practical.

During the Industrial Revolution people flocked from the land to the growing cities based on the coalfields in the Midlands and the north. This flow of population necessitated the setting up of a number of additional sees. New cathedrals were created, usually by upgrading existing parish churches – as at Manchester, Liverpool, Wakefield and elsewhere – but also from scratch, as at Truro. After World War II, some modern cathedrals were constructed: the one at Coventry replaced a building destroyed by enemy bombs, while that at Guildford was the product of an architectural competition.

Architectural Styles

The majority of English cathedrals are Gothic in style, but none has the purity of one specific period – indeed, it is often possible to find elements of Norman, Early English, Decorated and Perpendicular styles within a single cathedral.

It is frequently thought that English cathedral architecture originated in France and was brought over by the Normans, but this is an oversimplification: the Anglo-Saxons had imported the Norman style before the Conquest. Thereafter, English masons developed their own styles – for example, the Perpendicular, a style not seen among the French, who were then still experimenting with the Flamboyant, a development of the earlier Decorated style. Shape and form also differ between English and French cathedrals. The naves of French cathedrals soar to great heights, while English cathedrals tend to be long and low, with height gained by towers and spires. The extra length of English naves has two explanations. First, in monastic cathedrals the monks and townspeople were kept apart: the congregation occupied the nave and the monks the choir and presbytery, the two areas being separated by a *pulpitum* (screen). Second, the nave often had a non-religious use, such as the collection of tithes or the administration of justice, requiring a sizeable area. Another difference between English and French cathedrals can be found at the east ends. The French buildings are noted for their apse, a semi-circular structure within which was an ambulatory or processional way, often for pilgrims to pass by shrines. English cathedrals, on the other hand, are more likely to have a stepped or cliff-like east end, perhaps marked by a Lady Chapel.

Although one finds the occasional example of Anglo-Saxon work (such as Ripon's crypt), for convenience we can divide the medieval architectural styles into four.

Norman

The Norman style actually appeared (in parts of Westminster Abbey) during the reign of Edward the Confessor, but for simplicity's sake the start can be dated as 1066 at the beginning of the Norman Conquest. It lasted until approximately 1190. Known properly as Romanesque, it was common throughout Europe. In English cathedrals much of the Norman work has been replaced, but sufficient remains in buildings such as Durham, Ely, Gloucester and many others to recognise the essential elements. It was during the Norman period that the idea of three horizontal layers was introduced – the main arcade, the triforium (or tribune) and the clerestory – and their relative proportions are a key to the aesthetic appearance of the interior. The piers or pillars tend to be massive and cylindrical, with engaged shafts and occasionally, as at Durham, etched or chevron decoration. Arches are invariably rounded, sometimes with zigzag or dog-tooth mouldings. Sometimes, as at Ely, the arches interlock. Windows are small and narrow and splayed only on the inside. Roofs were initially wooden and highly decorated, although vaulting put in an appearance towards the end of the period, particularly in the aisles. Few Norman towers survive – they dropped like ninepins and were

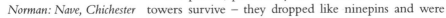

Norman: Nave, Chichester

Early English: North Transept, Salisbury

often replaced in later periods. Sculptural decoration was minimal, although exceptions are the west door at Rochester, the Prior's Door at Ely and the capitals in the crypt at Canterbury.

Early English

The Early English style marked the start of Gothic architecture and began in England around 1175, overlapping the end of the Norman period. It was to last until 1265. (It is interesting to note that the term 'Gothic' did not appear in the literature until the late 17th century). The Early English style had a lighter and more elegant appearance than the Norman. Pointed arches appeared and windows were tall and narrow, known as lancets after the surgeon's knife. Trefoils and plate tracery were used for the first time. Piers were often formed of columns with detached shafts (often of Purbeck Marble), united at the capitals, which frequently had stiff-leaved foliage. The Early English style probably first appeared in the choir at Lincoln and there are particularly fine examples to be seen at Exeter, Wells, the south Transept at York, Southwell and Peterborough.

Undoubtedly the most comprehensively Early English construction is at Salisbury, the English cathedral that comes nearest to having a single style; building started in 1220 and was more or less completed 38 years later.

Decorated

A further period of transition came with the Decorated style, which appeared *c*1250 and reached its zenith in the middle of the following century. (Architectural historians often divide the Decorated period into Geometrical or Early Decorated and Flowing or Late Decorated.) The style takes its name from the window tracery, which became extremely complex. The moulded stone mullions in the upper part of the windows formed graceful circles and other intricate designs. Piers came to have closely joined shafts, not detached as before, while capitals, bosses and other stonework were ornately carved with free-flowing foliage, animals and heads. All this work was expensive and labour-intensive, but this was no problem: it was a prosperous time and the Church was receiving considerable income form the land it owned. Examples of the Decorated style are plentiful in our cathedrals; there are particularly fine examples in the chapter houses at Southwell, Wells and Salisbury, in many parts of York Minster, in the Angel Choir at Lincoln and in the nave at Lichfield.

Decorated: Lady Chapel, Exeter

Perpendicular

The final stage of the Gothic, the Perpendicular, lasted 200 years, from 1350 to *c*1550. The Perpendicular, which has been described as the 'architecture of vertical lines', is best observed in window tracery, where the mullions carry straight on up to the head of the framework. The areas of glass became larger and the rectilinear spaces became more suitable for stained-glass renditions of stories and parables. Pillars were more elegant and led up to superb fan vaulting or the astonishing *pendant lierne* vault such as that at Oxford. Rose windows appeared, usually in the transepts. Shallow panels in the solid masonry of walls were another hallmark of the period.

Perpendicular: Lady Chapel, Gloucester

The earliest extant cathedral Perpendicular is probably that in the choir at Gloucester, but Southwell, Winchester and others have some striking west windows in the style. The crowning glory of the Perpendicular is to be found in Henry VII's Chapel at Westminster Abbey.

The subsequent Renaissance period saw a revival of the Classical and Roman styles of architecture. During this period – the 16th and 17th centuries – there was very little cathedral (or church) building in England, so the styles are little represented, the remarkable exception being St Paul's Cathedral. The huge Old St Paul's, a Gothic edifice, was destroyed in the Great Fire of 1666. The replacement – designed by Sir Christopher Wren (1632–1723) – with its massive dome, is totally unlike any other English cathedral.

The Gothic influence, however, would not go away. There was a strong revival of Neo-Gothic during Victorian times, often with unfortunate results; the replacement west front at St Albans is one example.

Early Cathedral Life

The medieval English cathedral was a very different place from what we witness today. Before the Reformation the cathedral was often a very wealthy establishment, particularly if it had an important shrine and thus attracted pilgrims. It would be a riot of colour, with abundant statuary, a bejewelled and gilded altar, rich tapestries and paintings.

Life in a medieval monastery or cathedral might seem very harsh to us, but by comparison with the lot of most of the common folk of the time it was fairly comfortable. Each day a monk would have to spend about four hours in public worship, about four in study or private prayer and perhaps another six engaged in work for the benefit of the monastic community – cooking, perhaps, or the tending of vegetables. The abbot's rule was supreme within the community: he could be as totalitarian as any despot if he wished, although most abbots had more sense.

The day was divided up by acts of worship. With Matins immediately after midnight, Prime at sunrise, Terce at about 9am, High Mass at about 10am, Sext at noon, None in midafternoon, Vespers in the early evening and Compline at sunset – with other services thrown in on special occasions – the monks were not left much time for such activities as sleeping! In fact, they retired to their dormitories to sleep twice each night, between Compline and Matins and between Matins and Prime.

While some monks would live, grow old and die within a single monastery – this was the life of the Benedictines (followers of St Benedict of Nursia [*c*480–*c*547]) – members of many orders would frequently move from one to the next, preaching in towns and villages en route, helping the poor and needy, and living off alms. Such was the practice of, for example, the Dominicans (adherents of St Dominic [*c*1170–1221]; called the Black Friars because of their garb), the Carmelites (gaining their name from Mount Carmel, France, where the order was founded; the White Friars) and the Franciscans (adherents of St Francis of Assisi [1181–1226]; the Grey Friars). Members of military orders, such as the Knights Templar, were likewise unbound to a single monastery.

At the Reformation, Henry VIII's men plundered the sacred shrines of orders such as the Benedictines, smashed the statues and removed much of the plate, jewels and hangings. The monasteries were closed down and their stonework was often stolen by townspeople for building purposes. Further vandalism occurred during the Civil War, with soldiers often using cathedrals as barracks. Then followed ages of neglect. The Victorians strove to rectify this, not always happily. Nevertheless, our cathedrals still retain much of their ancient beauty and charm and few of us can remain unmoved by them.

Life Today in England's Cathedrals

Life in today's – Church of England – cathedral is in some ways not so dissimilar from that of the medieval monastery. Although such activities as the tilling of fields have been superseded by their modern counterparts, the priests nevertheless still divide their time between religious and pastoral concerns – typically there are five services on a Sunday and two or three on each of the other days. Choral music remains an important aspect of cathedral life, with various first-rate choir schools attached to cathedrals.

Also unchanged since early times is the need to raise funds for the upkeep of the cathedral and other expenses involved in running it on a day-to-day basis. While large-scale benefactors play their part in this, the dean and chapter are also heavily reliant on contributions from the general public; thus, while it may grate on the sensibilities to be asked on visiting a cathedral for either an admission fee or a 'recommended donation' – which is very much the same thing! – do bear in mind that without such measures the cathedral would very soon decline into the kind of rack and ruin that was likely its condition for centuries before the Victorian era.

With their many visitors, their shops, their information desks, their audiovisual displays and so forth, it might seem that today's cathedrals lack the stillness and tranquillity – the space for contemplation – that one might expect in a house of God. To a great extent this can be true, especially in such popular venues as St Paul's and Westminster Abbey. Yet even in such places, as one gazes in awe at a stained-glass window or steps for a moment into the cool silence of a side chapel, one can discover the transcendent peace that lies at the core of us all.

English Cathedrals in Historical Context

Rulers of England and the UK		Cathedral History	
Edwy	955–959	600–1000	Many English cathedrals, e.g. Canterbury and Winchester, had their foundation in Saxon times, often attached to monasteries.
Edgar	959–975		
Edward the Martyr	975–979		
Ethelred the Unready	979–1016		
Edmund Ironside	1016	1066	Norman Conquest. Many Saxon cathedrals demolished or rebuilt.
Canute	1016–1035		
Harold I	1035–1040	c1066–1190	Norman or Romanesque style of architecture, well exemplified in Durham and Ely cathedrals.
Hardicanute	1040–1042		
Edward the Confessor	1042–1066		
Harold II	1066	1170	Archbishop Thomas Becket murdered in Canterbury Cathedral.
William I (the Conqueror)	1066–1087		
William II	1087–1100	c1190–1300	Early English style of architecture, seen, for instance, at Wells and Lincoln.
Henry I	1100–1135		
Stephen	1135–1154		
Henry II	1154–1189		
Richard I	1189–1199	c1250–1380	Decorated Gothic style of architecture, typified by Exeter and York.
John	1199–1216		
Henry III	1216–1272		
Edward I	1272–1307	c1350–1550	Perpendicular Gothic style of architecture, as seen at Gloucester.
Edward II	1307–1327		
Edward III	1327–1377	1532	Henry VIII begins the Reformation in England, separating the English church from Rome. Many statues and stained glass windows destroyed in the cathedrals.
Richard II	1377–1399		
Henry VI	1399–1413		
Henry V	1413–1422		
Henry VI	1422–1461		
Edward IV	1461–1483		
Edward V	1483	1536–1540	Dissolution of the Monasteries by Henry VIII. Many were refounded as cathedrals.
Richard III	1483–1485		
Henry VII	1485–1509		
Henry VII	1509–1547	1642–1650	English Civil War. Troops used cathedrals as barracks, causing considerable damage.
Edward VI	1547–1553		
Mary I	1553–1558		
Elizabeth I	1558–1603	1666	Old St Paul's Cathedral burnt down in the Great Fire of London.
James I of England and IV of Scotland	1603–1625		
Charles I	1625–1649	17th century	English Renaissance style of architecture.
Oliver Cromwell, Lord Protector	1653–1685	1675–1710	St Paul's Cathedral rebuilt in Classical style
Richard Cromwell	1658–1659	18th century	Period of decay for most English cathedrals
Charles II	1660–1685		
James II	1658–1688	19th century	Victorian times saw English cathedrals heavily restored, often badly.
William III and Mary II (Mary died 1694)	1689–1702		
Anne	1702–1714	Late 19th century	Gothic revival. New cathedral built at Truro in this style.
George I	1714–1727		
George II	1727–1760	1914–1918	World War I. English cathedrals largely unscathed.
George III	1760–1820		
George IV	1820–1830	1939–45	World War II. Many English cathedrals damaged in air raids, but only Coventry destroyed.
William IV	1830–1837		
Victoria	1837–1901		
Edward VII	1901–1910	1955–1962	Coventry Cathedral rebuilt in modern style.
George V	1910–1936		
Edward VIII	1936		
George VI	1936–1952		
Elizabeth II	1952–		

Cathedral Architecture — Glossary of Terms

APSE. A polygonal or semi-circular end to a cathedral chapel. It is usually vaulted.

ARCADE. A row of arches, usually between the nave and the aisles, supporting the main wall.

BALUSTER. A carved column supporting a handrail. A series of balusters is known as a balustrade.

BALL FLOWER. Stone ornament consisting of a globe shaped design with folded back petals, typical of the Decorated period.

BOSS. Located at the intersection of ribs in a vaulted roof. Usually carved with foliage or figures, it may be gilded or coloured.

BUTTRESS. A vertical area of stonework supporting a wall. An exterior buttress containing an arch is known as a 'flying buttress'.

CAPITAL. The moulded or carved block on the top of a column on which the superstructure rests. Often richly ornamented.

CHANTRY. A small chapel within a cathedral, in which prayers were 'chanted'. Usually named after a donor.

CHAPTER HOUSE. An assembly room for meetings of the chapter, who are the governing body of the cathedral.

CHOIR. The part of the cathedral east of the screen and west of the presbytery, in which the service is sung.

CLERESTORY An upper range of windows, below the eaves and above the aisled roof. Sometimes known as the 'clear storey' as distinct from the triforium or 'blind storey'.

CORBEL. A stone block projecting from a wall to provide horizontal support to various features. Often grotesquely carved.

CROSSING. The square space at the intersection of the nave and transepts, usually beneath the tower.

CRYPT. An underground chamber, usually vaulted, beneath the chancel. May contain an altar.

CHANCEL. The part of the cathedral east of the crossing.

DIOCESE. The area under the jurisdiction of a bishop.

FAN VAULTING. A type of vault in which the ribs (which are decorative rather than structural) are of equal length and curvature. Typical of the Perpendicular period.

GALILEE. A chapel or porch at the west end of a cathedral, usually included in the processional route.

GARTH. The area enclosed by cloisters.

HAMMER BEAM. A horizontal beam projecting at right angles from the top of a wall providing support for a wooden roof.

LADY CHAPEL. A chapel dedicated to the Virgin Mary, usually located at the east end of the cathedral.

LANCET. A tall, narrow window with a pointed head and no tracery. Typical of the Early English period.

LANTERN. A tower with windows designed to give light to the crossing beneath.

LIERNE. Short vault ribs, which are purely decorative. Typical of the Perpendicular and late-Decorated periods.

MISERICORD. A bracket beneath a hinged seat in the choir stalls. When the seat was tipped up it gave some support during lengthy periods of standing. Often engagingly carved.

MULLION. A vertical stone bar sub-dividing a window into 'lights'

NAVE. The main body and western arm of a cathedral. May have aisles.

OGEE. A double S-curve found on arches and typical of the late Decorated period.

PIER. A solid stone vertical support. May be carved or moulded.

PRESBYTERY. The area east of the choir where the high altar is located.

PULPITUM. A screen dividing the choir from the nave. The gallery or loft supported by the pulpitum often provided the location for the organ.

REBUS. A pictorial play on words often linked with the name of the bishop.

RETROCHOIR. In the eastern arm of the cathedral behind the high altar, but not including the lady chapel.

ROOD SCREEN. A screen, usually just west of the pulpitum and generally made of wood.

ROSE WINDOW. A circular window in which the tracery resembles a rose.

SANCTUARY. The area of the cathedral containing the high altar. Synonymous with the presbytery. In medieval times, fugitives from justice could shelter here after using the sanctuary knocker.

SEDILLA. A row of 3 canopied seats for the clergy on the south side of the chancel.

SPANDREL. The roughly triangular space between the outer curve of an arch and the mouldings enclosing it. Usually elaborately carved with, for example, foliage.

TIERCERON. A type of vaulting where minor ribs spring from the main rib and lead to the ridge rib.

TRACERY. Slender stone ornamental ribwork on the upper part of gothic windows. Also found on walls and screens.

TRANSEPT. The short arms running north–south in a cruciform church or cathedral.

TRIBUNE. A gallery extending along the roof of an aisle.

TRIFORIUM. An arcaded or walled passage at the intermediate level between the main arcade and the clerestory. Often known as the 'blind storey' because of its lack of windows and light. If there are windows, the term 'tribune' is preferable.

VAULT. Ceilings or roofs with load-bearing arches.

Key to Maps

Each of the cathedral tours and city walks in this book is accompanied by a detailed map on which the route is shown in purple. Places of interest along the walks – such as churches, pubs and historic houses – are clearly identified. Opening times are listed chapter by chapter at the back of the book, starting on page 166.

The following is a key to symbols and abbreviations used on the maps:

Symbols

route of walk

railway line

major building

† church

public toilets

park

Underground

railway station

Abbreviations

APP	Approach	PDE	Parade
AVE	Avenue	PH	Public House
CLO	Close		(Pub)
COTTS	Cottages	PK	Park
CT	Court	PL	Place
DLR	Docklands	RD	Road
	Light	S	South
	Railway	SQ	Square
DRI	Drive	ST	Saint
E	East	ST	Street
GDNS	Gardens	STN	Station
GRN	Green	TER	Terrace
GRO	Grove	UPR	Upper
HO	House	VW	View
LA	Lane	W	West
LWR	Lower	WD	Wood
MS	Mews	WHF	Wharf
MT	Mount	WLK	Walk
N	North	WY	Way
PAS	Passage		

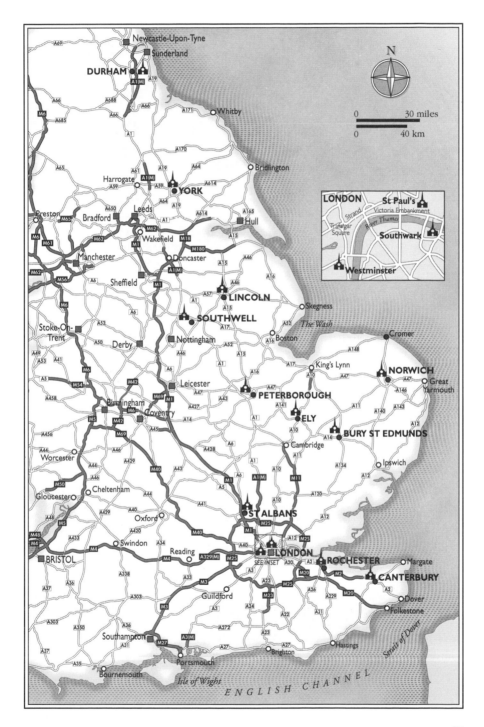

London: St Paul's

Access: Nearby railway stations include Farringdon, City Thameslink, Blackfriars, Cannon Street and Liverpool Street. The most convenient tube station is St Paul's (Central line). London Transport buses 4, 8, 22B, 25, 26, 56, 141, 172, 501 and 521.

The first cathedral on this site dated from early Saxon times; made of wood, it was built in 604 for Mellitus, Bishop of the East Saxons, and founded by Ethelbert, King of Kent. It burnt down and was rebuilt several times.

When the Normans conquered Britain, Maurice, Archdeacon of Le Mans, was declared Bishop of London. Two years later, after the Saxon cathedral had fallen prey to fire yet again, he decided to build a new cathedral, one that would reflect the importance of the capital of the new Norman territory. This stone building, now referred to as Old St Paul's, was built in cruciform shape in the Gothic style, with the nave and choir of equal length and each having twelve bays. The third largest cathedral in Europe, and dominating medieval London, it had elements of Norman, Early English and Decorated design. Flying buttresses were prominent. The spire, one of the tallest ever built – it exceeded the present one by some 165ft (50m) in height – attracted lightning strikes on more than one occasion.

Old St Paul's became a popular meeting place and social centre, containing law courts, workshops and a marketplace. It also witnessed many important historic events. Prince Arthur was married here to Catherine of Aragon in 1501. During the Reformation it was, of course, stripped of images and crucifixes. Elizabeth I is said to have stood up here and shouted at a dean with whose sermon she disagreed. In 1588 a public notice was read on the steps giving news of the defeat of the Spanish Armada. Guy Fawkes (1570–1606) and the other Gunpowder Plot conspirators were hung, drawn and quartered on the cathedral steps. The poet John Donne (c1572–1631) was an active dean here.

By the mid-17th century the cathedral was in a sad state. The choir was used as stables by Cromwell's troopers, monuments were desecrated and windows were smashed. It was perhaps fortunate that the Great Fire of London razed old St Paul's to the ground in 1666, allowing a fresh start.

King Charles II was instrumental in the planning of the new cathedral, providing money himself and raising further funds by taxing coal coming into the city; additional cash came from a public appeal. In 1669, Sir Christopher Wren (1632–1723) was appointed architect; his design approved by the king, work began in 1675. The construction took thirty-five years, being completed in 1710, and spanned five reigns – those of Charles II, James II, William and Mary, Queen Anne and George I.

St Paul's is the only major English cathedral in Classical style, or 'Wrenaissance'. The building is dominated by the imposing dome, 102ft (31m) in diameter, surmounted by a lantern – Wren's uncle was Bishop of Ely, and the architect was clearly influenced by the octagon at that cathedral. The west end has a fine pair of Baroque towers.

Despite these Classical features, the plan and structure owe much to Gothic design. There is a wealth of flying buttresses, for example, although Wren concealed these by screens so that they are virtually invisible from the ground. The stone used comes from Portland in Dorset, and recent cleaning has emphasized the excellent carving, much of it by Grinling Gibbons (1648–1721). The west end approach is marked by a steep rank of steps, and this can cause problems on state occasions – as when the aged Queen Victoria found herself too infirm to enter the cathedral for her Silver Jubilee celebrations, which had to be held outside the cathedral while she sat in her carriage.

St Paul's survived the heavy bombing which London received during World War II and continues to be the main venue for state occasions like royal weddings, funerals and remembrance services. It no longer dominates the London skyline, however, being increasingly hemmed in by office blocks, but it remains an important national symbol and a major attraction for visitors from all over the world.

TOUR OF THE CATHEDRAL
Start: The west front.
Finish: The southwest door.

Before you climb the steps to the entrance, pause by the statue of Queen Anne, which makes a good observation point from which to view the **west front** (1). Like the rest of the cathedral, this is built in two storeys, separated by a bold cornice. The Classical columns that dominate it are topped by a pediment containing a bas-relief of the conversion of St Paul. The statue itself is attributed to Francis Bird (1667–1731), as are the statues of the Apostles which appear at roof level around the building.

On each side of the building is a tower in Baroque style, with pillars, urns and cupolas; these two towers were the last parts of the cathedral to be built. One contains the clock and the other is the belfry. The clock, which has three dials, is known as Big Tom – it is of similar design and size to Parliament's Big Ben – and dates from 1893, although the present mechanism is more recent than that. The belfry's most used bell, Great Tom, dates from 1716 and is used for striking hours. The largest bell, Great Paul, is at 16 tons (17 tonnes) the heaviest swinging bell in the country.

Impressive as the west front is in daylight, do try to see it at night, when it is floodlit and incredibly beautiful.

A Famous Secretary of War and an Early Archbishop
Climb the steps and enter the cathedral through the side of the great west doors (the main doors are opened only on important state occasions).

Immediately on your left is the **Chapel of All Souls** (2), which contains the Kitchener Memorial, dedicated to the servicemen who died in World War I. Lord Kitchener (1850–1916), whose face is still familiar from old recruiting posters, was Secretary of War from August 1914; he drowned when HMS *Hampshire* was mined off Orkney.

Next along is the **Chapel of St Dunstan** (3), named after Dunstan (*c*909–988), a Bishop of London, during the days of the Saxon cathedral and later Archbishop of Canterbury. Note here the wooden entrance screen carved by Jonathan Maine and also the Richmond mosaic fresco behind the altar.

19

For further progress into the cathedral you have to pay an entrance fee – unlike the case in many other cathedrals, this is nothing new: St Paul's began charging in 1707, before the construction of the building was even complete! Choose here whether or not you want to pay also to visit the galleries.

The Military Connection

There is now a vista along the full length of the **nave** (4) towards the dome and high altar. In length the nave and the choir balance each other – it is this symmetry of the building which is so impressive. The large rectangular pillars have fluted pilasters with Corinthian capitals, while the arches, as elsewhere in the cathedral, are round-headed.

Proceed along the **north aisle** (5) and note on the right, filling an arch, the **Duke of Wellington Monument** (6). This imposing memorial, completed in the 1870s, is composed of contrasting white limestone and black marble. The sculpture of Wellington (1760–1842) on his horse Copenhagen was added on top of the monument earlier this century. The funeral of Wellington was a remarkable affair, with some 13,000 mourners occupying the cathedral, which was draped everywhere with black cloth.

Passing the Lord Mayor of London's Vestry on the left, move on into the **north transept** (7). Here you find the **font** (8) – unusually, because in most cathedrals it is at the west end. Carved by Francis Bird in 1727, the font is of Italian marble, cream with subtle blue veins. On the opposite side of the transept is the **north transept chapel** (9), which contains the colours of the Middlesex Regiment. The carved door shows a pelican pecking its own breast to succour its young – a recurring symbol in the cathedral.

Also in the transept are two notable statues: a modern terracotta Virgin and Child by Josephine Vasconellos and a white marble figure by John Flaxman of Sir Joshua Reynolds (1723–1792), the artist and first president of the Royal Academy.

The Dome and the 'Box of Whistles'

Go next into the crossing and stand under the **dome** (10). Believed to be the second largest dome in the world (after that of St Peter's in Rome), and estimated to weigh about 64,000 tons (65,000 tonnes), this is undoubtedly the great glory of St Paul's. Although Wren never went to Italy, he was obviously influenced by the great architects of the Renaissance such as Michelangelo (1475–1564), and he produced a dome which dominated the London skyline.

There are actually three layers to the dome: above the inner dome is a cone-shaped brick structure, followed by an outer dome of light wood covered with Derbyshire lead. The brick cone supports the beautifully designed Baroque-style lantern, which balances the Classical dome and the clearly Baroque west towers.

Back at ground level, note the marble floor, designed to represent a compass, in the centre of which is a circular brass grille, one of several around the cathedral constructed to allow hot air up from the original stoves in the crypt.

Also in the crossing are the lectern and the pulpit. These are totally different from each other in design. The lectern is in the form of a traditional brass eagle on a pedestal, likewise of brass, the whole done by Jacob Sutton in 1719. In contrast, the huge pulpit is of oak and limewood. It was installed in 1964 to celebrate the 250th anniversary of the opening of St Paul's. Interestingly, Wren's original pulpit had wheels and could be pushed around to allow sermons to be delivered in any part of the building.

The crossing is the best place to have an initial view of the **chancel** (11), which is often out of bounds to visitors, and a convenient location to view the organ and the choir. The present **organ** (12) is not the original, which was built by 'Father' Shmidt and installed in 1695. What Wren used to refer to as a 'box of whistles' has been rebuilt and modified on countless occasions. There are today five keyboards, each with sixty-one keys, plus a pedalboard with thirty-two pedals. The organ has 138 stops. The casing, which you can see on both sides of the chancel, is unusual in that it is richly carved with animated figures, again by Grinling Gibbons.

Around the East End

The **choir** (13) once more shows Gibbons's artistry, in the beautifully worked stalls and the screen behind. Gibbons, the son of a London draper but brought up in Rotterdam, was responsible for most of the cathedral's interior wood carving and also some of the exterior stonework.

Here in the crossing you can also get your first view of the mosaic ceilings. By contrast with those of the dome, which are mundane, these are breathtaking,

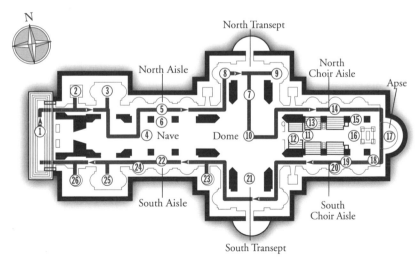

Key

1. West Front
2. Chapel of All Souls
3. Chapel of St Dunstan
4. Nave
5. North Aisle
6. Duke of Wellington Monument
7. North Transept
8. Font
9. North Transept Chapel
10. Dome
11. Chancel
12. Organ
13. Choir
14. North Choir Aisle
15. Tijou Gates
16. High Altar
17. American Memorial Chapel
18. Lady Chapel
19. South Choir Aisle
20. Effigy of John Donne
21. South Transept
22. South Aisle
23. Entrance to Galleries
24. The Light of the World
25. Chapel of St Michael and St George
26. Geometrical Staircase

particularly on the three saucer domes. Made in Whitechapel and dating from the late 19th century, they are the work of Sir William Richmond. The theme of the mosaics over the choir is wildlife – animals, fish and birds; in the apse over the high altar we see Christ flanked by cherubim and seraphim, while around the dome are prophets and evangelists. The impetus for the mosaics was provided by Queen Victoria, who in a letter to the bishop described St Paul's as 'most dreary, dingy and undevotional'. She herself never saw the completed mosaics, by then being too frail to climb the cathedral's entrance steps.

The **north choir aisle** (14) forms, with the south choir aisle and the apse, the ambulatory, or walk around the chancel. Otherwise the least interesting part of the cathedral, the north choir aisle is used as a display area. At its far end is a superb modern sculpture by Henry Moore (1898–1986) of the Madonna and Child. At this point stunning wrought-iron gates separate both aisles from the high altar; these are known as the **Tijou Gates** (15) after their maker, Jean Tijou, a French ironworker who from 1689 was almost continuously in Wren's employ. Both strong and intricate, the gates are considered Tijou's best work. The gilding was probably added later.

If you peer through the gates you can see the features of the east end of the chancel. Dominating the area is the **high altar** (16), the third to occupy this spot. Wren's original was controversially replaced by a Victorian high altar, but this was bomb-damaged during World War II. The present altar, dating from 1958, is similar to a sketch Wren made for what he clearly intended to be a focal point in the grand design. A massive slab of Italian marble supports a cross 10ft (3m) high that is flanked by candlesticks of similar size. Over this is a canopy or baldacchino of carved oak, heavily gilded and topped with a statue of the risen Christ. At the side of the altar is the bishop's throne, with sumptuous carving that includes the arms of Bishop Compton (1632–1713), whose term of office stretched from the ruins of Old St Paul's to the completion of the new cathedral.

The whole of the apse is taken up with the **American Memorial Chapel** (17). This end of St Paul's was badly damaged during World War II and was completely restored after the conclusion of hostilities. One of the architects involved was Stephen Dykes Bower, who was heavily concerned with work at Bury St Edmunds – see page 84. The chapel was dedicated to the 28,000 US servicemen based in Britain who lost their lives during the war; their names are recorded in an illuminated roll of honour. Note the panels and stained glass, both of which have US themes.

At the corner of the apse and the south choir aisle is the minute **Lady Chapel** (18), which dates from 1959. Some of the items here were retrieved from earlier features; the woodwork around the Virgin and Child statue, for example, came from Wren's first organ screen, and the oak altar table was his original high altar.

The **south choir aisle** (19) starts with the pair to the Tijou screen of the north choir aisle. Then follow two monuments of interest. On the chancel side of the aisle, a bronze of Bishop Mandell Creighton (1843–1901) rests on a plinth of green porphyry. Opposite is the marble **Effigy of John Donne** (20), by Nicholas Stone (1586–1647); Donne was dean here for a number of years. This was the only figure from Old St Paul's to survive the Great Fire; it did so because it fell through into the crypt. Careful inspection reveals scorchmarks.

The South Transept and the Galleries

The **south transept** (21) is distinguished by a number of white marble memorials, many with a nautical theme, such as those commemorating Lords Nelson (1758–1805), Howe (1726–1799) and Collingwood (1750–1819). Look also for those of Robert Falcon Scott (1868–1912) – Scott of the Antarctic –, J.M.W. Turner (1775–1851) and the prison reformer John Howard (1726–1790). Certainly the most impressive artwork in the south transept is the doorcase – yet another masterpiece by Grinling Gibbons. Also in the south transept is the entrance to the crypt (see below).

You now come to the **south aisle** (22). Immediately on your left is the **entrance to the galleries** (23). If you visit all the galleries you will have to negotiate over one thousand steps, so think carefully before you commit yourself!

The first gallery you reach is the **Whispering Gallery**, which runs around the interior base of the dome; it gets its name because a whisper against the wall can be heard on the opposite side of the gallery, some 140ft (42m) away. Try it if you like, but normally the place is too noisy for you to have any chance of success. A further spiral of steps brings you to the **Stone Gallery**, which goes around the dome's exterior and affords exceptional views over the rooftops of London. Masochists can tackle a further 150 steps up to the **Golden Gallery** at the base of the lantern; here you get even better panoramic views. It is an alarming thought that Wren was hauled up in a basket to this level two or three times a week to inspect the progress of his plans!

There are few outstanding works of fine art in the cathedral, but an exception is to be found in the south aisle once you've descended, doubtless breathless, from the galleries: *The Light of the World* (24) by William Holman Hunt (1827–1910), who is buried in the cathedral crypt. The (poorly lit) picture shows Christ knocking at a door, and has been described as a 'sermon in a frame'. In fact, this is a copy Hunt painted fifty years later of an original that hangs in Keble College, Oxford.

Next on your left is the **Chapel of St Michael and St George** (25), dedicated to those who have been knighted for service to the Commonwealth.

Before you leave, by the southwest door, take a look at the **geometrical staircase** (26) designed by Wren and built and carved by William Kempster, with iron banisters by Jean Tijou.

Tour of the Crypt

Start and finish: The main entrance to the crypt, *via* the stairs in the south transept.

The main purpose of a crypt is as a burial place. However, although St Paul's boasts the largest crypt of any cathedral in Europe, there have been no burials here for some time, but as you will see there is an extraordinary number of tombs and memorials of the great and the good, with two tombs dominating – those of Nelson and Wellington. The architecture throughout is basic and the stonework has benefited from recent cleaning.

From the foot of the access steps, note the memorial to the British who died in the Falklands conflict of 1982, then turn right and go to the east end, where you will find the **OBE Chapel** (1), dedicated to the holders of this award. This was

Crypt

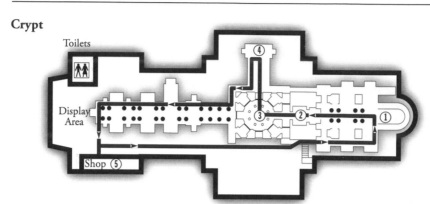

Key

1. O.B.E. Chapel
2. Wellington's Tomb
3. Nelson's Tomb
4. Treasury
5. Cathedral Shop

originally called St Faith's Chapel in recognition of a parish church demolished when Old St Paul's was extended in the 14th century. To the right are monuments to Reynolds, Wren and William Blake (1757–1827). Wren's tomb bears an inscription composed by his son: '*Lector, si monumentum requiris, circumspice*' – 'Reader, if you seek his monument, look around.'

The aisle to the south, often called Artists' Corner, has the tombs of or memorial slabs to painters like Reynolds, Turner and Sir John Millais (1829–1906).

Go down the central aisle to the **Tomb of Wellington** (2): a rather severe block of brown Cornish porphyry inscribed 'Arthur Duke of Wellington' rests on a limestone plinth. The walls around the tomb have memorial plaques to field-marshals of World War II – Alanbrooke, Wavell, Dill, Wilson, Auchinleck, Gort, Montgomery, Slim, Alexander and Warwick.

Nearby, and immediately under the dome, is **Nelson's Tomb** (3). After he died at Trafalgar in 1805, Nelson's body was preserved in a keg of rum and brought *via* Gibraltar to Britain. His funeral, in 1806, was a notable state occasion, with a flotilla of state barges and other craft sailing from Greenwich to St Paul's, where the procession inside the cathedral was led by the Prince of Wales, the future George IV.

Next turn right into the **treasury** (4), which was opened by the Duchess of Kent in 1981. This contains a comprehensive collection of liturgical plate. Among the vestments on display the star exhibit is the Jubilee cope worn in the service to commemorate the 25th anniversary of Elizabeth II's coronation. The treasury's impressive steel gates are apparently very necessary – also among the display items are two ancient locks and keys which failed to prevent an audacious robbery in 1810. Near here are two scale models, one of Old St Paul's, the other showing an original design by Wren for the cathedral.

The west end of the crypt has little of permanent interest but is worth a quick look: it is used largely for informative displays. Also at the west end are the well stocked **gift shop** (5) and the toilets.

Plate 1: *The dome of St Paul's, London. Designed by Sir Christopher Wren and built between 1675 and 1710, St Paul's is the only major English cathedral in the Classical style (see page 18).*

Plate 2: *St Paul's – view from the choir towards the high altar. Wren used the best craftsmen available, including Grinling Gibbons, whose magnificent wood carvings can be seen in the choir (see page 21).*

Plate 3: *Dr Johnson's House in Gough Square, where he lived from 1747 to 1759 (see page 27).*

Plate 4: *Westminster Abbey serves as a venue for royal weddings and funerals (see page 29).*

Plate 5: *The Houses of Parliament, more correctly the Palace of Westminster. Viewed from Parliament Square, Big Ben stands on the left and St Margaret's Church is on the right (see page 36).*

Plate 6: A guard of the Household Cavalry, outside the Horse Guards building (see page 38).

Plate 7: Southwark Cathedral's 19th-century nave was built in Early English style (see page 42).

Plate 8: The New Globe Theatre was completed in late 1997, making use of the same materials and design as the Old Globe, which was closed by the Puritans in 1642 (see page 50).

WALKING TOUR FROM ST PAUL'S CATHEDRAL

The tour looks firstly at the cathedral exterior and then follows a circular route taking in landmarks of the former printing, publishing and newspaper industries. Other features include Dr Johnson's House, the Old Bailey and some Wren churches.

Start and finish: The cathedral's west front.
Length: 1½ miles (2.4km).
Time: 1 hour, but allow longer if you want to visit the churches and other buildings.
Refreshments: Numerous pubs, restaurants and sandwich bars. Two pubs are strongly recommended – the highly atmospheric Ye Olde Cheshire Cheese, just off Fleet Street, and the unique Blackfriar near Blackfriars Bridge.

Before you start the walk proper, take a little time to stroll around the outside of the cathedral, going first along the south (Cannon Street) side.

This area is the **Churchyard** – not a graveyard but the precincts of the cathedral. Particularly in the days of Old St Paul's, this was a meeting place, a market, a place to preach and plot, the site of workshops and the haunt of prostitutes and thieves. In the 18th century, the Churchyard was the centre of the book trade. Today, the area is less frenetic and is a popular place for office workers to relax at lunchtime.

Look out for two statues. St Paul's Memorial Cross, in the northeast corner, dates from 1912 and stands on the spot where open-air sermons were preached. The other statue, more modern, shows the recumbent figure of Thomas à Becket (1118–1170).

Having circumnavigated the cathedral, walk up the broad steps into **Paternoster Square** (paternosters were strings of prayer beads). This area, flattened during the Blitz, was rebuilt in Modernist style as a pedestrianized square surrounded by office blocks. During the 1980s the architecture of Paternoster Square was the subject of a heated debate in which Prince Charles joined enthusiastically. The Corporation of the City of London has now decided to demolish the area and start again. For the moment, though, you needn't bother to explore the square – the office blocks are largely empty and there is little to see apart from one modern sculpture.

The Father of Fleet Street, and a Wren Church

Turn immediately left and walk down a sloping ramp into Warwick Lane. Cross the road and head up a short alleyway towards Amen Court – a private area, mainly offices and residences of cathedral staff. Just before you reach the gateway, turn left under a modern office block and then right into the forecourt of **Stationers' Hall**. This is the livery hall of the Stationers' and Newspaper Makers' Company, one of hundreds of livery companies descended from the craft guilds of the Middle Ages who administered apprenticeships and who were responsible for quality control. Many of the guilds became extremely wealthy and built extravagant halls for their lavish ceremonies. The officers of the guild wore elaborate uniforms or 'livery' – hence the name. Look on the front of Stationers' Hall for the plaque to Wynkyn de Worde (died c1535), the so-called Father of Fleet Street, who in c1500 set up his first printing press nearby.

Leave the forecourt along the alley by the Citizens' Advice Bureau and turn right on reaching Ludgate Hill. Lud Gate, one of six gates built in the old city walls, was finally pulled down in 1760.

A few yards to your right you'll see the unimposing entrance of the **Church of St Martin-within-Ludgate**. It is believed that a church was first built on this site about 1300 years ago, by King Cadwal, and some of the remains of that building may exist in the crypt of the building that stands here today. A medieval church (completed 1437) was destroyed in the Great Fire of 1666. The present church, built by Wren, was completed in 1684. Wren designed the spire to complement the view towards St Paul's; despite subsequent building it still carries out this function. St Martin's survived the Blitz intact, and its simple cruciform interior is today well maintained by several guilds and liveries. You can admire some more of Grinling Gibbons's carving while listening to the popular lunchtime concerts.

If you decide not to stop, keep going past the church until you cross **Old Bailey**, which runs inside and parallel to the old City walls. This street gives its name to the Central Criminal Court, which is 220 yards (200m) to your right from where you're crossing. Old Bailey was also the site of Newgate Prison, where large crowds turned up to witness public hangings.

Fleet Street and Environs

Cross Ludgate Circus and enter **Fleet Street**, named for a small stream, the Fleet, which rises on Hampstead Heath and which once marked the western boundary of the Roman city. For many years the Fleet was little more than a foul sewer. Wren attempted to tidy it up, canalizing the lower reaches and building four Venetian-style bridges – the foundations of one of these was recently discovered beneath Ludgate Circus. His scheme failed because habits die hard: people continued to use the Fleet as a receptacle for sewage, rubbish and dead dogs, along with entrails from Smithfield meat market. The stream was eventually covered up in 1766, reputedly after an inebriated butcher froze to death after becoming stuck in the mud. Also located here was the notorious Fleet Prison, where John Donne was obliged to spend some time, allegedly for marrying without his father-in-law's permission.

Fleet Street is, of course, famous for its connections with the newspaper industry. Printing came to the area with Wynkyn de Worde, who exploited the proximity of St Paul's and the inns of court. Two hundred years passed, however, before the first daily newspaper was produced here – the *Daily Courant*, a forerunner of *The Times*. The newspaper industry has now largely relocated to Docklands after an acrimonious dispute involving the print unions, whose craft had been rendered largely obsolete by new technology. Evidence of the industry remains, however. Look for the former *Daily Telegraph* building, with its Art Deco frontage – it is now occupied by a French bank – and the famous black-glass facade of the old *Daily Express* building. Opposite the latter is one of the very few of Fleet Street's remaining working links with the newspaper industry – the offices of the Reuters/Press Association news agency, housed in a sturdy stone building designed by Sir Edwin Lutyens (1869–1944) in 1935.

Continue west along Fleet Street until, on the right, you reach Wine Office Court, in which stands **Ye Olde Cheshire Cheese**. One of the most famous pubs in London, it dates from 1667, having been rebuilt after the Great Fire. The court is named for the excise office that was here until 1665. The pub is full of atmosphere – low ceilings, intimate corners, dark oak panelling – and provides excellent lunches and bar meals. It was the haunt of Samuel Johnson (1709–1784) and other literary

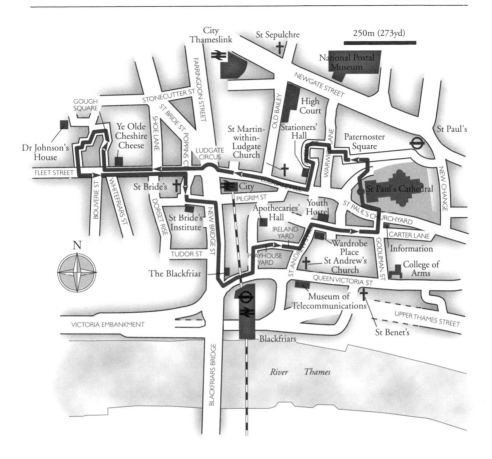

figures such as Alexander Pope (1688–1744), James Boswell (1740–1795), Lord Macaulay (1800–1859) and, more recently, Mark Twain (1835–1910).

Take the alleyway to the left of the tavern and fork left into Gough Square, a cobbled courtyard whose neo-Georgian buildings are mostly legal chambers. The one genuine 17th-century building is **Dr Johnson's House**, at 17 Gough Square; here Johnson lived from 1747 to 1759 while he compiled the first known dictionary of the English language. The house is full of memorabilia concerning both Johnson and his biographer Boswell. Look for the copy on display of the first edition of the dictionary. Don't miss the attic, where Johnson and six helpers compiled the dictionary.

Printing History

Leave Gough Square, pass through Johnson's Square and follow an alleyway back into Fleet Street. Cross the street and walk back towards St Paul's. Just before you come to the Reuters building, turn right to reach **St Bride's Church**.

Sometimes known as the 'printers' cathedral', the present church is the eighth to have been built on this site during the past 1500 years; its steeple (which is supposed to have inspired the tiered wedding cake) is the highest Wren built. Bombing badly damaged the church during World War II but also helped reveal the crypt, which has Roman mosaics, some medieval walls and the remains of previous churches. The crypt has a small chapel and a large display of artefacts discovered on the site. Alongside is a presentation of Fleet Street history. It was next to St Bride's that Wynkyn de Worde moved Caxton's printing firm in order to take advantage of the trade offered by the Churchyard book market and the law courts. Today there are frequent and popular lunchtime concerts in the nave of St Bride's.

Take the path alongside the churchyard to Bride Lane. Turn right and walk towards **St Bride's Institute and Printing Library**, which was opened by the Prince of Wales, the future Edward VII, in 1894 as a cultural centre. It stands on the site of the old Bridewell Abbey, and today includes a small theatre.

Blackfriars

Turn left at the institute, walk to New Bridge Street, turn right and head towards Blackfriars Bridge. You are now in the Blackfriars area, named after the Dominican monastery which existed here from 1278 until the Dissolution. This once-fashionable region is nowadays well off the tourist trail, but has a number of interesting buildings.

On the left, just before the bridge, is the unique **Blackfriar** pub, decorated in Art Nouveau style with a statue of a jolly black monk over the front door. Inside are friezes showing inebriated monks. This is a one-off – don't miss it.

Leaving the pub, go under the railway bridge and turn immediately left into Blackfriars Lane. Straight ahead is **Apothecaries' Hall**, dating from 1688 and arguably the most attractive of the City Livery Company buildings. The delightful courtyard is open to the public, but you can see the other attractions only if you have made a prior written application.

Just before you reach the hall, turn right into **Playhouse Yard**. Once the refectory of the monastery, the building here was converted into an indoor theatre, the Blackfriars Playhouse. William Shakespeare (1564–1616) was a partner in this theatre, which had three galleries and over six hundred seats, and functioned mainly in winter – summer performances were held in the open-air Globe Theatre, south of the Thames.

Fork right into **Ireland Yard**. On the left of the passageway was the Provincial Hall of the Dominican Monastery. After the monastery was dissolved in 1538, the Parish Church of St Ann Blackfriars was built on the site. The church was destroyed during the Great Fire and never rebuilt, the parish being amalgamated with the nearby St Andrew-by-the-Wardrobe. Gravestones can still be seen in the yard, which got its name from a haberdasher, William Ireland, whose shop was in the monastery gatehouse. Shakespeare is said to have bought the shop in 1613 and left it on his death to his daughter Susannah.

At the end of the yard, turn left into St Andrew's Hill and then immediately right into Carter Lane. On your left, the City of London Youth Hostel has an interesting pink and grey frontage. Immediately opposite is the delightful little courtyard of **Wardrobe Place**. This was where the Master of the King's Wardrobe, responsible for all the monarch's ceremonial robes, had his premises from 1359 until the Great Fire of 1666.

Continue along Carter Lane and take the next turning left, which brings you back to the west front of St Paul's, where the walk began.

London: Westminster

Access: The nearest mainline railway terminals are Victoria, Charing Cross and Waterloo. The most convenient underground station is Westminster (District, Circle and Jubilee lines). Victoria Coach Station is five minutes' walk away. London Transport buses include 3, 11, 12, 24, 53, 77A, 88, 109 and 211. Most London open-top bus tours pass by and allow you to jump on or off.

Although strictly speaking not a cathedral (it claimed this title only during the period 1540–50), Westminster Abbey deserves inclusion for various reasons. First, as the 'nation's church' it has provided the venue for the majority of royal coronations and burials throughout its history. Second, though it was, like many of the great cathedrals, based on a medieval monastery, it survived the Dissolution of the Monasteries almost intact, probably because of its royal connections. And third, it is one of the main tourist attractions in Britain; there are as many as 15,000 visitors a day, so do not expect to find the usual tranquillity of an English cathedral!

To many who come to the abbey, the building seems somewhat like a gigantic mausoleum, the recent introduction of hourly prayers being little more than a token and the frequent admonitory notices – NO PHOTOGRAPHY, NO VIDEOS, NO LECTURES HERE, WALK ONLY ON THE CARPET, etc. – an irritation. There is, nevertheless, much of interest here if you can manage to visit the abbey at a quiet time, for the building is in many ways a religious and historical record of the country.

A number of stories tell of early religious buildings on the site of the present one, but none can be verified. What is certain is that a Benedictine monastery was set up here by St Dunstan (*c*909–988) in 960. When Edward the Confessor succeeded in 1042 the monastery was still small, having only twelve monks, but under his patronage it grew, and a large abbey was built in the French Romanesque style. The Bayeux Tapestry gives us a tantalizing glimpse of its architecture. The building, of cruciform shape, had arcades with tall, rounded arches, above which was a clerestory. A high tower had corner turrets. Edward was unable to attend the consecration in 1065, having become seriously ill; he died shortly afterwards and was buried by the high altar.

Edward was succeeded by Harold, who was defeated by William the Conqueror at the Battle of Hastings in 1066. On Christmas Day the same year William rode up the aisle of the abbey on horseback to be crowned king, thereby establishing the tradition of royal coronations in the building. Since then only two monarchs have not been crowned at Westminster – Edward V and Edward VIII.

The Confessor was canonized in 1161 and his shrine became a popular place of pilgrimage. In the next century his great admirer Henry III decided the shrine should have a more suitable building as its home. He therefore demolished the old abbey and constructed a new building in Gothic style, strongly influenced by Rheims Cathedral in northern France. (The master mason was Henry de Reyns.) Work began in 1245 and, by the time money ran out in 1267, the apse, transepts and choir were complete, plus some bays in the east end of the nave. The materials used were varied. Much of the stone came from Reigate in Surrey, while many of the pillars were made from Purbeck marble. The more ornate work was carved from stone brought from Caen, Normandy.

For over a century the Norman nave – and the parishioners who used it – saw little change, but in 1348 Simon de Langham (d1376), Archbishop of Canterbury, bequeathed some money to the abbey, and work recommenced under the patronage of Richard III. Progress was slow: not until 1506 was the west end reached. The height of the nave matched that of the east end, attaining over 100ft (30m); the nave was supported on the exterior by flying buttresses. The master mason was Henry Yevele, who kept closely to Henry de Reyns's original plan, so that the whole building seems to have been constructed as one.

An important later addition to the church was the Lady Chapel, at the east end, built in the time of Henry VII in Perpendicular style. Henry VII intended it to honour his uncle, Henry VI, but, as the latter was never canonized, it in the event became the last resting place for himself and his family.

The Benedictine monastery was dissolved on the orders of Henry VIII in 1540, and the abbey became the cathedral of the diocese of Westminster. For the next ten years there were two London cathedrals, the abbey and Old St Paul's – indeed, the abbey contributed money to the repair of the latter (hence the saying 'rob Peter to pay Paul'). Meanwhile the old abbey buildings became Westminster School, a public school which still exists today.

In the 18th century the two towers that dominate the west front were added by Nicholas Hawksmoor (1661–1736), a pupil of Christopher Wren (1632–1723). This completed the structure of the building. Today, the abbey is less a place of worship than a venue for large state occasions, while the great and the good of the nation are buried or commemorated within its portals.

TOUR OF THE ABBEY
Start and finish: The west end.

Viewed from the square outside, the overall impression of the **west end** (1) is of verticality, putting it firmly in the Perpendicular style. With its two dominating towers and its huge central window, this part of the abbey is largely the work, as previously mentioned, of Hawksmoor in the early 18th century. Unfortunately, the symmetry is ruined by the squat Jerusalem Chamber on the south side. In 1998 the ten niches over the door, which had been bare of statues since the Middle Ages, were filled with effigies of 20th-century martyrs. Some of the subjects are well known – e.g., Martin Luther King (1929–1968) – but others are less well so. None – and this has caused much debate – are English.

Walk through the main entrance and look back at the interior of the west end, dominated by the west window. The stained glass dates from 1735 and was designed by Sir James Thornhill (1675–1734). The top layer shows Abraham, Isaac and Jacob, while on the two rows beneath are fourteen other prophets. The lowest row of windows is made up of coats-of-arms, including those of Elizabeth I and George II.

Look next for the **Tomb of the Unknown Warrior** (2). This takes the form of a simple black slab fringed by red poppies. The idea for such a memorial came from a British World War I chaplain and was taken up by the then Dean of Westminster. Working groups went to the six main battlefields and each brought back the exhumed body of an unknown British soldier. One corpse, chosen at random by the Director of the War Graves Commission in Flanders, was taken back to Britain. Here it was reburied at Westminster Abbey with full pomp on 11 November 1920. The three main allies on the Western Front all contributed to the memorial: an English oak coffin is surrounded by French soil and covered by a slab of Belgian black marble. Nearby is a memorial slab to Sir Winston Churchill (1874–1965).

Now look at the **nave** (3). If you're accustomed to the long low vistas of most English cathedrals, Westminster Abbey's nave will remind you much more of a French cathedral. The general impression is of height and narrowness. In fact, at 102ft (31m) the nave is the loftiest medieval vault in England, and its proportions are what make it so visually satisfying: the main arcade, at 51ft (15.4m), forms half the height; the tribune, at 17ft (5.2m), is one-sixth of the height; and the clerestory, at 34ft (10.4m), makes up the remaining one-third. When you look at the nave from the outside you can see that this prodigious overall height is supported by three layers of flying buttresses. The architectural style largely represents a transition between Early English and Decorated (built later, but done to match the older part of the abbey). The windows at tribune level take the form of an equilateral triangle filled with three trefoil circles of bar tracery. Finally note the roof chandeliers, made of Waterford glass and installed to mark the abbey's 900th anniversary.

On the north side of the nave you find a pay desk. Unlike many English cathedrals, where paying for entry is a recent phenomenon, Westminster has been requiring an admission fee for centuries. The cloisters are free (but are best seen towards the end of the tour), while the chapter house, pyx chamber and Undercroft Museum, all run by English Heritage, require further payment.

The tour now continues along a set route – if you stray from it one of the numerous staff will promptly set you right.

Musicians, Fighter Pilots and the Virgin Queen

The first part of the north aisle is known as **Musicians' Aisle** (4). Graves and memorials here include those of three of the abbey's organists – Henry Purcell (1659–1695), John Blow (1649–1708) and Orlando Gibbons (1583–1625). More recent memorials remember Ralph Vaughan Williams (1872–1958), Benjamin Britten (1913–1976) and Sir Edward Elgar (1857–1934).

The north aisle leads you to the **north transept** (5), where there is an excellent rose window, again by Thornhill, displaying eleven Apostles – the one missing is, inevitably, Judas. The north transept, sometimes called 'Statesmen's Aisle', is cluttered with the marble statues of 19th-century politicians like Sir Robert Peel (1788–1850), William Pitt the Elder (1708–1778) and William Gladstone (1809-1898).

Go back towards the central aisle where, in the crossing and in front of the high altar, you'll find the **sanctuary** (6), the focus of coronation ceremonies. The high altar and the reredos behind it were the work of Sir George Gilbert Scott (1811–1878) in the mid-19th century. Beneath the high altar is one of the abbey's most prized treasures – the Cosmati Pavement. Made by the Cosmati family from Rome, it was laid in 1268. In essence, it is a mosaic of coloured glass inlaid into

Purbeck marble. Unfortunately it is in such a delicate state that it is usually covered by a carpet, being revealed only on state occasions.

The set route now takes you into the east end of the abbey. Look out on the right for the side of Henry III's tomb, which displays further Cosmati work, giving you a fair indication of what the pavement looks like. Regrettably, much of the mosaic work – up to the height of a raised arm – has been removed by souvenir hunters.

The north aisle is also the location of the **Tomb of Elizabeth I** (7). This monument, in black and white marble and heavily gilded, shows a reclining effigy. Buried beneath Elizabeth is her half-sister Mary Tudor (Bloody Mary). The memorial was erected by James VI & I, who, aware of the ill-feeling between them, provided a Latin inscription which, loosely, reads: 'Consorts both in throne and grave, here rest we two sisters, Elizabeth and Mary, in the hope of one resurrection.'

The route now leads you to the apse at the extreme east end of the abbey and to the **Royal Air Force Chapel** (8), dedicated to members of fighter squadrons killed in the Battle of Britain. The zigzag window contains modern stained glass by Hugh Easton showing some of the men who died plus the badges of the squadrons.

Tudor Tombs and the Confessor's Shrine

You now enter the main part of the east end, which is **Henry VII's Chapel** (9). Completed in 1519, this is a riot of the Perpendicular and is justifiably considered the abbey's architectural showpiece. The fan-vaulted ceiling, with its circular designs, is particularly impressive. The choir stalls are intricately carved, with tall canopies over which is an extraordinary collection of nearly one hundred stone statues of saints. Above hang the banners of the Knights of the Order of the Bath, to whom the chapel is dedicated. The order goes back to the Middle Ages, and derives its name from the custom of bathing before receiving the knighthood – an installation ceremonies being performed every four years, usually at the Tower of London.

While in the choir area, look for the beautifully carved misericords beneath the choir seats.

At the other end of the chapel is the altar, actually a copy (but using two of the original pillars) of the first, 16th-century structure. The canopy has Henry's coat-of-arms; beneath it is a 15th-century Madonna and Child by Antonio Vivarini. Henry's tomb, which is also that of his wife Elizabeth, was made by the Florentine sculptor Pietro Torrigiani (*c*1472–1522), a pupil of Michelangelo (1475–1564) who fled to Britain after breaking his master's nose in a fight. Most of the other Tudor monarchs, princes and princesses are buried in the vaults under the chapel.

The official route now takes you over a glass 'bridge' into the abbey's most sacred core – the **Shrine of Edward the Confessor** (10). This has been altered considerably over the years. In the days of the monastery it had three parts: a stone base decorated with Cosmati work; a gold feretory (bier) which contained Edward's coffin and a wooden canopy which could be raised or lowered in order to protect or reveal the bier. During the Reformation the shrine was dismantled and the feretory removed, although in the reign of Mary Tudor some restoration took place. What you see today is a rather battered stone base with remnants of the original decoration, on top of which rests the restored canopy. In front is a small, discreet altar. Proximity to the shrine was important in medieval times, so you'll find nearby the tombs and effigies of five kings and four queens, including Richard II and Edward III. Look for the grooves in the stonework where countless pilgrims have knelt.

The shrine is separated from the west end of the abbey by a 15th-century stone screen showing scenes from Edward's life. Also on this side of the shrine is the coronation chair of Edward I, which has been used at every coronation since. The gap beneath the chair once contained the Stone of Scone, the coronation stone of Scotland before it was looted by Edward in 1296. Scottish Nationalists briefly stole it back in the 1950s, and it was officially returned to Scotland in 1996.

Poets and an Inspiration to Poets

The official route now leads you, almost backtracking, to the **south aisle of Henry VII's Chapel** (11), the site of the tomb of Mary, Queen of Scots, who was beheaded at the behest of Elizabeth I. Mary's body was brought here from Peterborough Cathedral by her grandson, James VI & I, and installed in this eight-poster tomb. Nearby is the tomb of Lady Margaret Beaufort (1443–1509), Henry VII's mother, known for her charitable works. Her effigy, showing her in old age, is by Torrigiani.

The south ambulatory now goes past the Chapel of St Nicholas (Santa Claus – patron saint of children) and the Chapel of St Edmund, King of the East Anglians,

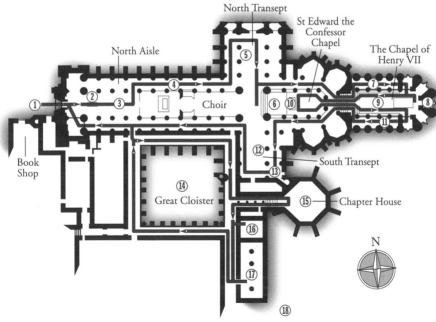

Key

1. West End
2. Grave of the Unknown Warrior
3. Nave
4. Musicians' Aisle
5. North Transept
6. Sanctuary
7. Tomb of Elizabeth I
8. Royal Air Force Chapel
9. Henry VII's Chapel
10. Shrine of Edward the Confessor
11. South Aisle of Henry VII's Chapel
12. South Transept
13. Poets' Corner
14. Great Cloister
15. Chapter House
16. Pyx Chamber
17. Undercroft Museum
18. College Garden

before reaching the **south transept** (12). The architecture here is pure Geometrical Decorated Gothic; the glass of the superb rose window is Victorian. Note the carvings beneath the window, in the angle of the arches and the 13th-century wall paintings. Look for the stairs next to the south side of the transept; these were part of the night passage from the monks' dormitory to the choir.

Also in the south transept is **Poets' Corner** (13). The first to arrive was Geoffrey Chaucer (*c*1345–1400), who was buried here apparently because he lived near the abbey and had been clerk of works to the Palace of Westminster. No other poets were buried here for nearly two centuries, until Edmund Spenser (*c*1552–1599) was interred nearby. It is said that his contemporaries wrote elegies and threw them, with their pens, into the grave. There are now slabs, busts, statues and other memorials to a vast number of poets and writers, including Samuel Johnson (1709–1784), Robert Browning (1812–1889), Alfred, Lord Tennyson (1809–1892), Charles Dickens (1812–1870), Lord Byron (1788–1824), Ben Jonson (1572–1637) and W.H. Auden (1907–1973). In among them, strangely, is the grave of George Friedrich Handel (1685–1759), whose music was often heard at Westminster Abbey. It was at a performance of the *Messiah* here that George III mistakenly rose to his feet during the 'Hallelujah Chorus'; everyone else did likewise, so that the king would not be embarrassed. Thus was established the custom of standing whenever it is played.

Walk a few steps into the south choir aisle – where there is a monument to Admiral Sir Cloudesley Shovel (1650–1707) – and take the door into the **Great Cloister** (14), which has remained intact since the time of the monastery and is still in good condition. In those days it would have been, in effect, a series of four long rooms with glass windows and rush floors. The north cloister, once a reading and writing area, is now a popular brass-rubbing centre. Young novice monks were educated in the west walk. The south side, which has the tombs of three early abbots, led to the refectory – a building destroyed at the Dissolution.

The Chapter House, Pyx Chamber and Undercroft Museum
The area to the east of here is administered by English Heritage, and a further admission fee is required. The charge is worth it, for this part of the abbey has few visitors and many interesting features.

The **chapter house** (15) was where the monks met to discuss daily business and for the reading of a chapter from St Benedict's Rule. It was used also as a parliament house by the Commons 1257–1547, much to the annoyance of the monks – who complained about the noise! Dating from 1250, it is octagonal, with a central column supporting delicate roof vaulting. Around the walls are traces of medieval painting, while the windows above contain modern clear glass interspersed with coats-of-arms; much of the Victorian glass was destroyed during World War II. Without doubt the most fascinating feature is the original decorated tile floor, which has survived through being covered for much of its life by a wooden floor. At the Dissolution the chapter house became property of the Crown, and remains so: the dean and chapter of the abbey have no control over it – hence the English Heritage involvement.

Go back from the chapter house, turn left and then left again into the **pyx chamber** (16), which was also part of the monastic buildings. The simple stone altar and wall *piscina* (basin for the water used to wash the sacred vessels) suggest it was once a chapel; later it was certainly the monastic treasury. After the Dissolution it became Crown property, housing the pyx, a chest containing gold and silver pieces that were used annually as standards against which to test the coinage – this was known as the Trial of the Pyx. The large double door has six locks and is prevented from opening fully by a stone sill; these arrangements were apparently introduced after a burglary in 1303.

Exiting the pyx chamber, go left and left again into the **Undercroft Museum** (17), a vaulted part of the monastery beneath the dormitory; it probably dates from *c*1070 and was almost certainly used as a *calefactorium* – a commonroom where the monks could keep warm. It became a museum in 1908.

A Roman sarcophagus on display probably dates from the 3rd century AD; the cross on the stone lid shows it was re-used in Saxon times for a Christian burial. Probably the most fascinating items are the wax death masks and funeral effigies, the figures dressed in original costumes so you get a good impression of what these people were really like. Among those represented are Charles II, Henry VII, a surprisingly diminutive Lord Nelson (1758–1805), Elizabeth I, William and Mary (the former standing on a stone so that his wife wouldn't tower above him) and Lady Frances Stuart, who was the model for Britannia on coins and whose pet parrot rests at her feet. Also shown are funeral armour, medieval stained glass and coronation regalia.

Close to the museum, *via* a dark passage and the Little Cloister, is the **College Garden** (18). This was the infirmary garden where the monastery's physician grew the herbs with which he treated ailing monks. It is open to the public only on Thursdays, when it is a popular lunchtime venue for office workers – particularly in July and August, when bands occasionally play here.

Return through the cloisters back to the south aisle of the nave and on to the west end, where the tour began.

WALKING TOUR FROM WESTMINSTER ABBEY
This circular walk covers many aspects of the government of the country, including the Houses of Parliament, Whitehall, Buckingham Palace and one of the royal parks.

Start and finish: The west front of the abbey.
Length: 2 miles (3.2km).
Time: 1½ hours, but allow longer if you want to visit the church and museums.
Refreshments: Surprisingly few refreshment opportunities. The Cakehouse Restaurant in St James's Park can be pleasant in summer. The only two pubs of character are the Red Lion in Whitehall and the Two Chairmen in Dartmouth Street.

Leave the west front of the abbey and head across the grass to **St Margaret's Church**. Consecrated in 1523 and the third church to be built on the site, St Margaret's has long been known as the 'parish church of the House of Commons'. The architecture is almost entirely Perpendicular. The windows are of particular interest: one is dedicated to Sir Walter Raleigh (1552–1618), who is buried somewhere under the church (sans head, because that was claimed by his wife) and others are dedicated to John Milton (1608–1674) and William Caxton (*c*1422–*c*1491); the modern stained glass in a window in the south aisle is by John Piper (1903–1992).

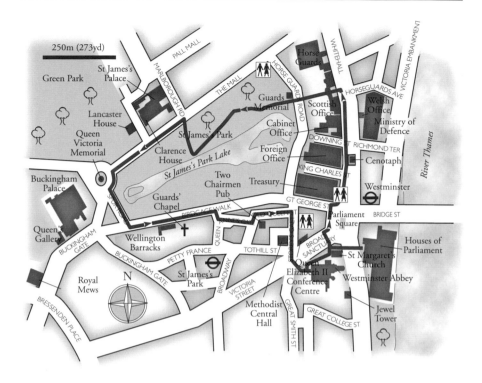

The east end of the church is the most fascinating part of the building. It has a fine reredos and a window with stained glass that may be the original Flemish material which was part of the 16th-century church; such is the value of the glass that it was removed for safety during the two world wars. The window commemorates the marriage of Henry VIII to Catherine of Aragon.

Leave the church and walk along its side to Parliament Street (the south end of Whitehall), where there is a fine view of the **Houses of Parliament**, with the clock tower of Big Ben prominent to the left. Although most people think only of the two debating chambers, there is much more to the Houses of Parliament – lobbies, bars, offices, libraries, over two miles (3km) of corridors, a police station, a travel agency and even an underground rifle range. Over 3000 people work in the building.

More correctly known as the Palace of Westminster, the original building burnt down in 1834, leaving only Westminster Hall and St Stephen's Chapel intact. The remainder of the extant parliament building was the work of Sir Charles Barry (1795–1860). Designed in ornate neo-Gothic style, it is undoubtedly the finest Victorian building in Britain and one of the best-known monuments in the world. Its honey-coloured stonework has recently been cleaned, so you see it in all its glory.

There are various ways of visiting the Houses of Parliament. For UK citizens probably the best is *via* one of the guided tours which MPs occasionally run for their constituents. To watch the proceedings in the debating chambers, join the queues for the public galleries. Note that the recesses, when MPs are on holiday, can be lengthy. When parliament is in session, a flag flies above the statue of Victoria on the south side of the building. You can also climb the tower of Big Ben and actually walk behind the clock face, and further entertainment can be had by strolling across to College Green, a favourite spot for publicity-conscious MPs to be interviewed by the media.

Now go back up one side of **Parliament Square** and cross the street by the pedestrian crossing. Laid out to give a vista of the Houses of Parliament, the square now resembles an extremely busy traffic roundabout. It contains the statues of five British prime ministers, including Disraeli (1804–1881) and Churchill, and of other notables such as Jan Smuts (1870–1950) and Abraham Lincoln (1809–1865).

Walk back down the other side of the square and into Parliament Street, which leads past the Treasury on the left and into **Whitehall**, a name synonymous with the bureaucrats who, behind the scenes, run the country.

Whitehall was named after the old Whitehall Palace, a royal residence in Tudor times that was destroyed by fire in 1698. In this building Henry VIII married Anne Boleyn, and here he died in 1547. The palace is said to have stretched for half a mile (800m) along the banks of the Thames and to have had nearly 2000 rooms. On its landward side were tennis courts, jousting yards, cockpits and other sporting venues. Today the broad avenue of Whitehall is occupied almost entirely by the offices of government departments.

First on the left is the large hulk of the Foreign Office, dating from the 1870s and built to a design by Sir George Gilbert Scott. Set back on the right is the Ministry of Defence, which contains in its bowels the old wine cellar of Whitehall Palace. Opposite is the Scottish Office (also known as Dover House), which has a porticoed entrance and a dome to its rear. Further north on the left is the Admiralty, whose splendid facade dates from 1726. The statues along Whitehall include Earl Haig (1861–1928), on horseback, Montgomery of Alamein (1887–1976), Lord Alanbrooke (1883–1963) and Raleigh.

In the centre of Whitehall, just opposite the Foreign Office, stands the **Cenotaph**, the focus of the annual Remembrance Day ceremony each November. The original memorial was designed in 1919 by Sir Edwin Lutyens (1869–1944) in plaster and wood, but it was replaced the following year by a more permanent structure in Portland Stone. It bears a simple inscription: 'The Glorious Dead.'

Just past the Cenotaph, on the left-hand side, is the short cul-de-sac of

The Cenotaph

37

Downing Street. The street is named after an Irish-born American, George Downing (c1623–1684), who came to Britain and became one of Cromwell's officials. He later supported the Restoration and by the time of his death he had built some fifteen houses in the street. No. 10 (including the large building behind it) was originally the home of the First Lord of the Treasury. An early holder of the post, Sir Robert Walpole (1676–1745), created for himself the role of Prime Minister and so No. 10 has since been the home of every PM except one. Next door, No. 11 has been the home of the Chancellor of the Exchequer since 1807, No. 12 is the office of the Chief Whip (interconnecting doors link all three), and the Cabinet Office is on the corner of Downing Street and Whitehall.

Downing Street was once open to the public, but when Margaret Thatcher was Prime Minister she had large wrought-iron gates erected at the entrance in a rather futile attempt to increase security.

A Royal Park and a Royal Palace

Continue along Whitehall until you reach the **Horse Guards building** on the left. Outside you'll see two mounted guards of the Household Cavalry (plus two unmounted guards), nominally to protect the building, which was designed by William Kent (1684–1748) in 1745. It actually contains little worth protecting, but the hourly changing of the two mounted guards is one of those curious English traditions which tourists arrive in flocks to see.

Pass through the archway (information boards here tell you about the guards regiments) and step into the open space called Horse Guards Parade. Once Henry VIII's jousting ground, this is now the square used each year for the Trooping of the Colour on the Queen's birthday.

Cross the parade ground and then Horse Guards Road, keeping the war memorial to the Household Division on your right, and enter **St James's Park**, one of London's royal parks. The land was acquired by Henry VIII, and the Court of St James was established. In 1603 James VI & I had a menagerie and a duck decoy here, and in 1660 Charles II had the park landscaped in a formal French style and opened it to the public. The first exotic birds, including pelicans, were introduced in 1667. Further informal landscaping was carried out in 1827 by John Nash (1752–1835) for George IV, and little has changed since. Today St James's Park is a popular lunchtime spot for office workers and tourists. Numerous kiosks sell snacks, and there is the popular Cakehouse Restaurant in the centre of the park.

Continue through the park with the lake on your left until you see a bridge. Turn right here and walk a hundred yards or so (100m) until you get to **The Mall**. This is the only London thoroughfare to resemble the boulevards of Paris. Look right to see Admiralty Arch, at the Mall's Trafalgar Square end, and left to see Buckingham Palace. Across The Mall are two of the royal palaces – St James's Palace and Clarence House. The former is the home of minor royals such as the Duke of Kent and Princess Alexandra, but for two centuries foreign ambassadors have been presented to the Court of St James here. Clarence House is the London home of the Queen Mother.

Walk left up The Mall towards Buckingham Palace, in front of which is the impressive **Victoria Memorial**. Made of white limestone and installed in 1911 by Edward VII in tribute to his late mother, this is one of the better statues of her. The enthroned Victoria is accompanied by Truth, Motherhood and Justice. Above her are gilded figures proclaiming victory, while some distance from the main monument are groups of figures in black bronze depicting scenes from the Empire.

Behind the memorial is **Buckingham Palace**, renovated by Nash in the 1820s and the main home of the monarch since Victoria came to the throne. It dates from 1702, when the Duke of Buckingham lived here and was briefly owned by George III in the 18th century. Despite its lack of charm it is usually thronged with tourists hoping to get a glimpse of a royal personage. The Changing of the Guard, carried out here by the Foot Guards, takes place every morning May–Aug at 10:30. Since the 1992 fire at Windsor Palace and the subsequent need to raise money for repairs, Buckingham Palace has been open to the public on an experimental basis (daily 9:30–17:30 Aug–Sep; tickets from box office in Green Park at west end of The Mall). Note that only small areas of the palace may be seen and the queues can be long.

From the palace turn left into **Birdcage Walk** – the royal aviary used to be here. On your left is St James's Park and on your right is a series of buildings associated with the Guards. The first is the rather severe Wellington Barracks, where most of the guardsmen are billeted. This building also houses the Guards Museum. This is a good place to sort out the different Guards regiments and their uniforms. Next along Birdcage Walk is the unexpectedly modern Guards' Chapel, which replaced an earlier building destroyed by a V1 rocket in 1944.

An Historic Pub and Some Culture

At the first set of pedestrian traffic lights, turn right and then immediately left into **Queen Anne's Gate**, one of London's architectural gems. All the houses were built during the reign of Queen Anne and many feature ornately carved wooden canopies over the doors. Queen Anne's Gate is actually an amalgamation of two streets once separated by a wall; the position of the wall is now marked by a small, well eroded statue of Queen Anne – a far less grand affair than that outside St Paul's Cathedral (see page 19). The street has had a number of distinguished residents; blue plaques record Lord Haldane (1856–1928) and Lord Palmerston (1784–1865; he was born in No. 19).

At the end of Queen Anne's Gate turn left into Dartmouth Street, noting the **Two Chairmen** pub and possibly – who knows? – popping into it. The name derives from the sedan chair trade, which reached England in 1634. Each chair was operated by two 'chairmen', who would carry passengers between fixed points in the city – one being at the site of the Two Chairmen. Nearby are the Cockpit Steps, where cockfights were held in Henry VIII's time.

Carry on *via* Old Queen Street to Storey's Gate, named after Charles II's gamekeeper. Turn right into this street. It is flanked by two very contrasting buildings. On your left is the modern granite-and-glass **Queen Elizabeth II Conference Centre**, while on your right is the **Methodist Central Hall**. Built in 1912 in grey limestone – and in what can only be described as Edwardian Beaux Arts style – the latter is distinguished by its huge dark-grey dome. Its organ is claimed to be one of the best in the country. The United Nations Organization held its very first meeting here in 1946.

Now cross Victoria Street and return to the west front of Westminster Abbey, where the walk began.

London: Southwark

Access: Nearby mainline railway stations include London Bridge and Cannon Street. The most convenient underground station is London Bridge (Northern line). Numerous London Transport buses serve the area: 17, 21, 22A, 35, 40, 42, 43, 45, 47, 48, 63, 78, 133, 149, 172, 188, 344, 501, 505 and 521.

At first glance this cathedral does not appear very inspiring, with its flint and stone walls covered with the grime of centuries, and hemmed in by office blocks, a railway viaduct, a busy main road and a fruit and vegetable market. But do not be deterred by this initial impression: the cathedral and the district are rich in history, both ancient and modern.

There may have been activity at Southwark in Iron Age times, but it was during the Roman occupation that the first settlement of any size came into being. The Romans selected this spot as an ideal point for bridging the River Thames. The river was wider and shallower in Roman times, and a series of low marshy islands on the south bank allowed a wooden bridge to be constructed to link up with the city of Londinium (London), which lay on a low hill on the north bank.

Southwark, then, developed as a suburb of Londinium. Two roads from the south met here – Stane Street from Chichester and Watling Street from Dover – while the route across the causeway over the marshes is now Borough High Street.

After the Romans' departure there was a period of decline, but by the 10th century the new London Bridge had been built and Southwark was being listed as a 'burgh', a designation which usually meant fortifications, in this case to protect trade. The bridge was the effective head of navigation and Southwark developed as a commercial centre.

In 1106 the Normans, assisted by the Bishop of Winchester, William Giffard, built a church at Southwark, St Mary Overie ('over the river'). This church was serviced by the Augustine priory located on its north side. Giffard's successor, Henry de Blois, set his palace just west of the church, and subsequent bishops of Winchester continued to give patronage to it.

The Norman church was ruined by fire in 1212 and the present cathedral has only a few arches and doorways to remind us of this architectural period. Peter des Roches, Bishop of Winchester at the time of the conflagration, speedily began to rebuild the priory church in what has become known as Early English style, with long lancet windows and pointed arches. Work began in 1220; by 1270 the retrochoir, sanctuary, choir, aisles, tower and part of the nave were finished. Construction then stopped, probably for financial reasons, and was not resumed for another fifty years. In 1390, when the building was almost complete, yet another fire took its toll. St Mary Overie had to be rebuilt again, this time by Cardinal Henry Beaufort (1377–1447), an illegitimate son of John of Gaunt (1340–1399).

A further disaster occurred in 1469 when the vaulted stone roof of the nave fell in. It was rebuilt in wood; a few of the original carved stone bosses are on display at the west end of the present cathedral. An early 16th-century addition was the carved stone altar screen, donated by the then Bishop of Winchester, Richard Fox.

Meanwhile Southwark, being outside the jurisdiction of the City of London, became the playground of Londoners, who flocked across the river for bear-baiting and cockfighting and to visit the prostitute-ridden inns. A number of theatres were built here, including the Globe, where William Shakespeare (1564–1616) worked, the Rose and the Swan. Southwark has had connections with other great literary figures apart from Shakespeare, Geoffrey Chaucer (c1345–1400) and Charles Dickens (1812–1870) being among them.

During the Reformation the priory was dissolved and the building handed over to Henry VIII. St Mary Overie became the parish church of St Saviour, Southwark, incorporating the Chapel of St Mary Magdalene. Around this time Stephen Gardiner (1482–1555), the Bishop of Winchester, used the retrochoir for his consistory court. After his death it became a bakery and then a pigsty before falling into disrepair. The church survived the Civil War, but the Winchester Palace was badly damaged and quickly became a ruin. This marked the end of the patronage of the various bishops of Winchester.

The 17th and 18th centuries saw a number of improvements made to the structure of the church. The tower was completed in 1689 and in 1703 a wooden altar screen extended Bishop Fox's existing stone screen. In the 19th century there was much renovation and the Chapel of St Mary Magdalene was demolished. In 1841, the wooden roof was replaced and a temporary nave built.

The wharves and docks of Southwark and neighbouring Bermondsey thrived during the Victorian era and the borough became the centre of London's food industry. This period also saw the growth of the railways, replacing the coaches which had run from Southwark's inns. London Bridge Station, opened in 1836, was the capital's first railway terminus.

With the reorganization of dioceses due to the enormous growth in population in the 19th century, Southwark was transferred from the see of Winchester to that of Rochester. It was clear, however, that a new cathedral was needed in South London and Southwark was the obvious place. Funds were raised to build a new nave that would be more fitting to cathedral status; the foundation stone was laid by the Prince of Wales, the future Edward VII, in 1890.

The church was given pro-cathedral status in 1897 and in 1905 an Act of Parliament created the diocese of Southwark, so that the parish church became the Cathedral of St Saviour and St Mary Overie. The diocese is divided into three areas – Woolwich, Croydon and Kingston, each with their own area bishop – and contains over three million inhabitants.

Southwark suffered considerable damage during World War II, but the cathedral managed to survive. The last quarter of the 20th century saw the closure of the docks, as port activity migrated downstream to Tilbury. This gave a great opportunity to redevelop Thameside. The wharves have since been converted into apartments and office blocks, while historic buildings have been preserved; the final section of Riverside Walk was completed in 1994. Among all this redevelopment, Southwark Cathedral maintains its central position in the heart of the community.

TOUR OF THE CATHEDRAL
Start and finish: The west end.

The tour begins at the main entrance, just to the south of the **west end** (1). On entering, look up to see the west window designed by Henry Holliday as part of the Victorian restoration. Beneath it on the floor is a memorial to the fifty-one victims, mostly young, who drowned when the *Marchioness* riverboat sank in the Thames near Southwark Bridge in August 1989. Against the rear wall, and seeming surprisingly large, are twelve roof bosses, all that remain of the 150 or so of the late 15th-century roof, which was taken down in 1930. Look out especially for the boss depicting the Devil swallowing Judas Iscariot. Also in this area is the hideous Victorian font in black marble, with a gold carved canopy by G.F. Bodley. The modern wooden font cover does nothing to improve its appearance.

Walk into the **nave** (2) to take in the view towards the chancel. The three levels of arcade, triforium and clerestory are nicely proportioned and topped by a simple vaulted roof. The pointed arches fit well with the Early English of the east end of the building; this is generally considered one of the better Victorian restorations of an English cathedral.

An English Poet and an American Benefactor
Cross into the **north aisle** (3), noting the arch and recess built into the wall. These are part of what little remains of the Norman church built in 1106 and largely destroyed in 1206. The bases of the arch are, interestingly, 2ft (60cm) below the level of the present cathedral. Further east is the tomb of John Gower (c1325–1408), court poet to both Richard II and Henry IV and a friend of Chaucer. Gower was the first poet to write in English as opposed to Latin. The medieval wooden tomb is attractively coloured and canopied, showing the recumbent poet with his head resting on three books written in French, English and Latin and said to be his most highly regarded works, namely *Speculum Meditantis* (French), *Confessio Amantis* (English) and *Vox Clamantis* (Latin).

Nearby is a Norman doorway whose jambs may have been the entrance to the Norman chapter house. Step inside the doorway to see the illuminated bases – again the level is 2ft (60cm) lower than the present cathedral floor.

Walk into the **north transept** (4), where there are monuments to Joyce Austin, Lionel Lockyer and Richard Blisse. Although the design of the transept dates from the 13th century, the walls are believed to have a Norman core. A curiosity here is the sword-rest against the north wall; it is dated 1674 and, unusually, is made of wood. It came from the Church of St Olave in Southwark, demolished in 1926.

Now amble under an unusual stilted arch into the north choir aisle and turn immediately left into the **Harvard Chapel** (5), which has traces of Norman work. Originally the Chapel of St John the Evangelist, this was restored in 1905 and received a thorough renovation in 1975 thanks to funds from Harvard University. John Harvard (1607–1638) was born in Southwark in 1607, the son of a butcher. The cathedral's register shows that he was baptized in St Saviour's. He emigrated to New England, where he left his books and some money to a recently founded college at Cambridge, Massachusetts, which college later became Harvard University.

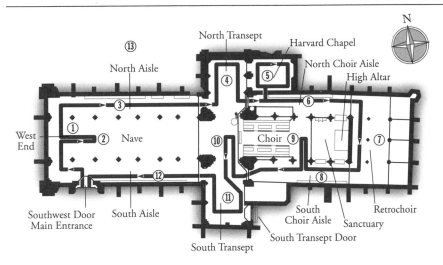

N

Key

1. West End
2. Nave
3. North Aisle

4. North Transept
5. Harvard Chapel
6. North Choir Aisle
7. Retrochoir
8. South Choir Aisle

9. Choir
10. Crossing
11. South Transept
12. South Aisle
13. Chapter House

'Gentleman Portar to King James I'

Go back into the **north choir aisle** (6), passing the organ (its case is in the south aisle) which dates from 1897; it has two tremolos, twenty-seven couplers, sixty-four speaking stops, and four manuals. Continue along the aisle, noting a series of monuments on the north wall.

The first is the **Trehearne Monument**, showing John Trehearne, 'Gentleman Portar to King James I' and his wife and beneath them a family at prayer. It is claimed that Trehearne was one of the four parishioners who bought St Saviour's from James l in 1614. Next comes a wooden effigy of a knight, thought to have been carved between 1280 and 1300. It is possibly a knight of the Warenne family, who were benefactors of the priory. Opposite the effigy is the beautifully carved **Nonesuch Chest**, believed to date from 1588.

Perceived Heresies

You now come to the 13th-century **retrochoir** (7), which measures four bays by three and is arguably the most fascinating part of the cathedral. The architecture is Early English almost throughout; particularly attractive is the blind tracery on the west wall. Memorials abound. One gruesome example shows a reclining figure, obviously a decomposing body in a shroud; this may have been one of the early priors. Note, too, the simple wooden modern sculpture in memory of John Robinson (1919–1983), the Bishop of Woolwich whose thought-provoking book *Honest to God* (1963) caused an uproar among more orthodox members of the Church of England.

The east end of the retrochoir is marked by four chapels dedicated, from north to south, to St Andrew, to St Christopher, to Our Lady, and to St Francis and

St Elizabeth of Hungary. On the south wall of the retrochoir is the Rider Memorial Window, built around the turn of the century in preparation for the designation of the church as a cathedral. The spacious area of the retrochoir was used at times as a consistory court by the various bishops of Winchester; the trial of the Marian Martyrs took place here in the time of Bishop Gardiner. Gardiner must have been a man who easily ignored his conscience. He acted as Henry VIII's advocate to the Pope when the king wanted a divorce, yet years later, in the reign of Mary Tudor, he was suddenly a good Catholic who approved the brutal persecution of Protestants.

Proceed now into the **south choir aisle** (8), which contains two notable memorials to former bishops. Immediately to your right is the tomb of Bishop Lancelot Andrewes (1555–1626). A flamboyant affair, dripping with gold leaf and coats-of-arms, it was restored by Sir Ninian Comper in 1930. Next to it is the monument to Bishop Edward Talbot, who in 1905–11 was the first Bishop of Southwark.

Architectural Delights

Turn immediately right into the **choir** (9). This area of the cathedral is another example of Early English at its purest, with a pleasing balance to the different levels. At ground level there are five bays. The piers, which alternate between octagonal and circular, lead to triple vaulting shafts. The triforium level has a row of pointed arches; the clerestory above has triple arcading.

Walk now towards the **sanctuary**, which is dominated by the superb altar screen. Built by Bishop Richard Fox or Foxe (c1448–1528) in 1520, it has three tiers of niches; the statues were added from 1905 onwards. The lower tier was gilded by Comper in 1930. Note also in this area the thrones for the bishops of the diocese.

Return to the south choir aisle and step into the **crossing** (10). The tower is supported by four 14th-century piers. Gazing up at the painted wooden roof of the tower, your attention is inevitably drawn to the Great Chandelier, which was given to the church by Dorothy Applebye, a brewer's widow, in 1680. Its main symbolic features are a crown, a mitre and a dove. The tower has twelve bells, eight of which go back to 1424 and the remainder to 1735. In recent years, four have been recast.

Walk into the **south transept** (11), which is usually full of chairs so that viewing is difficult. The transept was rejigged by Cardinal Beaufort in 1420 – look for his coat-of-arms on one of the shafts of the vaulting. There are also some mildly interesting busts of church benefactors.

The Bard of Avon

Finally you come to the **south aisle** (12). The most notable feature here is the Shakespeare Memorial, dating from 1911. It shows the Bard reclining in thoughtful pose with a Southwark scene carved in relief behind him. Above the memorial is the Shakespeare Window, designed in 1954 to replace an earlier one destroyed during World War II. Shakespeare lived in Southwark parish from 1599, working at the Globe and other theatres. Arguably his four greatest plays – *Hamlet, Othello, Macbeth* and *King Lear* – were written in Southwark for the Globe. He returned to his birthplace, Stratford, in 1611 and died there five years later. His brother Edmund was buried in this church in 1607, but the site of his grave is unknown.

Alongside the Shakespeare Memorial is a small plaque in memory of Sam

Wanamaker (1919–1993), the US actor and director who was instrumental in the reconstruction of the Globe Theatre.

Return now to the west end, where the tour began. You'll almost certainly, however, wish to visit the new **chapter house** (13). Composed of the same flint and limestone as the cathedral, and located on the site of the old medieval priory, this was opened in 1988 by Elizabeth II. Apart from the chapter room, the building includes a restaurant, bookshop, toilets and, on the upper floor, an art gallery.

WALKING TOUR FROM SOUTHWARK CATHEDRAL

The walk takes in a variety of riverside features, from HMS *Belfast* to old inns and the rebuilt Globe Theatre. Historic elements include the notorious 'Clink' Prison and the remains of Winchester Palace. En route you see plenty of examples of the way the riverside has been sympathetically redeveloped since the closure of the port facilities.

Start and finish: The cathedral.
Length: 2 miles (3.2km).
Time: 1½ hours, but longer if you want to visit the museums and places of interest.
Refreshments: Hosts of food outlets cater for the many office workers in the area. Modern riverside inns include the Horniman and the Founder's Arms, both on Riverside Walk; older establishments include the George in Borough High Street, the only galleried inn left in London, and the 18th-century Anchor Inn, the only survivor of the twenty-two inns which once lined Bankside.

Leave the cathedral's east end and climb the steps up to Borough High Street. Cross by the pedestrian crossing and head towards **London Bridge**.

The first bridge over the Thames was constructed by the Romans and made of wood. It was probably destroyed and rebuilt several times. The first stone bridge dates from 1176, and eventually houses, shops and a chapel were built on it; it had a drawbridge and gate at the Southwark end. Until 1750, when Westminster Bridge was built, this was the only bridge across the Thames in London. The old London Bridge was demolished in 1831 and replaced with a stone, five-arched structure that stood slightly upriver from the present bridge. In 1967 it was bought by a US entrepreneur, dismantled and reassembled in Arizona. The latest London Bridge dates from 1973.

The New Reveres the Old

Turn down the steps on the downstream side of the bridge. You are now on **Riverside Walk**, the final Southwark section of which was opened in 1994. In the days when the area was part of the Port of London this section was known as Hay's Wharf. Its old warehouses have been converted into apartments, offices, shops and pubs. Note on the left the London Bridge City Pier, whence people take riverboats upstream to Westminster or downstream to Greenwich.

Walk onto the pontoon which leads out to **HMS Belfast**. Launched in 1938, this cruiser saw distinguished service in World War II, taking part in the destruction of the *Scharnhorst* in the Battle of the North Cape and playing a supporting role in the Normandy landings. Recently repainted, it is now permanently moored at Southwark and you can see all of its seven decks.

45

Return along Riverside Walk. On the left is the **Horniman**, a modern riverside pub named after Thomas Horniman, the Victorian grocer who brought tea from many parts of the world to his warehouse on this site.

Turn left into **Hay's Galleria**, located on the site of Hay's Dock, built by Sir William Cubitt (1785–1861) in 1856 and designed for the speedy 19th-century tea clippers. Hay's Galleria is a thriving example of the way the riverside has been regenerated. The Victorian architecture has been maintained and the former dock area covered with a glass roof. There are shops, restaurants and bistros on the various levels, with the whole development dominated by a huge modern kinetic sculpture by David Kemp. Southwark Tourist Information Centre may be found on the basement level, next to the toilets.

Horrors!

Walk through the Galleria and out onto Tooley Street, to where the river's warehouses once extended. The name Tooley is believed to be corrupted from St Olave's Street, referring to the church demolished in 1926, itself named after King Olave of Norway, an ally of King Ethelred of England. Turn right in Tooley Street and head back towards London Bridge. On the south side of the street, under London Bridge Station, is the **London Dungeon** which, claiming to be the 'World's First Medieval

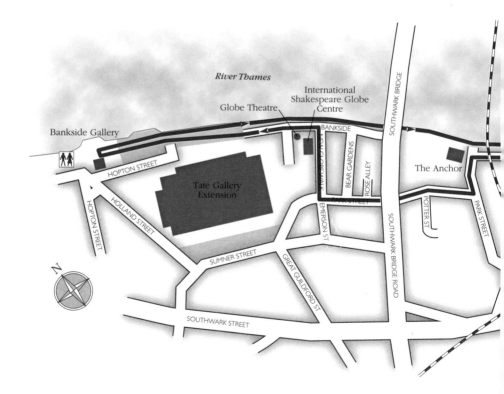

Horror Museum', uses frightening multimedia effects to present shows such as 'The Theatre of the Guillotine' and 'The Great Fire of London'. Not for the squeamish!

Fork left along Duke Street Hill, parallel with the arches of the railway, and turn left into Borough High Street, which marks the course of the old Roman causeway across the marshes. Turn briefly left into St Thomas Street, noting on the right the Bunch of Grapes, a Victorian-style pub which is full of atmosphere. On the left, at No. 9A, is The **Old Operating Theatre Museum**. This was rediscovered in 1956 in the roof of an 18th-century church and shows a genuine early Victorian operating theatre, with a wooden operating table and a number of simple instruments, which would have been used without benefit of anaesthetics. Also in this roof space is a herb garret, where the hospital apothecary cultivated his medicinal herbs.

On the north side of St Thomas Street are the extensive buildings of **Guy's Hospital**, founded by Thomas Guy (*c*1644–1724) in 1726. The son of a Thames boatman, he became a bookseller and publisher and, with the help of shrewd investments, became a wealthy man. He was a governor of St Thomas's Hospital, which once stood in the same road opposite Guy's (St Thomas's has now moved to Westminster). When he realized St Thomas's could not cope with the medical demands of the area he set up Guy's, leaving £220,000 in his will for its maintenance. He is buried in the hospital chapel.

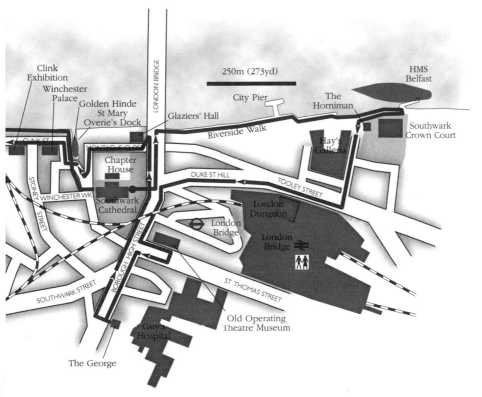

A Coaching Inn and Glaziers' Hall

Return to Borough High Street and turn left. After a hundred yards or so (100m) turn left into an alleyway where you'll find the long frontage of the **George**. Voted the 1995 Pub of the Year by the *Evening Standard*, the George is the only galleried pub left in London. Dating from 1676 and built on the site of an earlier inn, it originally stretched around three sides of a courtyard, but the north and west wings were demolished in 1899 to make way for railway buildings. It has been administered since 1937 by the National Trust. The George was one of a number of coaching inns in Southwark, each the starting point for destinations in southern England.

Cross Borough High Street and return towards London Bridge, passing on the left the cathedral and the appropriately named Barrow Boy and Banker pub. Immediately on the left and adjacent to the Thames is **Glaziers' Hall**. Built in 1808 as a warehouse, this had two floors and a Georgian facade added in 1850. It is the home of the Worshipful Company of Glaziers, who gained their charter in 1639. In more recent years it has become also the headquarters of the Worshipful Companies of Scientific Instrument Makers and Launderers.

Take the steps down from the hall into Montague Close, passing on the left the Mudlark pub, popular at lunchtime with office workers. You now have an excellent view of the exterior of the cathedral (note the flying buttresses along the side of the nave) and the **chapter house**. Prominent outside is a modern sculpture of an armoured knight by Alan Collins.

Mercantile Connections

At the end of Montague Close is the brick-and-glass Minerva House, the offices of a banking group. Just past Minerva House turn right into Pickford's Wharf and further right to **St Mary Overie's Dock**, where a notice tells you that the dock is still 'a free landing place at which parishioners of St Saviour's parish are entitled to land goods free of toll'. Floating in the dock today is a replica of the *Golden Hinde*, the ship in which Sir Francis Drake (*c*1540–1596) became the first Englishman to circumnavigate the globe (1577–80). This replica is not just a mock-up: it too has sailed around the world, clocking up over 140,000 sea miles. Five decks of the ship can be seen.

Opposite the ship is the Old Thameside Inn, located in a former warehouse; outside tables overlook the river. Just to the side is a viewing platform from where you can see a superb vista of the city from St Paul's in the west to the Tower in the east. The buildings can be located on a scenic plaque unveiled by Sam Wanamaker in July 1988 as part of the Riverside Walk.

The Clink

Return inland to Pickford's Wharf and turn right into Clink Street. On the left are the ruins of **Winchester Palace**, the remains of the town house of the bishops of Winchester. The site was bought by Henry de Blois, Bishop of Winchester 1144–9, and it became the administrative centre for much episcopal business. As well as the palace there were gardens, courtyards and a prison (the notorious Clink). The surrounding estate reared sheep and pigs.

The palace was sold in the middle of the 17th century and warehouses built on the site. The excavated remains – they were first exposed in 1814 when a fire destroyed a mustard factory built on the site – show part of the inner north court-yard. The three doorways in the surviving wall – the west end of the main hall – led to the kitchen and domestic quarters, with a stone cellar below. The most important surviving feature is the elaborate but heavily eroded rose window. Probably dating from the early 14th century, it is constructed from Reigate Stone and its geometric design probably contained painted *grisaille* glass.

You are now in the part once known, ironically, as 'The Liberty of the Clink' – an area of some 70 acres (28ha) under the Bishop of Winchester's jurisdiction which was the red light district of the time. The population of the bishop's prison reflected the region's diverse activities: erring priests rubbed shoulders (if nothing else) with prostitutes. Opened in the 12th century, the prison was destroyed in 1780. It was one of a number of Southwark prisons, probably located here to be outside the City of London's walls. Conditions were appalling, with torture common and lack of food the norm. Many of the prisons contained mere debtors, incarcerated there until someone could bail them out. Charles Dickens's father spent time as a debtor in Marshalsea Prison, which was not closed until 1842. The King's Bench prison, on the east side of Borough High Street, was another well known debtors' and military prison. The Horsemonger Lane gaol, built in 1791, was notorious for the public hangings outside its main gate, one of which was observed by Dickens.

Today's **'Clink Prison'**, located on the site of the original, aims to give you a realistic idea of the medieval conditions. Attractions include hands-on experience of torture devices!

Theatreland

Now go under Cannon Street Railway Bridge, turn left and then immediately right into **Park Street**.

On your left is the site of the old Anchor Brewery, marked by a plaque listing the names of the various brewers who operated there. The best known was Barclay & Perkins, dating from 1787. They were taken over in 1955 by Courage, who closed the brewery down in 1980 – signally failing to appreciate the growing movement in favour of real ale. Southwark had been a brewing centre since the Middle Ages, when hops were brought from Kent and Hereford and stored in warehouses before being sold to the brewers. The Hop and Malt Exchange can still be seen in Borough High Street; it dates from 1861.

Continue along Park Street into what in medieval times was the theatre district. On the left, now hidden by hoardings, is the site of the original **Globe Theatre**. At the time of writing there is considerable controversy about the site, which is awaiting development. Academics want a full-scale archaeological survey, but this is being resisted by the Department of the Environment.

Pass the *Financial Times* building and go under Southwark Road Bridge. Immediately on your right is the site of the Rose Theatre, concealed under a modern office block whose owners are obliged to allow visitors to see the remains. The Rose was built in 1587 by Philip Henslowe (d1616). Its leading actor was his step-son Edward Alleyn (1566–1626), who performed in many plays by Shakespeare and by Christopher Marlowe (1564–1593). The Rose did not last long, however, being demolished when Henslowe's lease ran out in 1605. The other two theatres in

Southwark were the Swan and the Hope, the latter having been converted by Henslowe from a bear-baiting arena.

Now turn right along New Globe Walk to the reconstruction of the **New Globe**. The first Globe Theatre opened in 1599 and was much larger than the other Southwark theatres, possibly holding as many as 3000 people. It burnt down in 1613 when the straw roof caught fire from a cannon shot used in a performance of *Henry VIII*. Legend has it that all escaped unhurt except a man whose trousers were ablaze; the flames were doused with ale! The Globe was rebuilt, this time with a tiled roof, and performances continued until the Puritans closed it in 1642.

The building of the New Globe was inspired by the late Sam Wanamaker. The design is as close as possible to what is known of the original building, and uses the traditional materials of the time – timber, wattle and daub, thatch, etc. The audiences sit on benches or stand in the yard in the open. Building was completed in late 1997 and the theatre is now the centrepiece of the International Shakespeare Globe Centre.

Bankside

You are now at **Bankside**. The original embankment was built to prevent the Bishop of Winchester's land from being flooded. On your left is a row of houses, Cardinal's Wharf, and in among them is Cardinal's Cap Alley. This alley once led to the Cardinal's Cap Inn, a favourite haunt of the Shakespearean actors. The inn was probably named after Cardinal Wolsey (*c*1475–1530), who was briefly Bishop of Winchester in the early 16th century. A plaque on the wall of No. 49 Cardinal's Wharf tells you that Christopher Wren (1632–1723) lived there during the construction of St Paul's Cathedral.

Continue along Riverside Walk, noting on the left the hulk of **Bankside Power Station**. This was the last work of Sir Giles Gilbert, grandson of the great Victorian architect Sir George Gilbert Scott (1811–1878). Sir Giles also designed the Bodleian Library, Waterloo Bridge and the chamber of the House of Commons. Bankside Power Station was built in 1948, with further additions and modifications in 1963. It is now redundant as a power station and the building is being converted into an offshoot of the Tate Gallery, specializing in modern art, to be opened in 2000.

Until then you could do worse than explore the **Bankside Gallery** in Hopton Street, close to the Blackfriars Railway Bridge. This small independent gallery is the home of the Royal Watercolour Society and the Royal Society of Painter–Printmakers. Most of the work is for sale.

Return eastwards along Riverside Walk until you see the **Anchor Inn** on the right. The only surviving inn of the twenty-two which once lined the river at Bankside, this has been in its time a chapel, a coffee shop, a brewery and a chandlery. Rebuilt in the 18th century, it is much older than it looks from the outside. Inside there is a minstrels' gallery, masses of oak beams and hiding places where customers could avoid the press gangs. Among the Anchor's customers have been Sir Joshua Reynolds (1723–1792) and Samuel Johnson (1709–1784).

Most of the Bankside inns were at one time or other brothels or 'stews' and, as the pubs came under the jurisdiction of the Bishop of Winchester, the prostitutes were known as 'Winchester Geese'. Henry VIII closed the stews in the mid-16th century.

From the Anchor, return along Clink Street to the cathedral, where the walk began.

Canterbury

Access: The M2 ends five miles (8km) short of the city; the M20, to the south, is the main route to the Channel ports. There are A-class roads from Margate, Maidstone, Whitstable, Herne Bay and Sandwich. National Express runs regular coaches from London, Gatwick and Dover. Buses to neighbouring towns are run by Stagecoach. Mainline trains from London stop at Canterbury East, five minutes' walk from the city centre. Canterbury West serves rural lines from Ashford and Ramsgate.

Few – if any – English cathedral cities have the attraction of Canterbury, the home of the mother church of the Anglican communion. The site of the most popular pilgrims' shrine in the country in the Middle Ages, Canterbury continues to attract visitors today; with the completion of the Channel Tunnel in 1994, a high proportion are now from the European mainland.

Archaeological work has confirmed there was a pre-Roman settlement on the site, but it was not until the 2nd century that the Romans began to build the formidable walled city, Durovernum Cantiacorum, which was to flourish for four centuries. Ironically, it was the Blitz which uncovered the great extent of Roman Canterbury, which had a huge D-shaped theatre, a forum and numerous temples.

At the fall of the Roman Empire during the early part of the 5th century the town was abandoned, although Danes and Jutes had small settlements in the vicinity. When St Augustine (d604) arrived in Britain at the end of the 6th century, full of Christianizing zeal, he found a thriving Kentish kingdom. He was well received by King Ethelbert and his wife Bertha and allowed to restore a church on the site of the present cathedral; Augustine became the first Archbishop of Canterbury. He later founded St Augustine's Abbey and Christ Church Priory at the cathedral; these two religious houses dominated Canterbury life for the next five centuries.

The martyrdom of Archbishop Thomas à Becket (1118–1170) in the Norman cathedral brought thousands of pilgrims to Canterbury over the succeeding 300 years and more. As a result of the building of inns and hostels for the pilgrims, the city began to expand outside the Norman walls. However, in the 1530s Henry VIII broke with Rome, dissolved the monasteries and removed Becket's shrine, and consequently Canterbury lost its prominence, particularly when the archbishop's seat was moved to Lambeth Palace in London.

Kent, however, began to receive religious refugees from mainland Europe. Among these were the Walloons, many of whom settled in the town and brought their textiles industry with them. There were English dissenters, too; it was in Canterbury that the Pilgrim Fathers planned the voyage of the *Mayflower*.

For the next three centuries Canterbury was, in essence, just a sleepy market town – even the Industrial Revolution did little to change this. The tranquillity was considerably disturbed, however, when in 1942 Canterbury became one of the targets of Germany's Baedeker Raids; in the fire-bombing of the city the cathedral remained relatively unscathed. The postwar years have seen the establishment here of the University of Kent and, more recently, the construction of the Channel Tunnel. Today, of Canterbury Cathedral's 2½ million annual visitors, more than half are believed to come from abroad.

As noted, the first cathedral was probably built *c*600, but later additions must have been impressive: excavations carried out in 1993 revealed the foundations of this building, one of the largest in the Western World at the time. The Anglo-Saxon cathedral suffered many indignities at the hands of marauding Danes, who on one occasion kidnapped and killed the archbishop. In 1067 the cathedral was almost totally destroyed by a fire which also swept through much of the town. The first of the Norman archbishops, Lanfranc (*c*1005–1089), rebuilt the nave within ten years and added a modest sanctuary. This work, in Romanesque style, was continued by his successor, St Anselm (1033–1109), who added the delightful staircase towers against the east transepts, the massive crypt and the quire above. Fire took a hand again in 1174, destroying the eastern end of the building. The crypt, which at that time contained Becket's tomb, was spared, as was the Norman nave.

By now the pilgrims were bringing considerable wealth to the cathedral, and it was decided that Becket's tomb needed a more worthy home. A French master-builder, William of Sens (d1180), was hired to rebuild the east end. Retaining the original outer walls and eastern towers, he constructed a new quire which pioneered the new Early English Gothic style in Britain. Unfortunately, William fell from the scaffolding and had to be replaced by William the Englishman, who completed the quire with the Trinity Chapel, where St Thomas's shrine was to be placed. The eastern end of the cathedral was finished off with the circular corona, giving this part of the building a 'continental' look that is unique among English cathedrals. The revenue from pilgrims also undoubtedly paid for the magnificent stained glass.

A succession of imaginative priors made some significant additions, such as the chapter house, with its stunning wooden wagon-vaulted roof, the stone choir screen and the great cloister, with its hundreds of bosses. Lanfranc's Norman nave was by now looking rather dated and in 1377 work began on its demolition. The designer of the new nave was Henry Yevele, fresh from triumphs at Westminster Abbey, who used the Perpendicular style to great effect. The final additions to the cathedral were the two west transepts and the west towers, all in Perpendicular style, followed in the 1490s by the dominating central tower, Bell Harry, the work of John Wastell.

Meanwhile the Priory of Christ Church and the neighbouring St Augustine's Monastery were facing hard times. Visited by Henry VIII's commissioners, the priory had to witness the spoliation of Becket's shrine and shortly afterwards, in 1540, the monks formally succumbed. Many of them, however, became members of the new cathedral foundation under the first dean, Nicholas Wotton.

There was a considerable amount of destruction during the Civil War, when Cromwell's troops inflicted enormous damage on the monuments and stained glass. The 17th and 18th centuries at Canterbury were, as with many English cathedrals, times of apathy and decay and it was not until the 19th century that the Victorians began to renovate. Fortunately, their efforts here were more sensitive than in many other similar buildings. A poignant, more recent scene was the visit of Pope John XXIII (1881–1963), who knelt in prayer with the then Archbishop of Canterbury, Robert Runcie (1921–) at the spot where Becket was murdered.

TOUR OF THE CATHEDRAL

Start: The Christ Church Gateway.
Finish: The southwest transept.

At the **Christ Church Gateway** (1) you must pay an entrance fee to gain access to the cathedral precincts and the cathedral itself. The gateway was built by Henry VII either to celebrate the marriage of his son Prince Arthur to Catherine of Aragon or as a memorial following Arthur's early death. (Arthur, the Prince of Wales, died aged 16. Catherine later was married to his brother, Henry VIII.) Perpendicular in style, it was restored in the 1930s. The many shields-of-arms are those of Henry VII's supporters, but the dominating feature is the copper-green statue of Christ, sculpted by Klaus Ringwald in 1990 to replace the original, lost to the Puritans in the 1600s.

Pass through the gateway and head towards the cathedral's Perpendicular **west end** (2). With two bell towers and a large central window, the west end is hemmed in by buildings and does not have the 'presence' you'd expect from a cathedral. Enter the cathedral through the southwest porch, a richly carved Victorian addition, and step into the **nave** (3). Designed and built by Henry Yevele between 1377 and 1405, the nave is a Perpendicular masterpiece. The first impression is of height: the tall, slender arcade has only a token clerestory above it and a triforium which is little more than a downward extension of the layer above. The main light comes from the aisle windows. The piers rise 80ft (24m) to a simple but pleasing *lierne* vaulting.

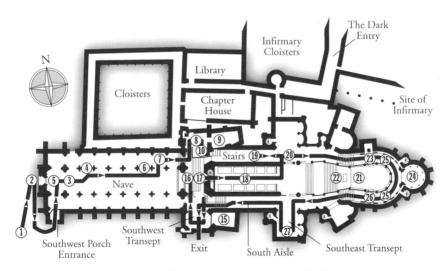

Key

1. Christ Church Gateway
2. West End
3. Nave
4. Font
5. West Window
6. Victorian Pulpit
7. Hales Family Monument
8. Martyrdom Chapel
9. Lady Chapel
10. No's 10-14 see map of Crypt
15. St Michael's Chapel
16. Bell Harry Tower
17. Pulpitum
18. Choir
19. Bible Windows
20. Chichele Tomb
21. Trinity Chapel
22. St Augustine's Chair
23. Tomb of Henry IV and Joan of Navarre
24. Corona
25. Miracle Windows
26. Tomb of the Black Prince
27. Modern Stained Glasss Windows

On the north side of the nave is the **font** (4), which dates from Stuart times; smashed by Cromwell's men in the 17th century, it has been carefully restored. Made of marble, it has figures representing the twelve Apostles around its base. The cover is raised and lowered by a pulley system.

Turn around to face the **west window** (5), which has some of the oldest stained glass in Europe, dating back to the beginning of the 13th century. At the centre of the bottom row you'll see Adam, expelled from Eden and dressed in an animal skin, busily digging. Above are Apostles, saints and 15th-century kings.

Two-thirds of the way along the nave, on the north side, is the **Victorian Pulpit** (6), which is finely coloured and carved in wood. To its right, on the slightly raised floor, is a compass rose placed there in 1988 to symbolize the worldwide communion of the Anglican Church.

Money and Martyrdom

Cross into the north aisle, where (as in the south aisle) there are monuments set into the wall. Of particular interest is the **Hales Family Monument** (7), placed here *c*1596. Sir James Hales was treasurer to the Portuguese Expedition of 1589 and the upper part of the monument, which is made of alabaster, shows his son being buried at sea, the weighted body dangling above the waves.

At the end of the north aisle the official route takes you into the most poignant part of the cathedral, the **Martyrdom Chapel** (8) in the northwest transept. It was here that Thomas à Becket was murdered on 29 December 1170 by four knights who believed they were obeying the wishes (and probably were) of Henry II. The spot where the deed was committed is marked by a simple modern altar, over which is a dramatically lit sculpture of swords and a cross. The north window of the transept is known as the Royal Window because of the fine stained glass showing a number of English kings.

Before leaving the transept, peep into the **Lady Chapel** (9), just to the left of the altar. Sometimes known as the Deans' Chapel, it has some superb 15th-century fan vaulting.

Norman Capital in the Crypt

The Crypt

Now go to the right of the Becket altar through a dogtooth Norman arch and down the steps into the **crypt** (10), which is generally agreed to be the finest in the country. Its western end is Romanesque, with rounded arches supported by stumpy pillars, every other one of which is carved. The capitals have some remarkable carving of animals and monsters, probably done *in situ*. In the centre of the crypt is the **Chapel of Our Lady of the Undercroft** (11), which has 14th-century delicately carved screens and painted stonework.

Walk along the north side of the crypt towards the eastern end, built by William the Englishman and marked by the slightly pointed arches. Becket's body lay here from his Martyrdom in 1170 until it was taken to the Trinity Chapel above in 1220. At the extreme east end of the crypt is the delightful Jesus Chapel, which has good stained glass.

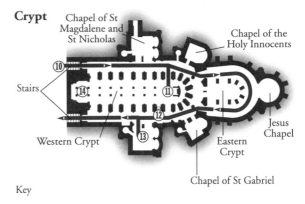

Crypt

Chapel of St Magdalene and St Nicholas

Chapel of the Holy Innocents

Stairs

Western Crypt

Eastern Crypt

Jesus Chapel

Chapel of St Gabriel

Key

10. From ground floor
11. Chapel of Our Lady of the Undercroft
12. Tomb of John Morton
13. Black Prince's Chantry
14. Cathedral Treasury

Return along the south side of the crypt, where the Chapel of St Gabriel is worth a look for its 12th-century wall paintings. On the other side of the aisle is the flamboyant **Tomb of John Morton** (12). Archbishop from 1486 to 1500, Morton was a zealous supporter of Henry VII's fiscal policy. Look at the gilded and coloured arch above the tomb, where the heads have been removed from all the statues, including those of the eagles! Almost opposite the tomb is the **Black Prince's Chantry** (13), founded in 1363 by Edward III's eldest son, Edward the Black Prince, in return for the papal dispensation that allowed him to marry his divorced cousin Joan, known as the 'Fair Maid of Kent'. The chantry is now used on Sundays by the Huguenot community, with the service spoken in French.

Before you leave the crypt, notice on your right the **cathedral treasury** (14), which contains the usual church plate and regalia, both from the cathedral and from churches in the diocese.

Warriors and Choirboys

Leave the crypt on the south side and climb the steps into the southwest transept. On its east side is **St Michael's Chapel** (15), sometimes known as the Warriors' Chapel. Hanging from the walls are the colours and other mementoes of the Royal East Kent Regiment – the Buffs. Dominating the centre is a massive tomb with three effigies – those of the influential Lady Margaret Holland and her two husbands, the Earl of Somerset and the Duke of Clarence.

Outside the chapel, to the left, is a model of the sailing ship HMS *Canterbury*. Below it is the ship's bell, which is rung daily at 11:00 while one page of the memorial book to the dead is turned over.

Go into the crossing, climb the steps in front of the choir screen and take a look up into the lantern of **Bell Harry Tower** (16). This was constructed between 1494 and 1504; beneath its stone veneer there are believed to be nearly a quarter of a million bricks. Designed by John Wastell, the lantern has some intricate fan vaulting interspersed with delicate carving. The central blue-and-white cathedral shield conceals a trapdoor through which stone was hauled up to complete the tower's exterior.

Turn towards the **choir screen** or **pulpitum** (17). This was built at the time of Prior Chillenden in the early days of the 15th century, when it was the practice to separate the people in the nave from the monks in the choir. The screen has statues of six English kings: Henry V, Richard II and Ethelbert to the left of the door and Edward the Confessor, Henry VI and Henry VI to the right.

Step through the pulpitum door, which has 15th-century iron gates, into the **choir** (18). Designed by William of Sens and completed by William the Englishman, the choir replaced the earlier Norman structure which was destroyed by the fire of 1174. Sens retained the outer Norman walls, but the interior is a pioneer work in the Early English Gothic style, with pointed arches. The Caen Stone piers are alternately octagonal and circular, rising to Corinthian capitals whence engaged shafts of Purbeck marble lead up to the base of the clerestory. The sexpartite vaulting is typical of the early Gothic in France, as in Notre Dame de Paris. The three levels of arcade, triforium and clerestory are in the classic proportion of 50:25:25, and are completely different from the nave, which was built later.

There is much to see in the choir, including the stalls carved by Roger Davis in 1682, the Victorian stone *cathedra*, the brass lectern (dating from 1663) and, at the east end, the simple high altar.

Leave the choir *via* the north side and walk into the north choir aisle. Immediately to the left are the world-famous **Bible Windows** (19), whose stained glass is among the finest in Europe. A series of squares and circles depict Bible stories and miracles from both Old and New Testaments. In past centuries many of the congregation could not read, and they relied on pictorial features like stained glass and murals for their religious instruction.

More stained glass can be seen in the **rose window** in the nearby east transept. Opposite the transept is the magnificently gilded and coloured **Chichele Tomb** (20). The tomb shows Archbishop Henry Chichele (*c*1362–1443) in his complete vestments; below this lies his *gisant*, or naked figure. Chichele founded All Souls' College in Oxford to commemorate those who died at the Battle of Agincourt.

Stroll now into the ambulatory, passing on the left St Andrew's Chapel, which has some recently restored medieval wall paintings. To the right is the **Trinity Chapel** (21), completed by William the Englishman for St Thomas's shrine, which rested here from 1220 until 1538, when Henry VIII had it destroyed. The actual site of the shrine is marked by a burning candle, while to the west is an intricate marble pavement, the **Opus Alexandrium**, dating from the 13th century and probably made in Rome. Notice, too, the zodiacal pavement, laid down at the same time. Next to the pavement and immediately east of the high altar is the 13th-century **St Augustine's Chair** (22). It is in this crude grey-green marble chair that archbishops are enthroned as primates of all England.

Tombs of Royalty

In prestigious positions alongside where Becket's shrine used to be are the only two royal tombs in the cathedral. Beside the north aisle is the **Tomb of Henry IV and Joan of Navarre** (23). Carved in alabaster, possibly by Robert Brown, the effigies lie under a canopy showing the royal coat-of-arms. Henry IV, who spent much of his life fighting, was finally stricken by leprosy and died while praying at Westminster Abbey.

The ambulatory now takes us to the extreme eastern end of the cathedral and to the **Corona** (24), a chapel added, like the Trinity Chapel but later, to house a Becket relic – in this case the top of the martyr's head, sliced off by one of the murderous knights. More recently rededicated to the Saints and Martyrs of our Own Time, it contains interesting 13th-century stained glass, some prominent shafts of Purbeck marble and the tomb of the last Cardinal Archbishop, Reginald Pole (1500–1558).

The ambulatory continues around the south side of the Trinity Chapel, passing a set of **miracle windows** (25) that show some of the events and miracles of St Thomas's times. Almost immediately opposite is the **Tomb of the Black Prince** (26). Edward the Black Prince fought gallantly in his father's wars against France. During a campaign in Spain he contracted an illness which was to last until his death at the age of 46. His armoured effigy is of latten, but the blackening was apparently done in Victorian times. More recent evidence suggests that he never did wear a black armour, his nickname coming instead from his prowess on the battlefield. In the 1930s, accordingly, the black paint was removed to expose the original latten.

Above the tomb are copies of the Black Prince's battle accoutrements, such as gauntlets, helmet and vest. (The originals can be seen in a cabinet further along on the south side of the aisle.) Note on the tomb the Black Prince's shields; the one with the three feathers was taken on the field of battle and has ever since been the crest of the princes of Wales.

From one of the cathedral's oldest set of treasures let's move on to some of its newest. The **modern stained glass windows** (27) in the southeast transept were made by a Hungarian refugee, Ervin Bossanyi, in the 1950s. The east window denotes deliverance and salvation from evil while the west window represents peace among the nations of the world. The brilliance of the colours is stunning.

The tour concludes *via* the southwest transept and a covered way into the cathedral precincts.

WALKING TOUR FROM CANTERBURY CATHEDRAL
The walking tour is divided into two parts. The first, shorter walk is around the cathedral precincts and certain sections of the old Christ Church Priory. The second, longer walk leads you around the historic core of Canterbury, taking in the castle, old gates and walls, and a variety of domestic architecture.

Start and finish (shorter walk): The door of the southwest transept.
Start and finish (longer walk): The Christ Church Gateway.
Length: Shorter walk 660 yards (600m). Longer walk 2½ miles (4km).
Time: The shorter walk should take you ½ hour at most. The longer one takes 1½ hours, but you'll probably want more time than this in order to visit the museums and churches.
Refreshments: A good selection of food outlets. Ambience and good bar meals are provided by a number of historic pubs and coaching inns, including the City Arms (Butchery Lane), the 15th-century Three Tuns (Beer Cart Lane), the Pilgrims' Hotel (opposite the Marlowe Theatre – good blackboard menu) and the Cathedral Gate Hotel, which predates the nearby Christ Church Gate.

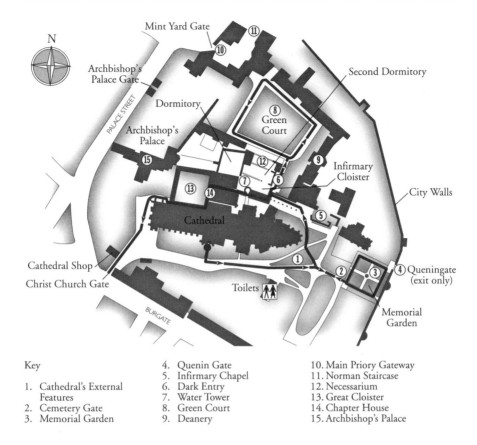

Mint Yard Gate
⑪
⑩
N
Archbishop's
Palace Gate
Second Dormitory
PALACE STREET
Dormitory
⑧
Green
Court
Archbishop's
Palace
⑮
⑫
⑨
Infirmary
Cloister
⑦
⑥
City Walls
⑬
⑭
⑤
Cathedral
①
Cathedral Shop
②
③
④ Queningate
(exit only)
Christ Church Gate
Toilets 🚻
Memorial
Garden
BURGATE

Key

1. Cathedral's External
   Features
2. Cemetery Gate
3. Memorial Garden

4. Quenin Gate
5. Infirmary Chapel
6. Dark Entry
7. Water Tower
8. Green Court
9. Deanery

10. Main Priory Gateway
11. Norman Staircase
12. Necessarium
13. Great Cloister
14. Chapter House
15. Archbishop's Palace

AROUND THE CATHEDRAL PRECINCTS

Walk eastwards onto the grassy area in front of the toilets, where there is a good view of the **cathedral's external features** (1).

Note first the Bell Harry Tower, rising to 235ft (72m) and completed *c*1500 by John Wastell. The Perpendicular style gives it a strong verticality, enhanced by the corner pinnacles. Complementing the main tower is the St Anselm Tower, hard against the southeast transept. The base dates from Anselm's time, but the upper parts, with their interlocking Norman arches, were added in 1160. This tower has its twin on the north side of the cathedral, the pair having survived the fire of 1174. Lastly, note the Corona at the east end of the cathedral; from the outside it looks almost completely detached from the rest of the building. On the grass near the east end is a modern statue, *The Son of Man*, by David McFaul.

Walk eastward towards the stone wall, passing over what was once the priory fish-pond. There are bee holes in the wall, reminding you that the monks produced much of their own food. Keep going until you reach the **cemetery gate** (2), with its impressive rounded Norman arch and dogtooth decoration. It is believed to have been built *c*1160, in the time of Prior Wybert.

Pass through the gate into the **memorial garden** (3). In the centre of the garden is a simple stone cross in memory of local soldiers who have died in times of war. The flint wall on the east side is part of the city walls and includes a large square bastion. An opening in the north corner leads to the **Queningate** (4). This was the route that Queen Bertha, wife of Ethelbert, took through the city wall when she went to pray in St Martin's Church. Today it presents a convenient way to get to the ruins of St Augustine's Abbey – or, at least, it *would* be a convenient way were it not for the fact that you're not allowed back into the cathedral precincts through the Queningate.

So turn back and head across to a line of old stone arches marking the ruins of the **infirmary chapel** (5). This chapel was provided for those monks who were too ill to attend the main mass. It was built *c*1150, but all that is left today are these Norman arches plus the occasional well carved capital and the remains of what must have been an impressive window on the north side.

A Haunted Alley

Walk past the spot where the infirmary itself stood and turn right into an alleyway known as the **Dark Entry** (6). This is reputed to be haunted, late on Friday evenings, by one Nell Cook. The tale is that during the days of Henry VIII a canon who lived by the Dark Entry had a servant, Ellen Bean, who was secretly in love with him; because of her skill in the kitchen he called her Nell(y) Cook. In time the canon's 'niece' came to stay with him, and Nell's jealousy was roused when she found out they were lovers. So she put poison in the pie they had for supper, and the cathedral authorities kept the deaths secret for fear of the scandal that might erupt. Nell vanished, and it was not until many years later that it was discovered she had dispatched herself by eating the rest of the pie.

This was revealed, so the tale goes, when three masons uncovered a skeleton and an incriminating piece of pie-crust! The three masons were dead within the twelve-month, one murdered and the other two hanged for the crime, and ever thereafter anyone who has seen the ghost of Nell Cook has likewise failed to live out the year.

Plumbing Matters

To reduce your chances of inadvertently sighting the ghost, look leftwards at the infirmary cloister, a grassy space once used for growing medicinal herbs. On its south side is the **water tower** (7) that once held the monastery's drinking water. The plumbing was evidently quite sophisticated. The water was taken from springs and put through settling tanks before coming to the monastery. From the water tower it was piped around the buildings; the dirty water was used to flush the monks' toilets.

Walk – briskly, if you're still worried about Nell Cook – along the Dark Entry, noting on your left the ruins of the old dormitories and on your right the Chequer Tower, all that survives of the priory's counting house. At the end of the passageway are the remains of the Prior's House and Prior's Gateway, the latter leading to the large grass-covered **Green Court** (8). This was the business centre of the priory, and some of the buildings around it have been sympathetically restored. Those still habitable are occupied by the King's School, one of the country's most highly respected public schools, whose foundation goes back to the time of Henry VIII. The buildings are not open to the public.

Turn right and walk round the square, passing on the right the old 12th-century bathhouse, now the **deanery** (9). Ahead is a row of buildings; from right to left these were the granary, the bakery and the brewery. In the far corner stands the **main priory gateway** (10). Behind this is the Mint Yard, the site of an old chapel which was the original building occupied by the King's School. To the right of the gate, is the **Norman staircase** (11); it once led to a hall that was part of the prior's guesthouse.

Continue your circuit of Green Court. On the south side are the ruins of the **necessarium** (12) – the monks' lavatory – reputed to seat fifty-six. Under it a large drain flowed continually.

The Great Cloister Area

Turn right to go back through the Dark Entry and at its end go right again along another gloomy alleyway, past the water tower until you reach the **Great Cloister** (13). Built in the late 14th or early 15th century, the present cloister is thought to be the fourth on this site. It is done in Perpendicular style; its fan vaulting is embellished with hundreds of roof bosses portraying the heraldic arms of people who contributed to the building of the cloister plus animals, monsters and religious symbols.

Turn left to find almost immediately the entrance door to the **chapter house** (14), the only monastic building to have survived fully intact. Almost 100ft (30m) long, it is the largest cathedral chapter house in Britain. The present building dates from the early 14th century and stands on the site of a Norman chapter house. The magnificent wooden (bog oak) roof dates to 1400. Note the impressive prior's 'throne' at the east end. Today, the chapter house is used mainly for concerts.

Leave the chapter house and continue round the cloister. In the southeast corner is the door through which Thomas à Becket entered the cathedral before his murder. Just by the cloister's exit look back at the chapter house, where the superb Perpendicular west end window, with its Victorian glass, is framed by what appears to be a typical 'Dutch end'.

Outside the cloister you can get a glimpse, to your right, of the **archbishop's palace** (15), built in the 19th century to replace one that burnt down in 1544; after a gap of almost 300 years, archbishops could once again reside at Canterbury.

Go back past the west end of the cathedral to the Christ Church Gateway, where this short walk ends. If you want, you can carry straight on into the longer walk.

Beyond Canterbury Cathedral

The Christ Church Gateway faces the **Buttermarket**, a small square which has always been at the centre of city life. The War Memorial in the middle marks the spot formerly occupied by a bull stake in the days when bull-baiting was popular. Leading off the Buttermarket is Mercery Lane, which has many old buildings with jettied walls; it was once full of pilgrims' inns and the shops of haberdashers and drapers. Note that many of the walls in Buttermarket are hung with 'mathematical tiles' to resemble bricks.

The Old Rush Market and the 'Leaning House'

Leave the Buttermarket by turning right into **Sun Street**, named after a pilgrim inn known as the Sun (now a shop); Charles Dickens (1812–1870) stayed at it when in

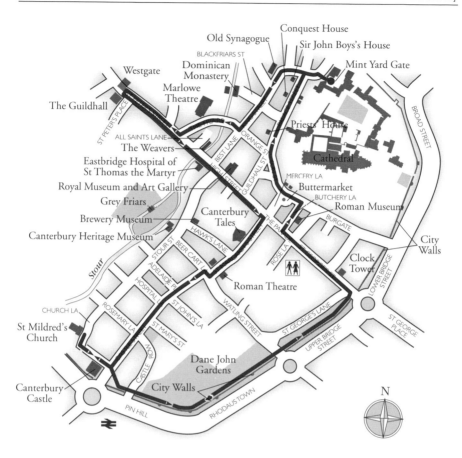

Canterbury. In medieval times Sun Street was the venue of the Rush Market – rushes were commonly used as a floor covering and for roofs.

Sun Street merges into **Palace Street**, named for the old bishop's palace, whose grounds stretched along its full length. This street is full of historic houses. The Pilgrim Fathers negotiated the hire of the *Mayflower* in a house on the right, now Beau's Creperie restaurant. Look on the left-hand side for the **Priests' House**, probably the oldest domestic building in Canterbury, a half-timbered Tudor building with jettied walls, carved beams and a grotesque in one corner. Further along on the left is **Conquest House**, another half-timbered house, now an antiques shop. It was in its 11th-century cellar that Becket's murderers are supposed to have plotted the deed. At the far end of Palace Street, on the corner with King Street, is **Sir John Boys's House**, now a bookshop. Sometimes known as the Leaning House, it was the home of Sir John Boys, a 16th-century lawyer and philanthropist. Note the crazy angles of the doors and windows and the fine carving on the timber posts.

Walk briefly to the right into The Borough to view the **Mint Yard Gate** of the former priory. The gate is a Victorian replacement of an earlier medieval gate, which was knocked down for redevelopment. The yard is named for an ancient coin mint discovered here. Inside the outer gate is the Almoner's Yard, where the poor of the town received alms from the priory. Further in is the main priory gate.

The Black Friars
Return now past Sir John Boys's House and fork left into King Street. If you look carefully on your right for a gap between the houses you should be able to spot the **Old Synagogue**. Behind pyramidal gateposts, the building is designed in Egyptian style, with prominent pillars and a balustrade. Built in the early 19th century, it is now owned by the King's School, who use it for music practice.

Further along King Street, stop at its junction with St Alphage Lane and Blackfriars Street. If you look left you'll find you have unexpectedly good views of the cathedral, while to your right are the surviving buildings of the **Dominican monastery**. The Dominicans, or Black Friars, came to Canterbury in 1221 and built a considerable complex of monastic buildings, of which only two survive. On the west side of the river is the old guesthouse or infirmary, while on the east side is the dining room, believed to date from the mid-13th century.

Walk to the end of King Street and turn right into The Friars. From the bridge over the Stour you get an excellent view of the friary. A little further along, on the right, you find the **Marlowe Theatre**, an unimposing building based in an old cinema. Christopher Marlowe (1564–1593), the author of *Doctor Faustus*, *Tamburlaine the Great*, *The Jew of Malta* and others, was born and educated in Canterbury; he died in a tavern brawl aged only 29. It has been claimed that he wrote some of Shakespeare's plays. The theatre puts on a varied programme, including music, dance and light entertainment. Opposite it are several convenient eating places.

Canterbury Tales
Continue to St Peter's Street (an extension of the High Street) and turn right, walking northeast towards the **Westgate**, which straddles an arm of the Stour. Of the eight gates around the city walls, this was the most important – it guarded the road to London, along which most of the pilgrims came – and has been rebuilt many times. The present Westgate dates from 1381 and was probably designed by Henry Yevele, also responsible for many parts of the cathedral. In the old days the Westgate contained a drawbridge and a portcullis, and was closed at night: pilgrims who did not reach the city in time had to sleep outside the walls – hence the many inns beyond the gate in St Dunstan's and London Road. It is claimed that the term to 'canter' originated when pilgrims spurred their horses on at 'Canterbury pace' to reach the city before the gate came down. The Westgate is now a museum, with displays concerning its time as a prison plus a comprehensive collection of Civil War weapons. There are superb views from the battlements.

Return along St Peter's Street towards the city centre. Just before you reach the bridge once more, make a quick diversion along **All Saints Lane**, a cul-de-sac on whose right-hand side is All Saints Court, a restored 15th-century half-timbered building with jettied walls and nicely carved grotesques on the support beams.

Return to St Peter's Street and look over the bridge at **The Weavers**, another half-timbered house, dating back to *c*1500. Flemish weavers worked here in the 16th and 17th centuries. A reproduction ducking stool protrudes out over the river.

Opposite is the **Eastbridge Hospital of St Thomas the Martyr**. Eastbridge was a hospital in the true sense of the word – i.e. it provided hospitality for poor pilgrims to the Shrine of St Thomas. Founded in 1180, it fell into decay but was refounded in 1342 by Archbishop John Stratford (d1348) and was probably busiest at the time when Geoffrey Chaucer (c1345–1400) was writing his *Canterbury Tales*. After Henry VIII ordered the destruction of St Thomas's shrine in 1538 there was another period of decline, but later archbishops arranged for the hospital to provide accommodation for the poor of the parish and it remains as almshouses today.

To the left of the entrance hall is a charming little chantry chapel. From here there are steps down into the Norman undercroft, which was used as a pilgrims' dormitory. Stratford decreed that only women over 40 (a good age at that time) should be appointed to be in charge, so that the pilgrims wouldn't be tempted! Stairs lead up to the refectory, built at the same time as the undercroft. The painting on the north wall, of Christ giving blessing, dates from the 13th century, having been hidden behind a chimney for many years. There is also a 'Minstrels' Gallery'; its panels are genuine late 16th-century, but the gallery was actually constructed in 1932. Finally, do not miss the 12th-century chapel, with its particularly fine wooden roof. Some of the sanctuary seats have misericords.

From the hospital, continue along the High Street. On your left is the imposing **Royal Museum and Art Gallery**, which is also the public library; it is sometimes known as the Beaney Institute, after its benefactor, a local doctor who made a fortune in Australia. The building is Victorian mock-Tudor. It is believed it may stand on the remains of the old Roman forum. The museum has a mixed collection of historical and archaeological artefacts and some military relics of the Buffs, while the gallery specializes in the work of the 19th-century local artist Sidney Cooper.

As you approach the modern part of the city, turn right into St Margaret's Street. On the right is **Canterbury Tales**, a theme museum based in the old St Margaret's Church. Chaucer's *Tales* are described with tableaux and realistic audiovisual presentations.

The crossroads at the end of St Margaret's Street marks the site of the **Roman Theatre**, believed to have been built c220 and to have thrived for the following 200 years. Traces of the foundations can still be seen in the basements of Alberry's Bistro and Slatter's Hotel.

All Saints Lane

Canterbury Castle

Continue southwest into Castle Street, which is lined with bistros, speciality shops and houses from all periods. On your left the Castle Gardens were once the churchyard of St Mary de Castro, long since disappeared. Eventually you get to **Canterbury Castle**, on your right. Construction of the castle began *c*1084. The finished structure consisted of a keep and a surrounding bailey, part of which included the Roman city walls. It was never a huge military success – it surrendered to the French Dauphin in 1216, to the Parliamentarians during the Civil War and was embarrassingly overrun by Wat Tyler's men during the Peasants' Revolt of 1381

All that remains today is the keep, which is the fifth largest in England. It acted as prison during the reign of Elizabeth I, while in this century it was a coal store for the local gasworks. There was an attempt to knock it down in the 18th century, but fortunately this got only as far as the top floor. The remains are now fully preserved.

You can make a short diversion here to **St Mildred's Church**, possibly the oldest parish church in Canterbury. Some 8th-century stonework can be seen in the south and west walls, and the south wall also has some reworked Roman tiles. St Mildred was the great-great-granddaughter of the Saxon King Ethelbert; after an education in Paris she became abbess of a convent at Minster-in-Thanet. Her body and relics were later acquired by St Augustine's Abbey in Canterbury.

Leave the church and walk back past the castle and across the carpark opposite to the steps which lead up to the **city walls**. Originally built by the Romans, the walls fell into decay before being rebuilt by the Normans. At their maximum extent they covered some 1½ miles (2.4km) and had eight gateways plus bastions and towers. Parts of the wall were destroyed during the Civil War and other stretches were taken down in the 18th century. Today about half of the original wall still stands.

We are going to follow part of the wall, going initially past the **Dane John Gardens**, landscaped during the 18th century when public executions were held here. Dominating the gardens is the Dane John Mound, thought to have been a Romano-British burial mound – if this is true the mound predates the wall. There is a small memorial dated 1803 to the gardens' benefactor, Alderman Simmons, on the top of the mound, which is reached by a spiral footpath.

Carry on along the wall past the bus station – which before 1956 was the site of the cattle market – until you reach the large roundabout with subways. This was the site of St George's Gate, demolished in 1801 when the New Dover Road was built. Descend the ramp and cross the road carefully into the pedestrianized St George's Street. This part of the city is modern; it was rebuilt after the Blitz. On the right is the **Clock Tower**, the only part of the Church of St George to survive German bombs.

Continue along St George's Street until older buildings start to dominate, then take a right turn into the narrow Butchery Lane. On the right, halfway along, is the **Roman Museum**. The Blitz actually helped reveal the extent of Durovernum Cantiacorum, hidden as it was under present-day Canterbury. The museum has a wide range of Roman artefacts, some authentic dioramas of Roman trades and professions and the latest hands-on computer reconstructions. The highlight is the large Roman pavement, which is actually *in situ*. Highly recommended.

Leave the museum and continue along Butchery Lane. Turn left at the end into Burgate, which takes you back to the Buttermarket.

Rochester

Access: Regular rail services from Victoria and Charing Cross (both about 45 minutes); station is ten minutes' walk from the cathedral. Regular coach services from Victoria Coach Station. M25, M20 and M2/A2.

The first religious building on the site of the cathedral at Rochester-upon-Medway may have been built by Christian soldiers at the settlement of Durobrivae, but evidence is scanty – although Roman building materials have been found in the walls of the old priory cloisters at the side of the cathedral.

Two hundred years later, in consequence of the evangelizing of Augustine (d604), King Ethelbert built a church at Rochester dedicated to St Andrew. Completed in the year of Augustine's death, this Saxon building could claim to be the second oldest cathedral in Britain. There is no trace today of this building above ground, but foundations have been revealed at the west end of the present nave.

It is believed the early Saxon building suffered continually from raiding Vikings. After the conquest of 1066, the Normans realized the strategic position of Rochester and built a large castle to guard both the river crossing and a new cathedral, begun in 1080 by the Norman bishop Gundulf (1024–1108), who laid out the west end, the nave and the quire. Gundulf also set up the Benedictine monastery, which is believed to have had around sixty monks by the time of his death in 1108. Work continued into the next century, being done in Early English Gothic style.

There is little of the Decorated period to be seen, although Bishop Hamo de Hythe's magnificent 14th-century chapter room doorway dates from this era. The important addition in the 15th century was the huge Perpendicular window in the nave. At the same time the original Norman windows in the clerestory were removed and replaced with larger ones, giving much more light to the nave. The building of the Lady Chapel in 1492 completed the cathedral.

When the monasteries were dissolved in the mid-16th century, Rochester's priory was speedily refounded as a cathedral and the prior became the first dean. Little remains of the monastery today, apart from a few of the cloister walls and some gateways.

During the 18th century several new buildings appeared in the cathedral precincts, including Minor Canon Row, Oriel House and the archdeaconry.

The following century was mainly concerned with restoration. There was serious subsidence in the south transept and an outward tilting of the quire, which were only halted by the construction of a large flying buttress close to the south door. The decrepit spire was pulled down, not to be replaced for sixty years. The removal of a pulpit in 1840 had the bonus of revealing part of a 13th-century wall painting. The ubiquitous Sir George Gilbert Scott (1811–1878) was involved in many of the Victorian renovations, replacing the roofs of the transepts, putting in some 'Early English' windows and designing a new high altar.

Today, work at the cathedral mainly concerns cleaning and restoration, with fund-raising a perpetual problem. The formation of the Rochester 2000 Trust and grants from English Heritage have helped in this conservation work, so that visitors (estimated annual figure: 200,000) see a busy and well cared-for cathedral.

TOUR OF THE CATHEDRAL
Start and finish: The west front.

Start by viewing the **west front** (1) of the cathedral from the outside – a good viewpoint is from the grassy slopes of the castle opposite.

The west front has recently been cleaned up, showing the Romanesque facade in all its glory. The overwhelming impression is of vertical lines, from both the tall, narrow Norman arches, dating from *c*1160, and the great Perpendicular window dating from 1470. Of the four turrets, two are attached and the two larger ones detached. Only the south turret is original; the others are accurate Victorian reconstructions. All demonstrate blind arcading.

Undoubtedly the best feature of the exterior of the west front is the Norman doorway, which reminds us of the carved Romanesque doorways of French churches – indeed, it may well be the work of a French sculptor. To view it, cross the road to the small green embellished by a catalpa – a North American bean tree. The door's tympanum shows Christ in Majesty, seated in a *vesica*. On each side are angels and beasts. The elongated figures on the inner pillars represent Solomon and the Queen of Sheba and are unique in Britain.

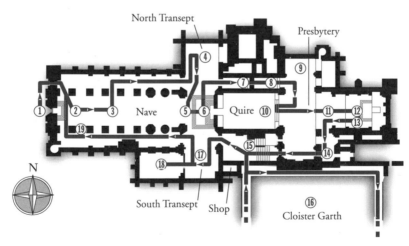

Key

1. West Front
2. Interior of the West Front
3. Nave
4. North Transept
5. Crossing
6. Nave Altar and Screen
7. Pilgrims' Steps
8. North Quire Aisle
9. North Quire Transept
10. Quire
11. East End
12. High Altar
13. Sedilia
14. Chapter Room Doorway
15. Crypt
16. Cloister Garth
17. South Transept
18. Lady Chapel
19. Font

Plate 9: *Canterbury Cathedral features some of the finest stained glass in the country, including the impressive Royal Window in the northwest transept (see page 54).*

Plate 10: *Canterbury Cathedral. Visitors walk towards the cathedral's west front, built in Perpendicular style (see page 53).*

Plate 11: *Conquest House, Canterbury – where Thomas à Becket's assassination is believed to have been plotted (see page 61).*

Plate 12: *Rochester Cathedral (opposite above). The cathedral was once the church of a Benedictine monastery, dissolved in the mid 16th century by Henry VIII (see page 65).*

Plate 13: *Chertsey's Gate, Rochester (opposite below). One of the old gates into the monastery's precincts. Dickens called it Jasper's Gate in* The Mystery of Edwin Drood *(see page 69).*

Plate 14: *St Albans Cathedral (above). Parts of the cathedral were built with Roman bricks plundered from Verulamium. The west front, however, is Victorian Gothic (see page 76).*

Plate 15: *The Clock Tower in French Row, St Albans (right). The tower was built in the early 15th century and contains a curfew bell dating from 1335 (see page 82).*

Plate 16: *Black Lion, St Albans. Once the main road from St Albans to the north, Fishpool Street is well provided with old coaching inns, such as this 18th-century building (see page 82).*

Plate 17: *Bury St Edmunds. The Statue of St Edmund outside the cathedral (see page 89).*

Plate 18: *Cupola House, Bury St Edmunds, dating from the late 17th century (see page 90).*

Enter the cathedral *via* the small door to the left. (Entrance is free, but a dona-tion is welcome.) Immediately inside the door, look for the curved line on the floor that marks the position of the apsidal east end of the original Saxon cathedral built for Justus, the first Bishop of Rochester, in 604; Justus was one of Augustine's fellow missionaries.

You can now see the interior of the **west front** (2), where two levels of Norman arcading on either side of the west door have been converted into a memorial to members of the Corps of Royal Engineers. The mosaic background to the names may not be to everyone's taste.

A Pious Baker and the Pilgrims' Steps

The **nave** (3) merits a lot of attention. Six bays of the original Norman survive, with subtle carved variations between each pier. At triforium level the symmetry continues, with two small arches within a larger one, all three being richly carved. The small Norman clerestory windows were, as we've seen, replaced by larger windows in the 15th century, bringing much more light into the nave. The wood-en roof is not the original, fires having destroyed its predecessors on a number of occasions.

Proceed now along the north aisle of the nave into the **north transept** (4), which is in Early English style with typical lancet windows. Against the main pil-lars, which are of cream limestone, rest thin pillars of Purbeck marble, a pattern repeated in other Gothic parts of the cathedral.

The north transept was the eventual location of the tomb – and later shrine – of William of Perth, a pious baker who stayed at the priory in 1201 en route to the Holy Land. He was murdered in the vicinity and his body brought back to the cathedral. Miracles at his tomb were soon reported and before long pilgrims started coming from all over the country. Unfortunately the shrine was destroyed in 1547, during the Reformation.

Walk now into the **crossing** (5). The ceiling is made of plaster and dates from 1840; it was restored in 1992 with the original colours. Above it is the 12th-centu-ry bell tower; campanological details are given by a small notice on the wall at the corner of the north transept. Immediately ahead of you is the nave **altar and screen** (6). The stonework has eight niches, four on each side of the central door, containing images of saints and other notables connected with the cathedral. On the left are St Andrew, King Ethelbert, Justus and Paulinus (d644), the missionary and first Archbishop of York; on the right Gundulf, William of Hoo, Walter de Merton (d1277) and John Fisher (1469–1535). Above the altar screen is the intricately paint-ed organ case, restored by Sir George Gilbert Scott in the 1870s. This unfortunate-ly obscures the view along the centre of the cathedral, making the nave and the quire two separate entities.

Move now to the left of the altar screen. On the left a small door marked PRIVATE leads to Gundulf's 12th-century bell tower. Carry on ahead to the **Pilgrims' Steps** (7), whose stonework was worn away by countless pilgrims' feet visiting William's shrine; the steps are now covered with wooden boarding to pre-vent any further erosion. They lead you to the **north quire aisle** (8) and the orig-inal site of the shrine. At the end of the aisle is the **north quire transept** (9), which features little of interest except a small patch of red-and-blue medieval tiled floor.

The Quire and the Dickens Memorial
Step into the **quire** (10), which is Early English in architectural style. The choir stalls have little in the way of carving and lack misericords, but the wall decorations are interesting, with an alternation of the French fleur-de-lys and the English leopard. Look for the painting called *The Wheel of Fortune*, discovered in 1840 when the pulpit was moved; it is believed to date from the 13th century. Opposite is the **bishop's throne**, well carved and with a number of coats-of-arms.

You now arrive at the **east end** (11). This area is notable for the lack of aisles or apse – so there is no processional walkway or ambulatory around the presbytery. The latter contains the **high altar** (12), one of Sir George Gilbert Scott's less impressive contributions. To the south of the high altar is a **sedilia** (13) – seating for officiating clergy set in the stonework of the wall – built in the time of Bishop Hamo de Hythe in 1343.

Flanking the presbytery are two small chapels: one is the Oratory, the other contains the Charles Dickens Memorial. Dickens lived at various stages of his life in the Rochester area, and began modelling his fictional locations on parts of the city as early as *Pickwick Papers*. As we shall see when we walk around Rochester, this practice continued in his later novels, notably including *Great Expectations* (1860–61) and *The Mystery of Edwin Drood*; Indeed, it is thought that he was planning to use Restoration House (already featured in disguise in *Great Expectations*) in this last, unfinished novel, for the day before his death he walked into Rochester and was seen standing in thought for a time at its gate.

Not surprisingly, Rochester-upon-Medway likes its alternative title: 'The City of Great Expectations.'

The Chapter Room Doorway, the Crypt and an Outdoor Excursion
Behind the Dickens Memorial is arguably the most important architectural feature of the cathedral – the mid-13th-century **chapter room doorway** (14), which would have been the monks' night entrance to the building. Carved in Decorated style, it shows standing figures representing the Church and the Synagogue. Higher up are the four Evangelists seated at desks, while at the apex of the arch is a human soul, apparently being rescued by angels. Altogether, a superb piece of carved stonework, which because of its interior position has escaped weathering. The oak door dates from the 19th century, but its carving is not of wood but of lead.

Now walk west and take the stairs down into the **crypt** (15), which lies under the quire.

The oldest part of the cathedral, the crypt is laid out in seven aisles, with simple heavy vaulting. At the east end, the crypt chapel is dedicated to Ithamar (d655), the first English Bishop of Rochester. Also of interest here are the traces of medieval graffiti and wall painting.

Go back up the steps to the main body of the cathedral and walk out through the south door into the **cloister garth** (16). Immediately on your left is the flying buttress constructed by L.N. Cottingham in the 19th century to support the quire. You can see some of the old cloister walls; a few of their Norman arches are interlocking.

Take a clockwise walk around the garth (garden). In the first corner are the remains of the old chapter house, built by Bishop Ernulf (1040–1124) in the early 12th century. Most of the stonework is at ground level. Note on the far side the 12th-century monastic dormitory doorway, the rough shafts of which are of Tournai marble from Belgium. Along the lintel is a heavily eroded tympanum showing Abraham about to sacrifice Isaac, while in the right-hand corner is a ram caught in a thicket by its horn.

In the opposite corner of the garth is the early-13th-century doorway that led to the monastic refectory and lavatory; it is made of Reigate Stone and Purbeck marble. On the lawn in the centre of the garth stands a modern sculpture, *Christ and the Blessed Virgin Mary* by John Doubleday.

Return through the south door and go leftward to the **south transept** (17), completed in 1280 in Decorated style. Adjoining the transept is the **Lady Chapel** (18), positioned here because the monastic buildings occupied the more usual site at the east end of the cathedral. It was completed in 1492 in late Perpendicular style. Its screen has more recently been moved through 90° so that the transept is less isolated.

Walk back along the south nave aisle, where the only item of interest is the Victorian **font** (19). Located under one of the Norman arches, it is made of marble. The carvings around the side are by Thomas Earp and represent scenes of baptism from the Bible.

The tour ends at the west front, where it began.

WALKING TOUR FROM ROCHESTER CATHEDRAL

The walk visits historical features such as the Norman Rochester Castle and some remains of the old monastic buildings. There is also a wide range of Kentish domestic architecture on view. Other features have close links with Charles Dickens.

Start and finish: The west front of the cathedral.
Length: 2½ miles (4km).
Time: 1½ hours, but allow longer if you want to visit the two museums and the castle.
Refreshments: Excellent cathedral refectory. Rochester has a number of old pubs and coaching inns offering lunchtime food in historic surroundings. Recommended: the Norman Conquest, the Eagle Tavern, the King's Head Hotel and the Royal Victoria and Bull Hotel, all in the High Street.

Leave the west front and head north towards the High Street.

On your right is the **Church of St Nicholas**, dating from the early 15th century but rebuilt two centuries later. In 1964 it was declared redundant and became the administration office for the Rochester diocese. Although the building is not officially open to the public, visitors are treated in friendly fashion and there are some interesting items, including the stained glass at the east end.

Proceed under the arch of **Chertsey's Gate**. Formerly known as Cemetery Gate (it featured as Jasper's Gate in Dickens's *The Mystery of Edwin Drood*), it was one of the old gates into the monastery precincts. It dates from the early 15th century, but had a rather unfortunate black clapperboard house slapped on top of it in the 18th century. It is not open to the public.

Treasures of the High Street

Turn left into the semi-pedestrianized **High Street**. Without the constant noise of traffic, this has become a delightful part of the town, with a wide range of shops, inns and restaurants among a number of buildings of historical and architectural interest.

Immediately on your right is the **Old Corn Exchange**, dominated by a huge moon-faced clock. The building was erected in 1698, and was originally the butchers' market. Its frontage was revamped by Admiral Sir Cloudesley Shovel (1650–1707) in 1706. Shovel was a fascinating character. A naval officer, he represented the town in three parliaments under William III and one under Queen Anne; he is buried in the south choir aisle of Westminster Abbey (see page 34). The circumstances of his death were somewhat bizarre, if the tales are to be believed. He survived a shipwreck off the Scilly Isles, when his crew became drunk and incapable, but on being washed ashore was murdered by a fisherwoman for his emerald ring.

Further along on the left is **Two Post Alley**, which separates two fine examples of domestic architecture. On the left a drunkenly tilting Elizabethan building, covered with weatherboarding, has a bookshop at street level, while on the right is a particularly fine Georgian residence, once a printing office. Notice the elegant ornamentation between its first and second floors.

On your right is the **Guildhall**, claimed as the best 17th-century public building in the county. The exterior is certainly impressive, with imposing pillars, Georgian windows and a rooftop cupola on which is mounted a weathervane in the form of an 18th-century warship in full rigging. The interior is equally impressive, with some fine decorated ceilings above the main chamber and the staircase – another gift from Cloudesley Shovel. If by now you've become a Shovel fan and wonder what he looks like, you can see his portrait hanging in the main chamber.

The Guildhall has been a museum since 1979; it was reopened in 1994 after major refurbishment and now has some state-of-the-art displays. The route through it is an historical journey starting with geology and archaeology and passing through various periods to Victorian times. The highlight for many people is the two-tier gallery, which recreates one of the Medway prison ships from the Napoleonic War. The audiovisual effects leave little to the imagination.

Opposite the Guildhall is the **Royal Victoria and Bull Hotel**. This 18th-century coaching inn was originally just the Bull, but Princess Victoria had to make an emergency overnight stop here the year before she became queen, and so the name was proudly altered. Note the impressive coat-of-arms over the main gateway – not Victoria's, but that of George III and Queen Charlotte. Dickens used the hotel in his books: it was the Blue Boar in *Great Expectations* and in *Pickwick Papers* Mr Jingle describes it as 'a good house with nice beef'.

Finally in the High Street you'll find behind a mundane shop front at No. 4, just before the bridge, **Draper's Museum of Bygones**. Covering three floors, this has

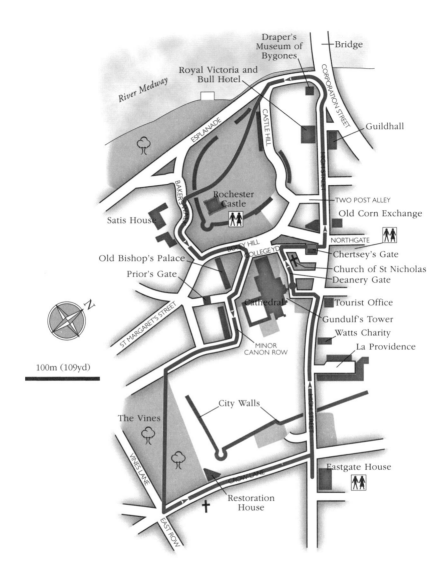

Draper's
Museum of
Bygones

Bridge

Royal Victoria and
Bull Hotel

River Medway

CORPORATION STREET

ESPLANADE

CASTLE HILL

Guildhall

BAKER'S WALK

Rochester
Castle

TWO POST ALLEY

Old Corn Exchange

Satis House

NORTHGATE

BOLEY HILL

COLLEGE YD

Old Bishop's Palace

Chertsey's Gate

Prior's Gate

Church of St Nicholas

Deanery Gate

N

ST MARGARET'S STREET

Cathedral

Tourist Office

Gundulf's Tower

Watts Charity

La Providence

MINOR
CANON ROW

100m (109yd)

City Walls

HIGH STREET

The Vines

Eastgate House

VINES LANE

CROW LANE

EAST ROW

Restoration
House

sixteen old shop sets such as a chemist, a toyshop, a haberdashery and a sweetshop. Absorbing to all ages, this is well worth a visit.

Rochester Castle

Ahead of you now is a **bridge complex** over the River Medway. This has been an historic crossing point since the Romans built the first stone bridge here to take Watling Street on its way to London. There have been five others since; the present (steel) bridge was built in 1914 to carry two roads and a railway. Oddly, it is

71

administered not by the Highways Authority but by the Rochester Bridge Trust, an ancient charity which pays for the upkeep.

Then turn left into the Esplanade. Ahead, on your left, is the entrance to **Rochester Castle**, *via* a mock Norman arch cut by the Royal Engineers in 1872. Walk up the steps through the 13th-century curtain wall. At their top is a cannon believed to have been fired in the Crimean War.

You are now within the grounds of the castle, originally fortified by the Normans shortly after the Conquest and initially con-sisting of earthworks and timber palisades. During 1088 Bishop Gundulf began the construction of a stone building, possibly the earliest masonry castle in the coun-

Prior's Gate

try. It remained in the hands of the Archbishop of Canterbury until in 1215 it was besieged by King John. The siege was lasted two months and succeeded only when the king's forces undermined the southeast corner turret by burning its wooden props with the fat of forty pigs. The rebuilt turret was round rather than square, like the originals.

Today, all that remains of the castle are the curtain walls and the massive keep, which must be one of the best preserved pieces of Norman architecture in England. It is over 100ft (30m) high and has walls 13ft (4m) thick. Within the keep a circu-lar staircase takes you to the battlements – a climb rewarded by superb views over the city and the river.

To the left of the castle and close to the toilets is a gap in the curtain walls which is probably the best spot from which to photograph the cathedral's west front.

Leave the castle grounds from the other side of the keep, where a small gate leads into Baker's Walk. Almost immediately opposite is a complex of buildings known as **Satis House**. The name comes from the Latin word meaning 'enough', said to have been Elizabeth I's comment on the hospitality she received when staying here in 1573. The buildings have changed considerably since then – the main building has a distinctly Georgian look – but Old Hall, to the left and once the east wing of the house, retains Tudor elements.

Ecclesiastical Dwellings

Turn left, in the direction of the cathedral, and then right into College Green.

Immediately on your right is the **Old Bishop's Palace**, a delightful 15th-century building of mellow brickwork. Bishop John Fisher, who was also chancellor of Cambridge University, lived here for thirty-one years before being put to death for refusing to acknowledge Henry VIII as head of the Church.

Just around the corner is the **Prior's Gate**, the best preserved of the three surviving 14th-century monastic gates. Today it leads pedestrians only into St Margaret's Street, where the Cooper's Arms was a favourite stop for pilgrims en route to Canterbury.

Turn left before you reach Prior's Gate into **Minor Canon Row**, a terrace of 18th-century houses built for the minor canons of the cathedral; originally there were six houses for the six minor canons, but a seventh was later added for the organist. The father of Dame Sybil Thorndike (1882–1976) was a canon at the cathedral, and so the actress lived here for several years.

The road now swings right past some of the buildings of the King's School. Just past the 18th-century Oriel House (note the fire insurance company marks on the wall) turn left into **The Vines**. This attractive public park was formerly the monks' vineyard. It is dominated by a row of plane trees, planted in 1880. A number were uprooted in the hurricane of 1987 and have been replaced. The trunk of one of the damaged trees has been carved into the figure of a Benedictine monk.

Secular Dwellings and the City Walls

On the far side of The Vines turn left into Crow Lane, where there is a variety of fine domestic architecture on view.

Immediately on your left, facing The Vines, is **Restoration House**. The name originated in 1666: this was the house, owned by Sir Francis Clarke, where Charles II stayed on the eve of his ascension to the throne. Dickens based the home of Miss Haversham in *Great Expectations* on this house, calling it Satis House – not to be confused with the real Satis House.

Continue down Crow Street until you once more reach the High Street. Turn right and immediately on your right, at No. 150, you see a magnificent half-timbered Tudor building with ground-floor shops. Dickens used this as the model for another building in *Great Expectations*, Uncle Pumblechook's shop.

Cross the High Street to **Eastgate House**, a timber and red brick mansion built in 1590 for Sir Peter Buck, once Mayor of Rochester. His coat-of-arms can be seen in one of the gables overlooking the High Street. In Victorian times the building was a boarding school for young ladies and well known to Dickens, who in *Pickwick Papers* called it Westgate House. It was the home of the city museum until in 1979 that moved to the Guildhall. Eastgate House then became the **Charles Dickens Centre**. It was refurbished in 1996 and now uses high-technology visual aids to illustrate the author's life and times.

Dickens (1812–1870) was born in Portsmouth, but when he was 5 his father got a job in the Navy Pay Office at Chatham and the family moved to the Rochester area, staying here until Charles was 11, when the family moved again, this time to London. Here things went badly for them, and Charles's father spent some time imprisoned for debt at Marshalsea; Charles himself had to give up his schooling and take a hellish job in a rat-infested blacking warehouse. He escaped to take various more congenial jobs, although his great ambition at the time was to become an actor – an ambition which, to an extent, he achieved towards the end of his life when he gave highly dramatic readings from his works both in Britain and in the USA. By then he was living again near Rochester, at Gadshill, which he had coveted in childhood and which he had bought in 1856 as a country house.

By the time he moved permanently to Gadshill, however, his private life was in turmoil. In 1836, three days after publication of the first part of *Pickwick Papers* (1836–7), he had married Catherine, the daughter of his friend George Hogarth, editor of the *Evening Chronicle* and a highly respected man of letters. Charles and Catherine had nine children but she became increasingly infuriated by his adulterous relationship, begun about 1857, with a young actress, Ellen Ternan, and the couple separated in 1858. There was a huge scandal when the matter became public – the similarly unorthodox lifestyles of his contemporaries Wilkie Collins (1824–1889) and William Makepeace Thackeray (1811–1863) for some reason caused nothing like the same furore – and Dickens retreated with Ellen to Gadshill, which he made his home for the rest of his life, although hereafter he spent a large part of his time abroad. He died of a stroke at Gadshill while working at his desk on *The Mystery of Edwin Drood* (1870).

In the garden at the rear of Eastgate House is the Swiss chalet from Dickens's home at Gadshill; he used it as a summerhouse and also wrote some of his later works in it. Unfortunately, the chalet is not open to visitors.

Return westwards along the High Street to the **city walls**. The defensive walls in Roman times were merely earth ramparts, but the Normans replaced these with stone walls and four gates enclosing an area of nearly 25 acres (10ha). The best surviving stretches today are by the carpark on the north of the High Street and on the opposite side of the High Street, where a short length can be seen behind the window of the City Wall Wine Bar.

Continue west along the High Street, until you come, on the right, to **La Providence**, also called the French Hospital, and founded by the Huguenots. Today it provides apartments for elderly local people of Huguenot descent.

Further along on the right is **Watts Charity**, a Tudor building with a Georgian frontage. The charity was endowed by Richard Watts, an MP for the town in the 1500s, to provide board and lodging nightly for 'six poor travellers'. Echoing this phrase, Dickens called one of his famous Christmas stories 'The Seven Poor Travellers' (1854).

Next on the right is the Tourist Information Office, newly ensconced in plush new surroundings. Cross the road here and walk into the War Memorial Gardens. Carry on towards the cathedral, where between the two north-facing transepts is the squat **Gundulf's Tower**. Once a free-standing bell tower, this was probably built after Gundulf himself had died. Today its main use is for choir practices.

Pass now through the **Deanery Gate**, a monastic inner gate dating from the 15th century, with original doors. Turn left at the end of the alleyway to reach the cathedral's west front, where the walk began.

St Albans

Access: Within four miles (2.5km) of exits from the M25, M1, M10 and A1 (M). The former A5 (now A5183) and A6 (now A1081) run through the city. St Albans Station is on the Bedford–St Pancras line; no InterCity services, but the Thameslink service operates and also connects with Luton and Gatwick airports. Greenline coaches no longer stop at St Albans, but the 724 service linking Heathrow and Stansted stops en route at St Albans.

Both the city and the cathedral take their name from the 3rd-century St Alban, probably the first Christian martyr in Britain.

Alban resided in Verulamium, an important town in Roman Britain. He sheltered in his house a Christian priest fleeing persecution – Christianity was proscribed in the Roman Empire. Impressed by the man's devotions and prayers, Alban was eventually converted. He then helped Amphibalus (as Geoffrey of Monmouth named the priest) escape, disguising him in his own cloak. Brought before the Roman magistrates, Alban refused to deny his new faith and was condemned to death. He was beheaded on the hill outside the Verulamium city walls in c209, c254 or c304, depending upon which authority you believe. A church later built on the site soon became known for miracle healing. Pilgrims began come, the first documented visit being that of St Germanus of Auxerre (c378–448) in 429.

King Offa of Mercia founded a Benedictine monastery on the site in 793. After the conquest of 1066, the Normans decided to build a vast new church. The first Norman abbot, Paul de Caen, brought a master mason from Normandy to supervise the Saxon workmen. Although there was no building stone in the local area, there was abundant brick, tile and flint in the remains of the Roman city, and these materials were widely used in the new church. When dedicated in 1115 the church was the largest in England.

Meanwhile the monastery went from strength to strength. Its wealth ensured that the abbey church was continually extended and reconstructed. At its zenith, the abbey had over one hundred monks and three times as many lay helpers. Its abbots included Richard of Wallingford, Thomas de la Mare and the future Cardinal Wolsey.

In 1539, however, the monastery was dissolved as part of Henry VIII's campaign. Most of the buildings were destroyed (an exception was the abbey gateway at the top of Abbey Mill Lane) and the treasures were looted. The local people saved the church to use as their parish church, buying it for £400. The population was too small to cope with the upkeep of such a building, however, and over the next three centuries it inevitably deteriorated. In the mid-19th century serious efforts were made to restore it, and the eminent Sir George Gilbert Scott (1811–1878) was appointed architect. The dominating force in the restoration was the wealthy barrister Edmund Beckett Grimthorpe, 1st Baron Grimthorpe (1816–1905). He imposed many of his own ideas, most of them controversial, but his financial contribution was invaluable. The abbey church was proclaimed a cathedral in 1877.

The most recent addition is the chapter house, opened by Elizabeth II in 1982 and built of handmade bricks – to blend in with the Roman tiles found in the older parts of the cathedral – on the site of the original chapter house where monks assembled daily to read a chapter of the Benedictine Rule. During the excavation of the new building the remains of many of the early abbots were found; they have been reburied in the presbytery. The new chapter house includes a visitor centre, refectory, shop and theological library.

TOUR OF THE CATHEDRAL
Start: The west door.
Finish: The new chapter house.

The **west end** (1) of the nave was reconstructed in Victorian Gothic style as part of the Grimthorpe renovations, and most experts today consider that it does not sit happily with the rest of the cathedral. The 19th-century work replaced what drawings show to have been an attractive Perpendicular construction, with a particularly eye-catching window. It was, however, in poor condition and the solution was to replace it completely with a design which was entirely Grimthorpe's. Inside his wooden draughtproof doors are windows and glass doors, with etchings which include the words of the Alban Prayer, 'I worship and adore the True and Living God who created all things'. The present glasswork dates from 1988 and is the work of David Pearce.

The **nave** (2) is impressive for its length (the second longest in England after Winchester) and for its variety of architectural styles. The eastern end, part of the original abbey church, displays typical round-ended Norman arches made largely of flint and bricks from the old Roman city and plastered to resemble stonework: the result is that the pillars are almost square. The pillars' west and south sides display a

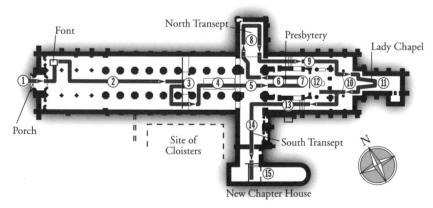

Key		
	5. Tower	11. Lady Chapel
	6. Presbytery	12. Chapel of
1. West End	7. High Altar	St Alban
2. Nave	8. North Transept	13. South Presbytery Aisle
3. Rood Screen	9. North Presbytery Aisle	14. South Transept
4. Choir	10. Retrochoir	15. New Chapter House

series of 13th- and 14th-century paintings showing saints and crucifixion scenes. The paintings were plastered over after the Reformation and rediscovered during the Victorian renovations.

The Norman columns are not duplicated on the south side of the nave as the originals collapsed during a service in 1323, killing two monks and a boy. They were replaced by five bays in Decorated style, made of 'clunch' from Tottenhoe in Bedfordshire, the work being finally completed in 1345. The triforium level is particularly ornate, and the sophisticated decoration of this style makes an interesting contrast with the more simplistic Early English work of the remainder of the western end of the nave.

The exterior of the nave on the south side shows some half-buried arcading, marking the site of the original abbey cloistering.

At the nave's eastern end is the 14th-century **rood screen** (3), which effectively divided the public nave from the monks' choir and presbytery. The screen is of stone and noticeably asymmetrical. Its many recesses are now empty, the statues having been removed during and after the Dissolution in 1539. At the base of the screen, above the nave altar, is a 16th-century Spanish cross composed largely of crystal.

An English Pope and the Magna Carta

Next proceed *via* the south aisle into the **choir** (4), where one of the stall nameplates is that of Nicholas Breakspear (1100–1159), who in 1154 became the only English Pope, Adrian IV. He had earlier been rejected by the abbey (where his father was a monk) because it was said that he was 'insufficient in learning'!

The present choir stalls are Victorian; the original monastic versions are thought to be those in the parish church in Leighton Buzzard. The wooden panels of the choir ceiling date from the late 14th century, with some Victorian restoration.

Go now into the crossing. The **tower** (5), with its impressive Norman arches, is the oldest cathedral tower in England. Its walls, 7ft (2m) thick, are made of Roman tiles which were probably 800 years old when the Normans constructed the tower in the late 11th century! The decoration of the wooden tower ceiling consists of red-and-white roses of the houses of York and Lancaster, who fought each other twice at St Albans. These wooden panels are replicas of the medieval originals, which are still in place above them.

Over the ceiling, the ringing chamber contains a peal of twelve bells of widely varying ages, the oldest dating from 1699 and the most recent from 1935.

Move into the **presbytery** (6), dominated by the **high altar** (7), erected by Abbot William of Wallingford and dedicated in 1484. Its purpose was to exclude visiting pilgrims from the choir. The stone statues were removed during the Reformation, but Lord Aldenham provided new figures of magnesian limestone in the late 19th century. The distinctive reredos, sculptured in marble and paua shells from New Zealand, was designed by Sir Alfred Gilbert (1854–1934).

In the floor of the presbytery you'll find a slate slab below which eleven abbots and four monks are buried. Their remains were found during excavations for the new chapter house and reburied in the presbytery with full Benedictine honours. The inscription on the slab tells us that one of the monks was Robert of the Chamber, the father of Nicholas Breakspear. The 13th-century wooden ceiling was painted over in the 15th century, and the shields were added during 17th-century restoration. Interestingly, there are no stone vaulted ceilings anywhere in the cathedral: it appears funds were lacking at crucial times, so wooden ceilings had to suffice.

On the north side of the presbytery is the chantry chapel of the 16th century Abbot Ramryge. Look for his rebus – a play on words, in this case involving the ram motif.

From the presbytery, step back into the **north transept** (8). Don't miss the painting on the west wall, which shows, to scale, the abbey church and monastery as they were prior to Dissolution. (You'll find this knowledge useful when walking around the city.) Nearby is a copy of the Magna Carta, which was compiled at the abbey before being presented to King John in 1215. Adjacent is a reconstruction of part of Abbot Richard of Wallingford's early-14th-century astronomical clock. Among the collection of busts is that of Lord Grimthorpe, while the tomb effigy is of the first Bishop, Thomas Legh Claughton.

The architecture of the north transept is Norman throughout apart from the rose window, installed during the Victorian restorations. Architectural purists may bridle, but it's a fine piece of work. The stained glass in the window was a gift from Laporte Industries of Luton.

The Shrine of St Alban

Walk on into the **north presbytery aisle** (9). The brass on the floor, for Abbot Thomas de la Mare (1349–1396), is believed to be of Flemish origin; since it does not record his death it may have been made during his lifetime.

On the south wall is one of the original panels from the ceiling of the tower. You can see the rear of the watching tower at the end of the aisle; you'll get a better view of it later, but notice here the carvings on the main beam, which show scenes of everyday life c1400. At the north end of the aisle are the stone remains of the Shrine of St Amphibalus, the mentor of St Alban.

From the **retrochoir** (10), your next port of call, you get a fine view into the **Lady Chapel** (11). Both were completed by Abbot Hugh Eversden c1320. After the Dissolution the Lady Chapel was walled off and a public passageway was made through the retrochoir. For the next 300 years the chapel was used as a boys' grammar school, with consequent wear and tear on its fabric. In 1870 the school was moved to the old abbey gateway and the chapel restored. There was a further renovation in 1958, when furnishings were added in memory of the Kent family.

Go now into the heart of the cathedral, the **Chapel of St Alban** (12). In the centre is the Shrine of St Alban. The relics of the saint, originally contained in an elaborate stone pedestal, gained a reputation for healing, and so attracted pilgrims from far and wide. After the Dissolution the reliquary was taken by the Crown and the stone of the pedestal used for building material when the chapel was walled off. The pedestal was reconstructed in the Victorian renovation, and a more complete reconstruction was finished in 1991.

Because of the value of the reliquary and the vast number of pilgrims which the shrine attracted there was constructed (c1400) a wooden watching chamber on the north side of the chapel, from which monks could maintain a constant vigilance.

On the south side of the chapel is the vault of the only royal person to have been buried in the cathedral, Humphrey, Duke of Gloucester (1391–1447), the youngest son of Henry IV and Protector during Henry VI's minority. He was a personal friend of Abbot Wheathamptead, and on his death it was requested that he be buried as near as possible to the Shrine of St Alban.

Leave the chapel by the retrochoir, taking note of the small Chapel of the Four Tapers, now used by the Mothers' Union, and proceed into the **south aisle** (13). On the right is the Chantry Chapel of Abbot William Wallingford (who built the altar screen), now reserved for private prayer.

Further along is a wall panel showing the martyrdom of St Alban.

Shrine of St Alban

The painting probably dates from the 17th century and is thought to have originally been the central panel of the north transept ceiling.

Our tour ends at the **south transept** (14), which merges into the **new chapter house** (15). The south wall of the south transept was entirely rebuilt in Early English lancet style during the Grimthorpe restorations. The original Norman arches are retained in the triforium; their baluster shafts have been turned, and may be Saxon in origin. Some of the crescents above the balusters are filled with Roman tiles. Look for the recesses in the transept walls; one of these was the original entrance to the cloisters. The wooden gallery and stairway are in memory of Bishop Greford Jones. The gallery provides a new location for the Sanctus Bell, which was formerly at the west end of the cathedral.

A Norman arch leads the visitor into the new chapter house, which has a bookshop, an information desk, toilets and a highly recommended refectory.

WALKING TOUR FROM ST ALBANS CATHEDRAL

This circular walk visits some of the city's Roman remains as well as remnants of the once thriving abbey, plus a working water mill and one of the best museums in the country. You can also see some varied domestic architecture in this Heritage Area of St Albans.

Start and finish: The west front of the cathedral.
Length: 2 miles (3.5km).
Time: 1¼ hours (allow longer if you want to visit the Verulamium Museum).
Refreshments: Excellent cathedral refectory. Numerous old coaching inns along the walking route provide excellent bar meals and pub lunches, notably the Fighting Cocks Inn (Abbey Mill Lane), the Tudor Tavern (George Street), the Rose and Crown (St Michael's Street), the Blue Anchor, the Black Lion and St Michael's Manor Hotel (all in Fishpool Street). The last two offer accommodation.

Walk towards the **Abbey Gateway**, sometimes known as the Great Gateway. Built of flint and Roman tiles, it is the only surviving monastic building. It is believed to have been built in the early 1360s during the abbotcy of Thomas de la Mare (1349–1396). In 1381, during the Peasants' Revolt, it was besieged by insurgents, between 1553 and 1869 it was the local prison, and since 1871 it has formed part of the adjacent St Albans Boys' School,

Cockfighting

Go down Abbey Mill Lane towards the River Ver, at the side of which is the historic **Fighting Cocks Inn**, which claims to be 'probably the oldest licensed house in England' – a claim supported by *The Guinness Book of Records*. The name refers to the cockfighting which took place here during the 17th and 18th centuries (after cockfighting became illegal in 1849, it was briefly renamed the Fisherman). The main part of the inn is octagonal, and built on what is thought to have been a medieval pigeon house, rebuilt for human habitation *c*1600. An information plaque on the wall claims that the inn accommodated Oliver Cromwell (1599–1658) for one night, his horse being stabled in what is now the bar area.

Opposite the Fighting Cocks, on the far side of the Ver, are the **Abbey Mills**, which once provided water power to grind corn for the monastery. The present building dates from 1800 and is a silk-weaving mill.

Walk westward into Verulamium Park, dominated by a large ornamental lake dug out in the 1930s to replace the fishponds which had provided food for the monastery.

The Roman Legacy

Now you have a choice. The path along the river leads directly to St Michael's and the Verulamium Museum (see below). The longer route to the left of the lake goes there too, but *via* a number of interesting features, including stretches of the **Roman wall** with the foundations of the London Gate. The walls are thought to have been built *c*200 to enclose about 200 acres (80ha) of the city. Follow the signs to take a leftward detour to the **hypocaust**, now housed in a brick building covering the remains of what was a large Roman townhouse, also dating from *c*200, with possibly as many as twenty rooms. The heating system, illustrated on wall panels, is well preserved.

Return to the path you left to visit the hypocaust and stroll along it to the carpark. You are now in the area known as St Michael's and in the heart of the old Roman city. Next to the carpark is the timber-framed **Glebe House**, a restored 16th-century building now the administrative and educational centre of the Hertfordshire and Middlesex Wildlife Trust. A small nature reserve nearby is open during the summer months.

Cross the carpark to the attractive **St Michael's Church**, one of three churches founded by Abbot Ulsinus in 948 (the others being St Peter's at the northern end of St Albans town centre and St Stephen's, to the south of the city). St Michael's has had much restoration – the tower, for example, was replaced by Lord Grimthorpe – but there is original Saxon work in the windows of the nave, which is largely Norman. Look for the statue of Sir Francis Bacon (1561–1626), who lived at the nearby Gorhambury Estate. The churchyard was the location of the Roman basilica or town hall and the adjacent forum. It has been suggested that the basilica may have been as large as the present cathedral nave. Today, only one small part of the foundations can be seen, between the Verulamium Museum and the carpark.

Carry on to Bluehouse Hill, the main Hemel Hempstead–St Albans road, and cross by the traffic lights. Enter the gates of the Gorhambury Estate. Some fifty yards (50m) to your left is the **Roman Theatre**. This was not an amphitheatre for glad-iatorial contests but a theatre with a stage for dramatic productions and possibly reli-gious rites, and is the only fully excavated example of its type in Britain. It is thought the theatre was built *c*150, with a final rebuilding *c*300. The main excavations were carried out in the 1930s, with some reconstructions on the basis of available evi-dence. The remains of tradesmen's shops and an extensive villa have also been uncovered. An official guidebook is available at the kiosk.

Retrace your steps across Bluehouse Hill to the Roman **Verulamium Museum**. No ordinary stuffy museum this, but a lively display of everyday life in Roman Verulamium. There are interpretative displays, abundant Roman and Iron Age artefacts, plus realistic audiovisual presentations. Not to be missed!

Old Coaching Inns

Proceed now along St Michael's Street towards the Ver, passing two old coaching inns to your left. The first, the Six Bells, is built over the remains of the Roman baths, which were destroyed during the Iceni revolt led by Queen Boudicca in

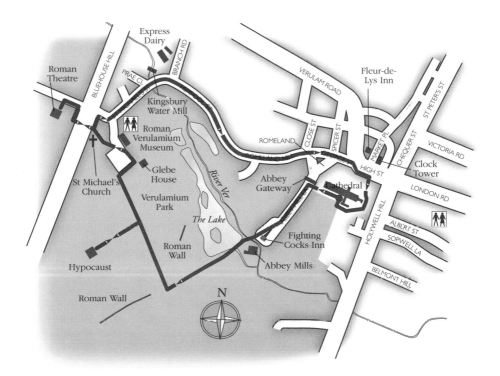

60–61. The carpark of the second pub, the Rose and Crown, is thought to lie above the old Colchester (or northeast) Gate to the Roman city.

After crossing the Ver you see on your left **Kingsbury Water Mill**. On the green in front of the mill is a large block of Hertfordshire puddingstone, an example of the local conglomerate which used by the Romans as a millstone. There has been a water mill on this site since at least Domesday times, although the present restored mill dates from the 16th century. It is open to the public, and you can see the water wheel and milling apparatus along with a fascinating collection of farming implements. There are also a shop, an art gallery and a restaurant, which sells delicious waffles.

Architecture buffs may wish to make a diversion into Branch Road, where a hundred yards or so (100m) along is the **Express Dairy**, which is pure Art Deco in style.

The main route now proceeds into **Fishpool Street**, named after the series of monastic ponds once close to the site. There are some superb examples of domestic architecture from timber-framed Elizabethan through Georgian to Victorian, with jettied walls, pargeting and fascinating memorial wall plaques dating from World War I.

This street was once the main road from St Albans to the north, and is well provided with old coaching inns. On the corner of Branch Road is the Black Lion, a timber-framed inn dating from the 16th century but refronted in brick in 1720. Further along on the right is the St Michael's Manor Hotel, once the home of the Gape family, who played a leading role in the life of the town for several centuries. The oldest surviving part of the hotel dates from the 1500s; the imposing porch, with its Doric columns, is from the 19th century.

The only other surviving inn is the Lower Red Lion, on the left near the top of Fishpool Street. Here you find a triangular walled area known as **Romeland** – probably from 'room land', meaning an open space. Fairs were once held here, and here the Protestant George Tankerville was burnt at the stake.

Continue up the hill into **George Street**, a marvellous medieval street named after the former George Inn. Most of the buildings are now specialist shops. The jewel is undoubtedly the **Tudor Tavern**, with its half-timber work and jettied walls. It is now a steakhouse; you can dine in its first-floor hall, which dates from 1400.

Moving towards the town centre, the next item of historical interest is the **Clock Tower**, built 1403–12 and 77ft (23m) high. Its medieval belfry, probably unique in England, contains the large Curfew Bell, dating from 1335. The tower was restored in 1866 by Sir George Gilbert Scott. Near it a cross once marked one of the resting places of Eleanor of Castile's body on its journey from Harby in Lincolnshire to Westminster; the cross was demolished in the 17th century.

At the side of the Clock Tower is the narrow pedestrianized French Row, which includes among its historic buildings the **Fleur-de-Lys Inn**, thought to date from 1440. A wall plaque claims this was the site of a building in which King John of France was held prisoner after the Battle of Poitiers in 1356. The present building has an interesting yard, with a 17th-century balustraded staircase which may have led to a gallery.

Leave the Clock Tower area and walk down the alleyway opposite. This leads you to Sumpter's Yard, at the east end of the cathedral. Here packhorses once unloaded supplies for the abbey. Walk along the south side of the cathedral to the west end, where the walk began.

Bury St Edmunds

Access: The A14, which bypasses the town to the north, links with the M11 and London. Other main roads connect with Thetford, Diss and Sudbury. National Express coach services from London Victoria: two coaches daily. Rail from Kings Cross (change at Cambridge) or from Liverpool Street (change at Ipswich). Both rail and coach journeys take about 2½ hours.

The cathedral at Bury St Edmunds is of the 'upgraded parish church' type, and thus not really within our scope. However, such is the historic interest of the town and in particular the ruins of the abbey that an exception has been made. Indeed, had the abbey church survived the Dissolution it would have compared favourably with the other East Anglian abbey cathedrals, Ely and St Albans.

The site of the present cathedral was occupied by a church – St Denis's Church, built 1065–98 – in early Norman times. This was demolished in the next century and replaced by a new church dedicated to St James. (It is said that the abbot responsible – Anselm – had hoped to make a pilgrimage to the shrine of St James at Compostella in Spain, but was too busy!) Most of the present building, however, dates from 1510–30 and is largely attributed to John Wastell. He was a local mason; his other work includes King's College Chapel in Cambridge, the fan vaulting in Peterborough Cathedral (see page 115), the Bell Harry Tower at Canterbury (see page 52) plus a number of Suffolk parish churches. Most of the rest of the cathedral is either Victorian or Modern.

The motto of Bury St Edmunds is *Sacrarium Regis, Cunabula Legis*, which approximately translates as 'Shrine of a King, Cradle of the Law'. The history of the town explains it all. Bury originated as a Saxon homestead, Beodricksworth, where *c*630 King Sigebert of the East Angles founded a monastery. Later, in 869, King Edmund was killed by the Danes (either in battle or as a martyr) on one of their frequent raids on Eastern England. His body was buried near Diss, but some time later, after miracles had been attributed to them, his remains were brought to the monastery at Beodricksworth, which changed its name to St Edmund's Bury, and the shrine became a place of pilgrimage. In 1032, King Canute, who had conquered the whole of the country, granted the monastery abbey status. Later, at the time of the Norman Conquest, the abbey was fortunate in having a French Abbot (Baldwin) who was able to ensure there was no destruction by the invaders.

Baldwin also constructed the abbey gates and walls and laid out the grid plan of the town's roads. It was in his time that work commenced on the abbey church. His successor, Anselm, continued the work afterwards, but on a much grander scale. A serious fire (*c*1150) held up progress, but the great west front was completed during the time of Abbot Samson, who held office 1182–1211, and pictorial reconstructions suggest it must have rivalled the west front of Ely (see page 93).

During King John's troubled reign, a group of barons gathered together at Bury ostensibly to celebrate St Edmund's Day but in fact to swear before the high altar of the abbey church that they would force the king to sign the Magna Carta. This he eventually did in 1215, so leading to the town's claim to be the 'cradle of the law'.

Relations between the abbey and the town were rarely peaceful. In 1327 there were riots that lasted for most of the summer, culminating in the destruction of a considerable part of the abbey and the abbey gateway, the abbot being abducted. Once peace was restored, the townspeople were reprimanded and obliged to rebuild the gateway.

The abbey was at its most powerful during the 15th century. The abbey church was among the largest in the country – at 505ft (154m) long it was some 15ft (5m) longer than Norwich Cathedral – and its style influenced the architecture of the other East Anglian cathedrals. Both of Bury's medieval parish churches, St James (now the cathedral) and St Mary's, stood within the abbey walls. In 1533 Henry VIII's sister Mary was buried at the abbey (although her body was later moved to St Mary's – see page 87). Shortly afterwards came the Dissolution of the Monasteries, and Bury St Edmunds Abbey was surrendered to the king in 1539. The abbey precinct was later sold to local people and the buildings became in succeeding years a quarry for the townspeople, so that today the Barnack and Caen stone has all but disappeared, leaving only the flint core to show the outline of the abbey church and buildings.

The town continued to prosper, its wealth based on the wool industry. A few medieval secular buildings, such as the Guildhall, survive. The original street plan, too, is largely extant between Market Square and Angel Hill, next to the abbey grounds. Prosperity continued into the 18th century, as shown by the numerous impressive Georgian buildings – e.g., the Athenaeum on Angel Hill and the Manor House on Honey Hill, the latter built for the family of the Earl of Bristol. It was during this period, in 1711, that the nonconformist Unitarian Meeting House was built.

The area lacks coal deposits, so during the Industrial Revolution Bury St Edmunds suffered little of the ugly development seen elsewhere in the Midlands and North. Its main industries were brewing, watch- and clockmaking and those related to agriculture. Victorian terraces are hard to find, and there are many gems of domestic architecture in the central area of the town.

The parish church of St James, Bury St Edmunds, became a cathedral in 1914 when the Diocese of St Edmundsbury and Ipswich was created; the bishop resides in Ipswich. Plans for extending the building were drawn up shortly thereafter, but two world wars and constant shortage of funds have rendered progress slow. The porch and the first part of the cloisters were completed by 1961, while the new choir and crossing were finished in 1970 (marking the 1100th anniversary of St Edmund's death). In 1990, the new cathedral centre and song school were opened.

Controversy rages regarding the continuing lack of a decent tower for the cathedral. Stephen Dykes Bower, who died in 1994, left a £2 million legacy in his will for the completion of his designs, which included a new tower to complete the pre-

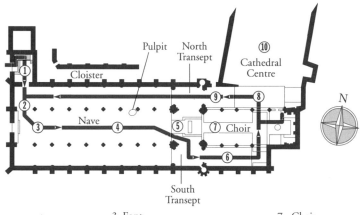

Key

1. Northwest Porch
2. West End

3. Font
4. Nave
5. Crossing
6. Lady Chapel

7. Choir
8. St Edmund's Chapel
9. Treasury
10. Cathedral Centre

sent unfinished stump. This sum was insufficient, and the authorities made an application for funds to the Millennium Commission. The application for a new tower and spire was rejected by the commission, who regarded the design as 'insufficiently distinctive'. A more recent design was submitted in 1997 involving a tall tower without a spire, the work of Hugh Mathew, who was Dykes Bower's assistant for many years.

Meanwhile, Bury St Edmunds is still a thriving market town and regional centre, with a particularly well preserved historic core. It prides itself on its cultural attractions and is well known for its flower displays, both in the Abbey Gardens and within the town itself.

TOUR OF THE CATHEDRAL
Start and finish: The northwest porch.

Although the cathedral is relatively small, it is certainly not without interest. Enter *via* the **northwest porch** (1) rather than the west door. Above the porch is the chapter house while to the north is a stretch of cloister; this complex was completed in 1960.

Go forward into the **west end** (2) and turn to note, above the porch on the inside, a cherub that once adorned the top of the old organ casing and was later retrieved from a Belgian antiques shop. If only the cherub could talk, so that it could tell us about all the adventures it had during its absence.

Dominating the west end is the **font** (3). The base is medieval and the rest Victorian, the work of Sir George Gilbert Scott (1811–1878). The ornate font cover, designed by F.E. Howard, commemorates servicemen who fell in World War I. Both base and cover were painted and gilded in medieval fashion by the Friends of the Cathedral in 1960.

In the wall, flanking the font, are the two Reynolds memorials. Sir James Reynolds died in 1739, having been the town's MP and Chief Baron of the Exchequer; the other memorial is to his wife, who died in 1736.

The windows of the west end, though Perpendicular in style, are in fact Victorian. The glass too is Victorian, an exception being in the Susanna Window on the south side, opposite the porch, which is composed of fragments believed to be from the old abbey church.

Proceed into the **nave** (4). Whereas the aisle roofs are original, the nave roof was designed by Sir George Gilbert Scott and completed in 1864. The hammer beams terminate with angels clutching shields which show either a scallop shell, the wallet and staff of St James, the Cross of St George or the crown and arrows of St Edmund. The colouring of the roof was begun in 1948 and took thirty-four years to complete. The nave roof's high pitch meant that Wastell's west end had to be modified – hence the Victorian windows. Note the kneelers in the nave; there are over a thousand of these, depicting local scenes or saints and made by parishioners in the diocese.

Walk on into the **crossing** (5). The rest of the cathedral to the north dates from 1970 onwards. Scott's chancel was inadequate for the demands of a modern cathedral, so a new east end was designed by Dykes Bower (1903–1994). He created an illusion of transepts, although the real things could never be built because of the proximity of the churchyard. The high altar, retained from Scott's chancel, is backed by modern ornaments. Note, close to the lectern, the old chair with the date 1600 carved on it.

Carry on to the south side and into the **Lady Chapel** (6) *via* impressive wrought-iron gates designed by Dykes Bower and made by a local craftsman (a septuagenarian indeed, so his was some achievement). The chapel was furnished by the women of the parish.

The Choir and St Edmund's Chapel

Return to the crossing and enter the **choir** (7). When this section of the cathedral was rebuilt to replace Scott's chancel an extra 36ft (11m) was added to the length of the building. Above the arches of the choir is a collection of shields representing the coats-of-arms of the barons who met at St Edmundsbury Abbey and agreed to force King John to sign the Magna Carta. The sedilia on the south side was resited there at the time of the extension. The *cathedra*, to the left of the altar, was designed by the same artist who produced the font cover; it has not, however, been coloured or gilded. The carving at the top of the throne depicts a wolf guarding King Edmund's decapitated head, as the well-known story of the saint describes.

The organ is an exceptional four-manual instrument with seventy-nine speaking stops. It is hoped to provide a suitable casing when funds allow.

On the north side of the choir is **St Edmund's Chapel** (8), completed in 1970, the 1100th anniversary of St Edmund's death. As part of the pageantry, local schools produced banners showing a visual history of the saint's life. These are now mounted on the wall of the chapel. The glass in the chapel's east window has been reworked from a window, thought to date from 1832, formerly in the east wall of the south aisle. The ugly brick wall on the north wall of the chapel will be removed when further funds become available – a situation all too familiar to cathedral builders past and present!

The Treasury
Near the chapel gates is a broad staircase to the **treasury** (9). An entrance fee is charged – drop your money into the early-19th-century poor box at the top of the stairs. As well as the cathedral's own valuable articles, the treasury contains gilt and silver plate from churches throughout the diocese.

Return now to the entrance porch, where a broad stairway leads down to the partially complete cloister and on to the **Cathedral Centre** (10), completed in 1990 and housing a lecture hall, committee room, sacristy, song school and refectory.

WALKING TOUR FROM BURY ST EDMUNDS CATHEDRAL
The walk begins with St Mary's Church, which has a magnificent hammerbeam roof. On the way to the city centre, with its public buildings, private houses and museums, we explore the remains of the Abbey of St Edmund. Along the way we encounter two museums and see domestic architecture from many periods.

Start and finish: The west front of the cathedral.
Length: 2 miles (3.2km).
Time: 2 hours, but allow longer if you want to visit the two museums and St Mary's Church.
Refreshments: The Alwyne House Tea Rooms in the Abbey Gardens are particularly enjoyable on a summer's day. A number of old inns of character offer good lunchtime fare, notably the One Bull and The Angel Hotel (both in Angel Hill), the Queen's Head (Churchgate) and the Olde White Hart Hotel (Southgate Street). The two hotels also offer accommodation.

Leave the west front and turn left past the Norman Bell Tower and then along Crown Street.

A Church to Remember
After a hundred yards or so (100m) you reach **St Mary's Church**. Regrettably, this is not always open (see page 168 for details). Try to arrange the tour around the opening times, as St Mary's is a gem – in many ways more interesting than the cathedral.

A church existed on the site in early Norman times, although no evidence of it survives. The oldest parts of the church, the crypt and the Decorated chancel, date from 1290–1350; the rest was built in the first half of the 15th century. The glass throughout is Victorian. The last century and a half has seen considerable restoration, which continues.

The nave roof is of hammerbeam construction, with eleven pairs of life-sized angels; unlike that in the cathedral, it has not been painted. The earlier chancel roof is of the wagon type, with some detailed bosses. There are five chapels or chantries; the North Chapel is the chapel of the Suffolk Regiment. St Mary's is also rich in monuments and brasses (mostly concealed under carpets).

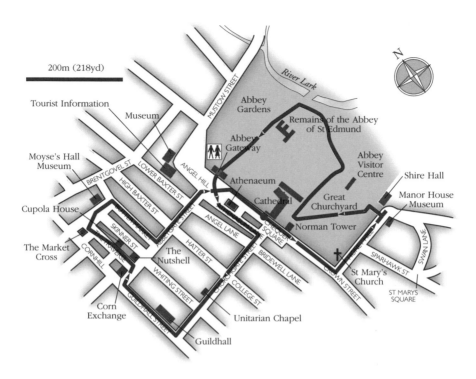

There are two other features of interest. First, on the north side of the sanctuary is the grave of Mary Tudor, who was a sister of Henry VIII and, through her marriage to Louis XII, Queen of France. She was originally buried at the abbey, but at the Dissolution her tomb was transferred to St Mary's. Second, at the base of the tower in the north aisle is a 'squint' – a slit in the wall through which the sexton (who lived in the first floor of the tower) could observe the service and see when to ring the sanctus bell.

Leave St Mary's by the entrance porch and turn immediately left into Honey Hill. About 150 yards (135m) along on the right is the **Manor House Museum**. The building dates from 1738, when it was built for Elizabeth Hervey, wife of the first Earl of Bristol. It later had several owners before being sold to the St Edmundsbury Borough Council in 1988 and being converted into a museum, which opened in January 1993. It has displays of costume, fine art, and horology (watch- and clockmaking was a local industry), plus temporary exhibitions.

The Abbey of St Edmund

Cross Honey Hill and fork obliquely left into the **Great Churchyard**, believed to have been created in 1120–48. This was the town's burial ground, rather than the abbey's, and over the centuries was a popular meeting place. The path through it gives you a good view of the north side of St Mary's Church and in particular the Notyngham Porch, which sits rather unhappily against the wall. The porch is named after a local grocer who in 1438 left £20 for the building of a south and west porch. These were never built, but in 1440 a porch was constructed, entering the north aisle through a re-used Decorated style doorway.

To the right of the path is the flint charnel house, where bodies and bones were piled up.

The path leads you on to a grassy square facing the **west front** of the old abbey. Incorporated into the huge arches are a number of former dwelling houses which appeared after the Dissolution. There were three arches in all, and they would have been even more impressive in the days before the ground was raised 4ft (1.3m) to ameliorate flooding. The front was completed by Abbot Samson, who built octagonal towers at each end. The remains of the south tower are now the home of the Abbey Visitor Centre. Before you leave the west front green, don't miss the statue of St Edmund, the work of the local Suffolk sculptress Elisabeth Frink (1930–1993).

From here there is an informative way-marked route to take you round the remains of the Abbey of St Edmund; at each stop you're supplied with information and also given concise directions to the next point.

Stop (1) is at the back of the Abbey Visitor Centre; here you find a model of the abbey as it would have been at its prime in medieval times. Stops (2), (3), (4) and (5) concentrate on the ruins of the abbey itself, including the position of the Shrine of St Edmund. Particularly impressive are the huge supporting pillars at the one-time crossing. The remains consist almost entirely of just the flint and rubble cores of the pillars and walls, the building stone having been robbed by the townspeople over the centuries. Stop (6) looks at some of the other monastic buildings – such as the prior's house, the dormitory and the infirmary. Stop (7) is at the abbot's garden, from where the 13th-century Abbot's Bridge can still be seen. Stop (8) is in the middle of the ornamental gardens which mark the location of the Great Court, whence the abbot administered royal justice. This was surrounded by other busy abbey buildings – e.g., the kitchen, brewery, bakery, granary and workshops. Stop (9) is at the magnificent Abbey Gate; as we saw, the Norman original was destroyed in the town riots of 1327 and the townspeople had to build a replacement, completed c1340, next to the ruins. Note that today's tower does not quite line up with Abbeygate Hill opposite. The final stop (10) is back at the Norman tower, built in 1120–48 and now used as the cathedral's bell tower.

A Prosperous City

You're probably a little 'abbeyed out' by now, so carry on into the city centre, which has a street plan laid out in a grid pattern. As in many medieval towns, there are two squares – one for God and one for the people. The people's square is the marketplace, while God's is **Angel Hill**, a gently sloping open space leading down to the Abbey Gate.

Angel Hill has a wealth of historic buildings, including the house known as Angel Corner, the Angel Hotel and the building which now houses the Tourist Information Office. By far the most fascinating building here, however, is the **Athenaeum**, a late-18th-century assembly house which has been serving that purpose for the townspeople ever since its completion. It has a fine ballroom, said to have been designed by the Adam brothers.

Take the alleyway, Angel Lane, on the right-hand side of the Athenaeum known. Turn right at the end into Churchgate Street. A couple of hundred yards (180m) along on the right is the **Unitarian Chapel** or **Meeting House**. Built in 1711 as a Presbyterian chapel, this is generally regarded as one of the finest nonconformist chapels in Britain. Recently restored, it is well worth a visit. Note in particular the double-decker pulpit.

Continue to the end of Churchgate Street and turn right into Guildhall Street. A few yards down it, on your right, is the **Guildhall** which was the St Edmundsbury Council Chamber until 1966. The central part of the building was built in the late 15th century, but a doorway inside the main porch is considerably older. The two wings were added in 1807.

Keep going along Guildhall Street until you get to the junction with Abbeygate Street. Immediately opposite is the **Corn Exchange**, an imposing building with a huge six-column portico and arched windows and pilasters on each side. This still operates as a corn exchange on market days. The ground floor is largely shops, while the upper storey is now a concert hall.

Go to the right of the Corn Exchange into a pedestrianized street, The Traverse. On the corner is the **Nutshell**, which claims to be the smallest pub in Britain. Admittedly it is far from unique in this, but certainly you couldn't swing a cat inside its single, minute bar, and often the drinkers have to resort to the pavement instead.

As you walk along The Traverse you'll notice **Cupola House** on the right. This dates from the late 17th century and was built by Thomas Macro, a well known local apothecary. It has a cupola, a belvedere and a second-floor balcony that projects over the street.

Market Square
The next building on the left is the impressive **Market Cross**, completed in 1780 and generally regarded as the city's most attractive post-medieval building. Designed by Robert Adam (1728–1792), it originally had a theatre on the first floor and an open market on the ground floor. The theatre later moved to its present site in the Corn Exchange and the first floor was made a concert hall; it has also functioned as the town hall. Today the ground floor consists of a number of commercial premises and the upper floor has become an art gallery.

Step now into Market Square which, despite the parked cars and garish shopfronts, still retains an historic air. The gem here is undoubtedly **Moyse's Hall**, one of the few surviving Norman domestic buildings in the country and certainly the oldest in East Anglia. The two rounded window arches you can see from the outside are typical of the period, while the interior is even more impressive. Moyse's Hall has had an interesting history, being successively a workhouse, a police station, a gaol and, during Victorian times, a railway parcels and enquiry office. Today it is a museum, concentrating on the historic and archaeological aspect of the area.

Leave Market Square *via* the Buttermarket and, on reaching Abbeygate Street, turn to the left. This will soon bring you back to Angel Hill and the west end of the cathedral.

Ely

Access: Ely is a focal point in the Fenland road system. It is situated on the A10, with easy access from the M11 *via* the Cambridge bypass. National Express coaches run from London to Cambridge; thereafter use the local Cambus services. Ely is a major junction on the recently electrified Kings Lynn–Liverpool Street line; there are connections with Norwich, Peterborough, Ipswich and the Midlands, and a new service to Stansted, the nearest international airport. The railway station is on the south of the city.

Ely derives its name from the Fenland setting. The place was once known as Elig or Elge, meaning 'island of eels', which were, and still are, prolific on the waterways of the Fens.

Ely owes its existence to St Etheldreda (d679). One of four daughters of Anna, ruler of East Anglia, she was twice unsuccessfully married, eventually fleeing her second husband to set up an abbey on land she had inherited on a low hill at what is now Ely. This was believed to be in 637. There was a small settlement about a mile (0.5km) to the north called Cratendune. On the founding of the abbey, the inhabitants abandoned their village and resettled close by.

In 870 the abbey, along with many others in East Anglia, was destroyed by raiding Danes. It was another century before Benedictine monks reestablished a monastery on the site. Meanwhile the remains of St Etheldreda had become a pilgrims' shrine; it is recorded that King Canute came to Ely with gifts of gold and jewels for it. The monks founded a school – at which Edward the Confessor received part of his early education.

During the Norman conquest, Ely and the Fens were a stubborn pocket of Saxon resistance, led by Hereward the Wake. Eventually William the Conqueror himself was obliged to come to the area in an attempt to overcome the rebels, an aim eventually achieved only with the help of treacherous monks.

The cathedral, to replace the old Saxon church, was begun soon afterwards, in 1083, under the stimulus of early abbots such as Simeon. The east end was completed by 1106, followed by the north and south transepts, the nave (1130) and the northwest and southwest transepts. The central and west towers are thought to have been finished c1189. The final result displays the full range of Norman/Romanesque architecture, particularly well seen in the southwest transept. The stone used was almost entirely Barnack limestone, brought by water from Lincolnshire.

In the interim, in 1109, the monastic church was made a cathedral and the existing abbot, Herve le Breton, became the first bishop while remaining the head of the monastery. Because of this dual role, there is no *cathedra* at Ely. (The bishop, as abbot, would have occupied a place in the stalls on the south side of the choir, while the prior had a similar seat on the north side.)

There have been only six additions to the cathedral since Norman times. In 1215 the Galilee Porch was completed at the west end in Early English style under the

91

direction of Bishop Eustace. His successor, Hugh de Northwold, demolished the Norman east end and built a presbytery of six bays, again in Early English style; completed in 1253 largely at his own expense, this presbytery was able to cope with the increasing numbers of pilgrims to the shrine of St Etheldreda. When the cathedral tower collapsed in 1322 it was replaced by the famous stone octagon topped by a wooden lantern, unique in British cathedral architecture.

Before the tower fell, work had started on the Lady Chapel, and after some delays it was completed in 1349. The final additions were the two chantry chapels at the east end – Bishop Allcock's Chantry was completed in the late 15th century and Bishop West's Chantry in *c*1534.

The monastery was dissolved in 1539 and, although the basic structure of the cathedral had been completed, many of the images, statues and shrines were destroyed at this time, including St Etheldreda's shrine. However, Henry VIII swiftly refounded the cathedral and school.

Oliver Cromwell (1599–1658) lived in Ely for a number of years before he became Lord Protector of England. In his capacity as MP and governor of Ely he had the cathedral closed for some seventeen years. The house in which he lived is now the Tourist Information Office. The 17th century also saw the first attempt at draining the Fens, an endeavour supervised by the Dutch engineer Sir Cornelius Vermuyden (*c*1595–*c*1683). Cromwell was initially opposed to this work as he believed it would deprive the Fenmen of their livelihood, but in fact the drained land was fertile and Ely became a flourishing market centre.

By the 18th century (as noted by Daniel Defoe in 1724) the cathedral was in bad shape. A thorough survey of the fabric was begun by the architect James Essex in 1750, and over the next twenty years a considerable amount of repair work (rather than restoration) was carried out.

Until the mid-19th century, produce to and from Ely was still waterborne and the Waterside area of the city sprouted hythes and warehouses to deal with the goods. All this changed with the arrival of the railway in 1845, linking Ely to Norwich and London. A new railway station built two years later gave further impetus to the south side of the town.

The general neglect of the cathedral continued, until in 1839 Dean George Peacock arranged for Sir George Gilbert Scott (1811–1878) to embark on a thorough restoration. This lasted thirty years and to a large extent returned the cathedral to its former magnificence. The city of Ely was meanwhile developing agriculture-related industries such as brewing and jam making, and a large corn exchange was built in the marketplace. In the 1920s the first sugarbeet factory appeared just outside the town.

In 1938 the Lady Chapel, which had been used as a parish church, was handed back to the dean and chapter and thereafter underwent a comprehensive cleaning and refurbishment. By the mid-1950s it was clear that a considerable amount of restoration was needed, and in 1986 a public appeal was launched to finance the work. Several million pounds were raised and restoration proceeded in all parts of the cathedral. The decision to charge an entrance fee did not meet with universal approval, but Ely is a small city – just over 12,000 inhabitants – and additional resources are needed to fund the ongoing restoration work.

Ely remains a market town, but the brewery, corn exchange and sugarbeet factory have all gone. A western bypass and a pedestrianized shopping centre have improved the quality of life, and there is a new emphasis on leisure and tourism based around the riverside and the cathedral – the 'Ship of the Fens', as it is sometimes called.

TOUR OF THE CATHEDRAL
Start and finish: The west end.

The **west end** (1) is best viewed from the Palace Green, where the lopsided nature of this part of the cathedral is clearly seen. The west end is unique among British cathedrals in that it has a west tower, originally with two transepts. One of these, the north, fell down some time during the 15th century and was never replaced. Despite this absence, the west front presents one of the finest Norman facades in the country, with numerous tiers of blind arcading. The west tower was completed *c*1200 and was later topped with a stone spire. This was replaced in the 14th century with an octagonal capping, which until 1801 had a lead-coated wooden spire.

Enter the cathedral through the **Galilee Porch** (2). Built 1200–1215, in the time of Bishop Eustace, this is a two-storey structure in Early English style with delicate shafts of Purbeck marble. Once you're through the doors of the Galilee Porch you find yourself under the **west tower** (3). The patterns of the tiled floor form a labyrinth; the distance from the entrance to the centre is 215ft (66m), the exact height of the tower.

Step now into the **southwest transept** (4), which includes St Catherine's Chapel. This area shows the full range of Romanesque architecture, starting with the classic rounded Norman arches, through interlocking and dogtooth to the pointed transitional windows at the top. The restoration programme in this area is now complete. Before you leave note the stone font, which shows the symbols of the four Evangelists.

From the Nave to the South Transept
To go into the rest of the cathedral you have to pay. Having done so, proceed into the **nave** (5), which dates from 1110–30. It gives the impression of being long, well lit and narrow, largely because the pulpitum – which separated monks from public – was pulled down during the repairs of James Essex in the 18th century. The proportions of the arcade, triforium and clerestory are exceptional. (The triforium is not blind and is probably better referred to as a tribune.) The wide galleries are best appreciated from the Stained Glass Museum, which occupies the south side at this level. Despite the strong Barnack limestone pillars, there is no vaulting. The wooden ceiling was boarded in during the Scott renovations in 1858 and painted by Henry Styleman le Strange from Hunstanton. His designs were based on those at St Michael's Church at Hildesheim in Germany. Unfortunately, le Strange died before finishing; the work was completed by his friend Thomas Gambier Parry from Gloucester.

Move now into the **south aisle** (6). Two doors led from here into the cloisters (which did not survive the Dissolution). The south (monks') door served as a processional entrance to the cathedral and is richly carved, but lacks a tympanum. The **prior's door**, which should be viewed from the exterior, is one of the most notable features of the cathedral. It is thought to date from 1150 and is significant for the elaborate stone carving in the pillars and rounded arch. The tympanum is filled with flat figure carving (the sculptors of the time had not yet mastered carving in the round) portraying, among other subjects, Christ in Majesty supported by archangels. Note, too, the particularly gruesome corbel heads. Following recent restoration, the prior's door has been enclosed to protect it from further weathering.

While in the south aisle look for **Ovin's Stone**, the base of a Saxon Cross commemorating Ovin, Etheldreda's steward. It was discovered in the 18th century in the village of Haddenham, where it had been used as a mounting block.

The **south transept** (7), one of the oldest parts of the cathedral, houses two of its most modern additions – two sculptures, both gifts: *Mary Magdelene Meeting her Risen Christ* by Davis Wynn and *Christus* by Hans Feibusch. On the east side of the south transept is the **Chapel of St Dunstan and St Ethelwold**. These two Benedictine monks revolutionized monastery life and music at Glastonbury. The chapel contains an interesting mosaic icon.

The Octagon and Lantern Tower

Walk on to the crossing, where you can appreciate the **Octagon and Lantern Tower** (8). The original Norman tower collapsed in 1322, remarkably without loss of life. The sacrist of the time, Alan de Walsingham, decide to replace it with something completely different. The remains of the four tower pillars were removed and he took one bay from each of the two transepts, the nave and the choir, to leave a vast central space linked by arches set at 45° to each other, giving an irregular octagon unique in British church architecture. The capitals on the eight pillars (binoculars are useful here) depict scenes in the life of St Etheldreda.

Roofing the octagon, which is 74ft (22m) wide, was clearly a problem. A stone vault was out of the question. The solution was a lantern tower built of wood faced externally with lead. It took fourteen years to build this under the direction of the master carpenter William Hurley. The vertical timbers, 63ft (19m) long and 3ft 4in (1m) thick at the base, were made from oak trees brought from Chicksands, Bedfordshire. The whole structure is remarkably successful, flooding the cathedral with light and marred only by the uninspiring Victorian glass.

The Choir and Presbytery

Proceed into the **choir** (9). Its first three bays were destroyed when the central tower fell, and were rebuilt in Decorated style. The stalls are 14th-century and were originally located beneath the octagon. The canopies are richly carved – look for the Victorian additions, done by a Belgian artist from Louvain, showing Old Testament scenes on the south side and New Testament scenes on the north. There are also some misericords of note.

Walk up three steps into the **presbytery** (10). Originally the east end of the choir had a Norman apse, but Bishop Hugh de Northwold (in office 1229–54), worried by the increasing number of pilgrims visiting the Shrine of St Etheldreda, demolished the east end and extended the cathedral by six bays with his fine presbytery made of Barnack limestone and Purbeck marble in Early English style. The proportions reflect those of the nave. Dogtooth ornamentation, deeply cut carving, tierceron-ribbed vaulting and strongly carved bosses and corbels make this one of the gems of British Gothic architecture.

The Shrine of St Etheldreda itself was destroyed during the Reformation, but the spot is marked by a commemorative slate. It is not the only thing missing. As we've noted, you can seek in vain for a *cathedra*. However, to the right of the high altar are two modern wooden 'thrones', which were occupied by the Queen and Prince Philip at the distribution of Maundy Money.

Former Bishops

Turn next into the **south choir aisle** (11), on whose floor you'll find a brass of the notorious Bishop Goodrich, who at the time of the Reformation was responsible for much of the destruction of statues, stained glass and ornaments here, and was later rewarded with the post of Lord Chancellor of England.

The **east end** (12) of the cathedral has two fine chantry chapels. In the south aisle is **Bishop West's Chapel**, completed *c*1538, a year prior to his death and just before the Dissolution. A wealthy man and on occasion Henry VIII's diplomatic envoy, West travelled widely in Europe, and the Italian influence in his chapel, with its early Renaissance ceiling, is clear to see. There are no figures in the numerous niches, and probably never were, reflecting the trend away from overadornment.

To reach the second chantry chapel, Bishop Allcock's Chapel, you must pass through the **Chapel of St Etheldreda**, dedicated in 1957 to those local people who lost their lives in World War II. **Bishop Allcock's Chapel**, facing the north aisle, was built 1488–1500 of soft chalky Cambridgeshire clunch, which was carved into ornate pinnacles. Here the numerous niches (in contrast to those in West's

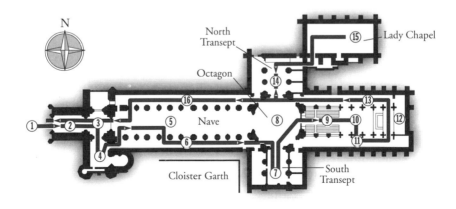

Key	5. Nave	11. South Choir Aisle
	6. South Aisle	12. East End
1. West End	7. South Transept	13. North Choir Aisle
2. Galilee Porch	8. Octagon and Lantern Tower	14. North Transept
3. West Tower	9. Choir	15. Lady Chapel
4. Southwest Transept	10. Presbytery	16. North Aisle

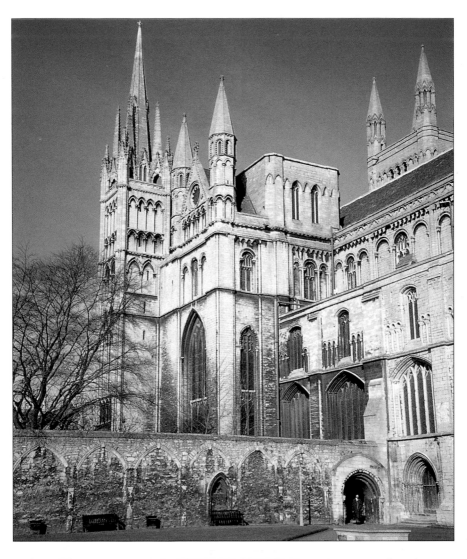

Plate 22: *Peterborough Cathedral. View of the south side from the remains of the old abbey cloisters, parts of which are older than the cathedral (see page 123).*

Plate 23: *The Guild Hall, Peterborough. Also known as the Buttercross, the upper floors of the Guild Hall have been used as a gaol, a magistrate's court and a schoolroom (see page 125).*

Plate 24: *Norwich Cathedral. The elegant 15th-century spire is the second highest in England. The cathedral also features wonderful lierne vaulting and impressive cloisters (see page 107).*

Plate 25: *Norwich. The Market Place is surrounded by features of interest, including the 15th-century Guildhall, the modern City Hall and the Victorian Royal Arcade (see page 113).*

Plate 26: Southwell. The Saracen's Head is a distinctive half-timbered coaching inn in the centre of the town. It dates as far back as the late 14th century (see page 132).

Plate 27: Southwell Minster – the west front, with its Germanic-looking spires (see page 127).

Plate 28: The central tower of Southwell Minster is Norman in style (see page 126).

The acoustics of the Lady Chapel are something special. The celebrated Six-Second Echo makes conversation difficult but is superb for singers. Choirs come from all over the world to sing here, and you may be lucky enough to catch one should you be here at lunchtime.

Return to the north transept and proceed into the **north aisle** (16) of the nave. You can see here one of several huge Victorian Gurney stoves used to heat the cathedral. Originally they used solid fuel, but they were converted to gas in 1982.

Towards the western end of the aisle is a large bell. This once hung in the tower of St Nicholas Church, Feltwell, but, as it had been dedicated to St Etheldreda (probably *c*1500), it was given to the cathedral.

Go to the end of the north aisle, and from there on to the west end, where your tour finishes.

Before leaving the cathedral, visitors may wish to see the Stained Glass Museum, which is located in the South Triforium. Access is via the southwest transept and a narrow spiral staircase. You might also like to try your hand at brass rubbing. This takes place in the north nave aisle, next to the shop.

WALKING TOUR FROM ELY CATHEDRAL

Two connected walks are described below. The shorter one looks only at the area of the college – the collection of former monastic buildings by the cathedral. The longer one continues from the college to take in some of the city's other historic buildings and its riverside life.

THE COLLEGE WALK
Start and finish: The west front of the cathedral.
Length: ¼ mile (0.5km)
Time: No more than 15 minutes.
Refreshments: Space in the cathedral refectory is at a premium; the cathedral-run Almonry is a better bet.

Leaving the west end of the cathedral, turn right into a grassy area known as **Cross Green** (1). This was the site of the former Church of the Holy Cross, which acted as a parish church from the mid-14th century until 1566. The green was a burial ground for some time. Opposite is **Steeple Gateway** (2), once the entrance to the burial ground and possibly the route pilgrims took to the monastery. The gateway has a Tudor framework built over a 14th-century undercroft.

Further along the path is the **sacrist's gate** (3), through which tradesmen came to the monastery; it is believed to have been built in 1325. Nearby is the **bell tower** (4), sometimes known as Goldsmith's Tower – the prior's goldsmith had a workshop here. All the buildings round here formed the offices and stores of the sacrist to the monastery.

Next to the sacrist's gate is the **Almonry** (5). The building once contained a school and its dormitories, and dates from the 12th century. The almoner was that official of the monastery who distributed alms to the poor. Nowadays, the Almonry is a restaurant run by the cathedral; in summer you can eat in the charming walled garden.

Medical Matters and More

Go to the east end of the cathedral along a path which gives good views of the Lady Chapel and, on the south side, the remains of the cloister walls. Turn into **Firmary Lane** (6), which used to be roofed over and was the monastery's infirmary. The arches forming the bays can still be seen in the walls.

The first building on the left is **Powcher's Hall** (7), named after an early prior. It was used as a 'bloodletting house' where monks were bled using leeches – a practice thought at the time to be healthy (and which has once again found favour in recent years in the treatment of hypertension).

Opposite is the **canonry** (8), which still retains some 12th-century features. Further on the left is the **Painted Chamber** (9), built in 1335 as a residence for Alan de Walsingham. On the opposite side of Firmary Lane is the **Black Hostelry** (10), used to accommodate visiting Benedictine monks (who wore black habits).

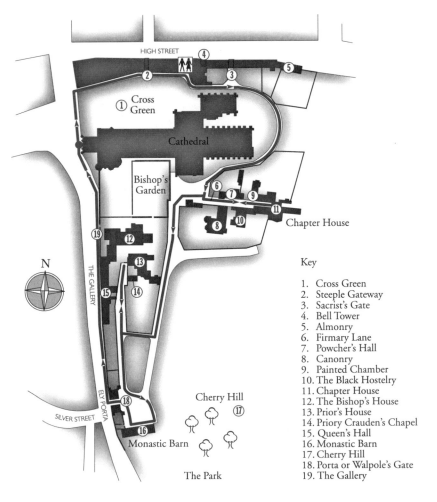

Key

1. Cross Green
2. Steeple Gateway
3. Sacrist's Gate
4. Bell Tower
5. Almonry
6. Firmary Lane
7. Powcher's Hall
8. Canonry
9. Painted Chamber
10. The Black Hostelry
11. Chapter House
12. The Bishop's House
13. Prior's House
14. Priory Crauden's Chapel
15. Queen's Hall
16. Monastic Barn
17. Cherry Hill
18. Porta or Walpole's Gate
19. The Gallery

Today, it continues to offer bed and breakfast; dress optional. At the end of the lane is the **chapter house** (11). Once the chapel of the infirmary, it is now the administrative centre of the cathedral.

Return along Firmary Lane and turn left. On your right is a further group of old monastery buildings, the first being the **bishop's house** (12). Formerly the great hall of the monastery, it was later the deanery. It was rebuilt in the 14th century, but retains a 13th-century vaulted undercroft. Next comes the **priory** (13) or prior's house, also rebuilt in the 14th century and now used by the King's School.

At the end of the priory garden, turn right into a lane which leads back to **Prior Crauden's Chapel** (14). This gem of Decorated architecture, dating back to 1324, has some medieval wall paintings and a fascinating tiled floor showing Adam and Eve with the serpent. Although it is now used as a chapel by the King's School, you can look around if you collect the key from the chapter house (weekday office hours) or from the headmaster's house (weekends).

Opposite the Chapel is the **Queen's Hall** (15), built to provide accommodation for Queen Philippa, wife of Edward III, and now the house of the headmaster of the King's School.

Returning southwards along the lane, you are confronted by the impressive **Monastic Barn** (16), a brick-and-timber building now converted into a dining room for the King's School. At its west end is the wooded **Cherry Hill** (17), which marks the site of a Norman 12th-century motte and bailey castle.

Outside the College

You now leave the area of the college through the **Porta** or **Walpole's Gate** (18) (named after the 14th-century prior). This was the main gateway into the Benedictine priory. On the ground floor was the porter's lodge, while other parts of the building housed the prior's prison. The Porta, like most of the other college buildings, is regrettably not open to visitors.

From the Porta turn right and proceed along **The Gallery** (19), named after the bridge which once led from the bishop's palace to the cathedral. This brings you back to the west end of the cathedral.

THE CITY WALK

Start and finish: The west front of the cathedral.
Length: 3 miles (4.8km).
Time: About 1¼ hours, but allow longer if you want to visit the two museums.
Refreshments: Few ancient inns en route apart from the Lamb Hotel in Lynn Road, a 13th-century coaching inn (accommodation). The Cutter Inn, on the riverside, can also be recommended.

Walk across to Palace Green. On the south side is the **Bishop's Palace**, an imposing brick-and-stone building begun in the 14th century and not completed until 400 years later. Prior to its construction the Bishops of Ely used as many as ten different palaces or manor houses scattered around the south of England. In its time the palace has been a convalescent home for servicemen, a school for handicapped children and a private residence. It is currently a Sue Ryder home.

Opposite the palace is a private house, The Chantry, built on the site of Bishop Northwold's Chantry Chapel. At the far end of the green is a **cannon** captured from the Russians during the Crimean War and given to the city by Queen Victoria in 1860.

Church and Commonwealth

Close to the cannon is **St Mary's Church**, a fine parish church dating from the time of Bishop Eustace in the 13th century and displaying a variety of architectural styles: the columns in the nave are Norman, the north door is Early English, and the spire and tower are Decorated. A curiosity is the tablet set in the southwest wall commemorating those executed for taking part in the Littleport and Ely famine riots of 1816. The church is usually open, although many of its more valuable artefacts are removed for safety during the week – a sad comment on modern society. A nursery school is tucked away at the rear.

Carry on to **Oliver Cromwell's House**, a beautifully restored half-timbered building some 750 years old. Cromwell lived here for eleven years, and two of his daughters were born here. The house was once the vicarage for St Mary's, and has also been a public house; it is now owned by the District Council and is used as a Tourist Information Centre. An audiovisual presentation describes many aspects of Cromwell's life.

Cross the road into St Mary's Street, noting the Old Fire Engine House, now a restaurant. Walking along the street you'll find on your left **Bedford House**, which was the headquarters of the corporation responsible for much of the drainage of the Fens. Note the coat-of-arms over the door – the Latin motto loosely translates as 'dryness pleases'!

Just past the end of the street is the 14th-century **Lamb Hotel**; many of the pilgrims to St Etheldreda's shrine would have been clients.

Cross into the High Street, which formed the northern boundary of the college. Close to the sacrist's gate is the **Ely Museum**, opened in 1974. Its present displays concern the archaeology and social history of the area, including the drainage of the Fens.

Continue along the High Street until you reach Market Square. Now you're in the main shopping area of Ely. Market day is Thursday and the square is the venue for the May Fair and for the Etheldreda Fair, held in October.

The Waterside and Riverside Areas

Continue past Market Square down Fore Hill and into **Waterside**. This area, once semi-derelict, has in recent years undergone some gentrification, a number of buildings having been restored with the help of the Ely Preservation Trust.

Keep going until you reach the river. The **Riverside** area, formerly known as Broad Hithe, is where goods were unloaded in the days when the Ouse formed the region's main transport artery. Many of the old warehouses remain, although their usage has changed; a particularly good example is the three-storey antique centre. The attractive Riverside Walk has been known in part as the Quai d'Orsay since 1981, when Ely was twinned with the French town of this name, just outside Paris.

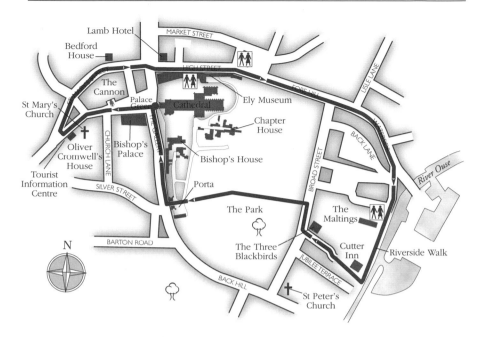

Among the historic buildings in this area are the **Cutter Inn** – named after not a boat but the men who 'cut' the arm of the River Ouse nearer the city – and the **Maltings**, formerly Harlock's Brewery and now sympathetically converted into a conference centre.

The recreational aspects of the area are clear to see. There is a flourishing pleasure-boat hire yard on the town side of the river, while the marina at Babylon, on the far side of the Ouse, has space for two hundred craft. Two boathouses provide rowing facilities for the King's School and Cambridge University.

By Way of The Three Blackbirds

To leave the Riverside area, take the footpath at the side of the Cutter Inn. This leads into a side street at whose end is **The Three Blackbirds**. Dating from the end of the 13th century, this house is probably the oldest secular building in Ely. Once belonging to a wealthy merchant, it was a public house in the 19th century. It has more recently been restored by the Ely Preservation Trust and converted into three dwellings.

Turn right into Broad Street. About fifty yards (50m) along, turn left through an ornamental gateway into the **Park**, which occupies the area between the college and Broad Street. The Park is owned by the dean and chapter of the cathedral, and originally contained the prior's vineyard and a number of fishponds, filled in at the middle of the last century.

Take the path up the hill, noting the old castle mound to the left; there are fine views of the cathedral to the right. Eventually you come once more to the Porta. Turn right here into The Gallery and return to the west end of the cathedral.

Norwich

Access: The nearest motorway (M11) is over fifty miles away (30km), but the city is the focal point of a network of A-class roads and trunk roads, linking it with all the major towns of East Anglia; allow at least 2½ hours from London, a little longer from the Midlands. National Express: five coaches a day from London Victoria to Norwich; one coach a day from Birmingham. Local bus services are largely run by the Eastern Counties Company. InterCity trains run from Liverpool Street to Norwich's Thorpe Station, a ten-minute walk from the cathedral and city centre. Norwich Airport, on the city's northern outskirts, has flights to other English cities, scheduled continental passenger services and tourist charter flights.

The ancient core of the' city of Norwich is located on a double bend of the River Wensum a little to the north of its confluence with the River Yare. Early settlement concentrated around the lowest fording point of the river, where there were nearby gravel terraces. These terraces have yielded flint axeheads which have been dated to the Palaeolithic, but it was not until Neolithic times that man began to seriously influence the form of the landscape as agriculture came to occupy the drier terraces.

The Romans preferred to develop their headquarters at nearby Caistor (Venta Icenorum). Their presence improved communications in the area, which helped Norwich grow as a route centre.

Saxons and Angles, originally arriving as raiders, now occupied the area and added their typical placenames to the area. A group of Middle Saxon villages near the Wensum coalesced to form a market town which took its name from one of them, Northwic. During this period numerous churches were built, with typical Saxon round flint towers. By late Saxon times development was still largely north of the river, centring on what is now Magdalen Street. The first defences – simple earth walls and ditches – were built, mainly as a protection from raiding Danes.

Huge changes came soon after the Norman invasion in 1066. William the Conqueror quickly put his stamp on the city and by 1075 the castle had been built. Of motte and bailey design, it stood on an artificial hill, replacing over ninety late-Saxon houses. The original building was of timber, but in 1120 work began on a new stone keep some 66ft (20m) high and faced with Caen stone.

The Normans also began the construction of a cathedral, following the transference of the see of East Anglia from Thetford to Norwich in 1094. On the same time work began on a Benedictine monastery for some sixty monks. The building materials used for the cathedral were local flints and white Caen limestone, shipped across the Channel, up the River Wensum and finally by a small canal from the river at Pulls Ferry to the site.

The cathedral was consecrated in 1278. The original roof and the tower, both wooden, were destroyed by a fire in 1463. Later in the 15th century a vaulted stone roof and a stone spire were added, along with the presbytery, which had exterior flying buttresses to support it. By now Norwich had become a cosmopolitan settlement, the Anglo-Danish population augmented by French, Bretons, Flemings and Jews.

Already by medieval times Norwich had become one of the wealthiest cities in the country. The population, which may have numbered 10,000, sustained over one hundred trades, of which weaving was the most important. The city was not without its problems, however. There was an intolerable gap between rich and poor, and conditions for the latter were generally dirty and unhealthy; the Black Death probably claimed as many as two-thirds of the population. Fires were a constant problem – eventually it was decreed that thatch roofs were to be replaced by tiles.

The gap between the urban poor and the wealthy families continued into the Tudor age, but overall prosperity was increased by the influx of refugees from the Netherlands. These so-called 'strangers' were mainly weavers but brought many other trades to the city.

There were no great upheavals when the monastery was dissolved in 1538 – the prior became the first dean and former monks became canons – except that the Lady Chapel was demolished. During the Civil War Norwich remained largely loyal to parliament. Although the city was outside the main area of fighting the war was a strain on resources and disrupted the woollen and other trades. The cathedral did not escape unscathed: rioting Puritans destroyed some of the artefacts.

Georgian times saw the woollen industry lose much of its influence to the textile towns of the North, but other industries continued to prosper. Georgian development remained within the city walls, but this changed in the 19th century, which saw Norwich's most spectacular expansion. By 1871 the population reached 80,000, swollen by farm labourers looking for work in the city and the development of the factory economy. The growth industries were now leather, brewing, soap-making, papermaking and a host of agriculture-related trades. The coming of the railways provided a great stimulus to economic development, while at the same time the lack of coal in the area prevented the ugly growth typical of the industrial cities of northern England.

The 20th century was marked by the coming of the tram car in the city centre. The suburbs had by now moved outside the walls. While World War I did not physically affect Norwich, one in nine of its servicemen were killed; most famously, the heroine Edith Cavell (1865–1915), a nurse from Norwich, was executed by the Germans for helping Allied prisoners escape. (A mountain in Alberta has been named after her by a grateful Canada.) During World War II the city experienced over forty air raids: 340 people were killed, 30,000 houses damaged and seven of the city's medieval churches destroyed. The cathedral was hit by a number of incendiary bombs.

The 1950s and 1960s saw major redevelopment, and unfortunately many of Norwich's historic buildings were demolished. By the 1970s sense prevailed, and the city's heritage became paramount. City authorities now work closely with charitable trusts, English Heritage and local groups such as the Norwich Society to ensure historic buildings are preserved.

Major recent changes have included the founding of the University of East Anglia, with its prestigious Sainsbury Centre for the Visual Arts, the opening of the Norwich regional airport at Horsham St Faiths, and the building of a new southern bypass. The city continues to develop as a regional centre for shopping, administration, sport, television and tourism.

The main activity at the cathedral has been a rolling restoration programme, while an important postwar addition has been the construction of the Visitor Centre, occupying the ancient monastic guest quarters over the cloisters.

TOUR OF THE CATHEDRAL
Start and finish: The west end.

The large Perpendicular window of the **west end** (1) has Victorian glass and is flanked by vertically grooved pillars, matching those on the tower – which, completed in 1145, is the tallest Romanesque tower in England. The door beneath the window is usually closed, so enter through the Norman arch on the west end's north side.

Go into the **nave** (2), completed *c*1120. The arcade and the triforium above it consist of rounded Norman arches. Look for two pillars with a spiral design; these

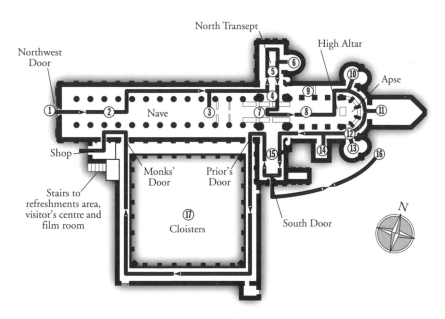

Key

1. West End
2. Nave
3. Pulpitum
4. Crossing
5. North Transept

6. St Andrew's Chapel
7. Choir
8. Presbytery
9. Reliquary Arch
   and Treasury
10. Jesus Chapel
11. St Saviour's Chapel

12. Stone Effigy
13. St Luke's Chapel
14. Bauchon Chapel of Our Lady
   of Pity
15. South Transept
16. Grave of Nurse Edith Cavell
17. Cloisters

are thought to have been prefabricated at the quarries at Caen. The clerestory was added in Perpendicular style in the late 15th century, in the time of Bishop Lyhart, and his rebus may be seen at the head of some of the pillars below it. At the same time a stone vaulted roof replaced the earlier wooden one, destroyed by fire. The vaulting is in tierceron, onto which *lierne* ribs have been added for purely decorative effect. The ribs on either side of the ridge produce alternating star and lozenge-shaped patterns – an effect continued throughout the choir, presbytery and transepts. There are countless bosses on the rib joints – over 300 have been recoloured and gilded in recent years. (Binoculars are useful for inspecting the bosses.) Despite the disparity in age between the Perpendicular clerestory and roof and the Norman arcade and triforium, the whole effect is oddly satisfying.

Flemish Lectern

Move along to the other end of the nave, to the stone screen or **pulpitum** (3), which with the ritual choir forms the last three bays of the nave; it divided the people's nave from the monks presbytery. Step to the side of the pulpitum and walk into the **crossing** (4), where a small altar has been placed for services. The main item of interest here is the lectern, which is Flemish and dates from 1380. Made of brass, it depicts a pelican feeding her young from her own breast.

From here, walk into the **north transept** (5). Note the private door for the bishop to reach his palace. On the east side of the transept is **St Andrew's Chapel** (6), the first of a number of chapels based on a double circle plan. This chapel is reserved for private prayer and meditation. The window is 13th-century, with later glass. The modern statue of the Madonna is by John Skelton, who was brought up in the city of Norwich.

The Choir and Presbytery

Now head eastwards and turn into the **choir** (7). It has stalls originally designed for the Benedictine monks, but recently renovated. Some stalls are kept open for visitors, so you can look at the misericords. One depicts an owl being mobbed by birds and a second shows a schoolmaster beating a small boy while others look on apprehensively.

Move further east into the **presbytery** (8), which continues the architectural scheme of the nave. The Norman arcade and triforium and the Gothic clerestory and vaulting give a height to the east end which is unusual in Britain - the comparison with some continental cathedrals is inevitable. The presbytery contains the bishop's throne which, unusually for an English cathedral, is placed behind the high altar. The main part of the throne is a simple medieval wooden chair. It rests on two ancient stones, all that is left of a stone seat brought to Norwich when the see was moved from Thetford in the 11th century.

Return to the north presbytery aisle, turn right and approach the **reliquary arch and treasury** (9). This was designed to display the cathedral treasures to pilgrims passing below as they went in procession round the ambulatory. Today the treasury contains not only cathedral artefacts but silverware lent by other churches in Norwich and the county. To reach it, pay a small fee (the proceeds go to charity) and climb the spiral staircase. Apart from its interesting silverware, the treasury is the best place in the cathedral to view the medieval wall paintings.

Returning to ground level, spend some time looking at the Erpingham Window, which contains a good collection of medieval glass from a variety of local sources, reassembled and leaded by the company of Kings of Norwich in 1963.

Continue around the ambulatory. On your left you will see the **Jesus Chapel** (10), dating from 1096 and cleverly restored. It has the remains of wall painting which probably covered most of the building. The prize feature of the chapel is the picture *The Adoration of the Magi*, painted in 1480 by Martin Schwarz. We are now in the apsidal east end of the cathedral, which was the site of the Lady Chapel, demolished during the Reformation. It was replaced in 1930 by **St Saviour's Chapel** (11), which is the regimental chapel of the Royal Norfolk Regiment, the honours of which drape the walls. The painted panels behind the altar come from the redundant Norwich church of St Michael-at-Plea.

Further along the ambulatory you'll notice in the wall a **stone effigy** (12) of what appears to be an early bishop giving his blessing with one hand and holding his pastoral staff in the other. The effigy was once thought to be of the cathedral's first bishop, Herbert de Lesonga, who died in 1119. Modern dating techniques, however, have cast doubt on this, as it is believed to have been made around 1100. It probably represents St Felix, who brought Christianity to East Anglia.

The Despenser Reredos
We now come to **St Luke's Chapel** (13), formerly dedicated to St John the Baptist and nowadays used as a parish church for the parishioners of St Mary in the Marsh. This chapel contains the Despenser reredos, said to have been donated by Bishop Despenser in 1381 and showing five scenes on painted glass panels. Claimed to be the greatest artistic treasure in East Anglia, this survived the Reformation only through being turned upside-down and used as a table top! The chapel is also the home of a rather battered medieval font, showing the Seven Sacraments.

Next you come to the **Bauchon Chapel of Our Lady of Pity** (14), named after the monk who built it in the 14th century. It has also acted as a consistory court. Don't miss its bosses; these tell the tale of an empress saved by the Virgin after being falsely accused by her brother, who had tried to seduce her.

The Grave of a Heroine
Leave the ambulatory at the chapter room (not open to the public) and go into the **south transept** (15). The south wall of this was entirely refaced at one stage to remove the traces of a 14th-century prison that used to be inside the building. Notice the Taylor Ramsden Window, which has 17th-century French glass in 16th-century Flemish style.

To visit the **Grave of Nurse Edith Cavell** (16), leave the south transept by the south door and turn left towards the east end of the cathedral. The simple grave is located between St Luke's and St Saviour's chapels on what was once the ancient burial ground of the monks. Prayers are said at her grave each Remembrance Day.

Return through the south transept and turn left through the **prior's door** to enter the cloisters. This door, which dates from *c*1310, is one of the most charming aspects of the cathedral and it is fitting that it leads to the largest cloisters of any English cathedral. Above its arch are seven figures in a radial arrangement. Behind them are gables, alternate ones in ogee form and liberally decorated with crockets.

The present **cloisters** (17) were built after the original Norman ones had been destroyed in a riot between the Norwich citizens and the cathedral staff in 1272. They are beautifully vaulted and have a fine collection of bosses, which have been skilfully recoloured and gilded. These bosses give a sociological account of medieval life and merit close attention. You may be glad of the movable mirror-topped tea trolley placed here to assist viewing. Look also for the monks' lavatorium (washing place) in the southwest corner and the various coats-of-arms which are scattered around.

Leave the cloisters by the monks' door in the northwest corner and return to the south aisle of the nave. Here you can visit the **Cathedral Shop** (18), which sells a variety of books, cards and other gifts. The tour concludes at the west end door.

WALKING TOUR FROM NORWICH CATHEDRAL

The amount of historic interest within the old city walls of Norwich is immense, and several walks of interest could be chosen. The figure-of-eight walk detailed below aims to give a general impression of the city's heritage. It includes a riverside walk and a look at a few of the city's medieval churches, some excellent museums and some specialist shopping areas.

Start and finish: The Cathedral Close at the west end of the cathedral.
Length: 2½ miles (4km).
Time: 2 hours; allow longer if you want to visit the museums.
Refreshments: The cathedral refectory is recommended for light snacks and coffee. Traditional pubs along the route offer bar meals, notably the Adam and Eve (Bishopsgate), the Red Lion (Bishop Bridge), the Louis Marchesi (Tombland), named after the man who founded the Round Table movement, the Wig and Pen St Martin (Palace Plain) and the Maid's Head Hotel (Tombland).

Norwich's **Cathedral Close** claims to be the largest of any English cathedral. It consists of an area of grass and trees, with statues of both the Duke of Wellington (1760–1842) and Lord Nelson (1758–1805). It is surrounded by buildings in a variety of architectural styles, including the Carnary Chapel (1316) and the Bishop's Palace to the north of the cathedral.

There are three gates to the Close, two by land and one by water. The oldest is St Ethelbert's Gate, to your south, built by the citizens of Norwich as a penance following the riots of 1272. The Erpingham Gate, to your north, was built in 1420 by Sir Thomas Erpingham who fought in the Battle of Agincourt (1415). A statue of him is in a small niche above the arch of the gateway.

If you're short of time, you can omit visiting sites 1–8 and start your walk from the Erpingham Gate (see page 107).

An Executed Rebel

Leave the Upper Close by St Ethelbert's Gate and take the roadway through the Lower Close, where there are some gems of domestic architecture. Note on the left the line of stables marking the course of the canal built to bring Caen stone to the cathedral site and eventually filled in during the 18th century. Eventually you come to **Pull's Ferry**, named after the last ferryman to ply his trade in this area. The present watergate dates from the 15th century, and the ferry house itself is probably 16th-century.

Take the Riverside Walk westwards, to your left. After a couple of hundred yards (180m) you reach **Bishop Bridge**. This three-arched stone bridge dates from *c*1340 and is the only surviving medieval bridge in Norwich.

If you feel energetic you can cross Bishop Bridge and take the road up the hill past the gasometers to **Kett's Heights**. There you'll be rewarded by a superb view across the city to the cathedral, castle and beyond. The hill is named after Robert Kett, a farmer from Wymondham, who in 1549 used the area as headquarters for his army of some 20,000 men protesting about the enclosure of common land. They were eventually defeated and Kett was hung in chains from the walls of Norwich Castle until he died.

Back on the Riverside Walk, pass behind the Red Lion pub and, after another two hundred yards (180m), you'll reach **Cow Tower**, at a bend in the river. For

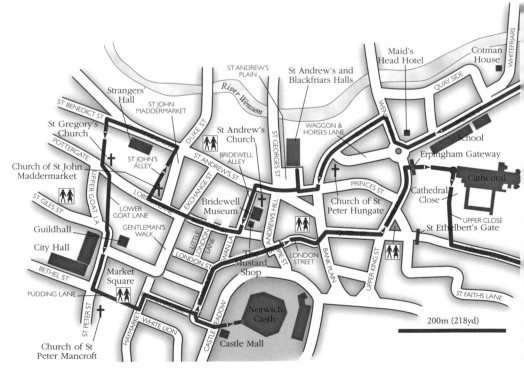

many years cows sheltered in this somewhat decrepit building, which dates from *c*1378 and was at one time part of the city's defences. It is built of flint and brick; if you can get inside you will see evidence of original roof vaulting. From here there is a good view of the cathedral tower and spire; the cathedral's original wooden spire fell in 1362 and was eventually replaced by a stone spire which, at 315ft, is the second tallest in Britain (after that at Salisbury).

Continue along the Riverside Walk for a further three hundred yards (270m) until you arrive at a new flint wall. Fork left here and pass through the wall to find in front of you the **Adam and Eve pub**. Claimed as the oldest pub in Norwich, the Adam and Eve was named after a wherry (one of the famous Norfolk sailing barges which plied the Wensum) and was a favourite wherrymen's inn. The brick-and-timber building dates from 1249 and has classic Dutch ends. There was a brewhouse on the site for over 700 years.

A City of Many Churches

Opposite the Adam and Eve are the new law courts. Further on, on the right, is the **Church of St Martin at Palace**, in whose graveyard many of Kett's men are buried.

There were once fifty-seven churches within the city walls of Norwich. Thirty-one remain, and of these only ten are used for worship. Sixteen of the redundant churches are cared for by the Norwich Historic Churches Trust, which restores and preserves these buildings – St Martin at Palace among them. The church – fittingly, because of its proximity to the probation office and law courts – is used today as a probation day centre.

In the small square opposite the church is **Cotman House**, once the home of John Sell Cotman (1782–1842), best-known of the 19th-century Norwich School of landscape artists.

Proceed now along **Palace Street**. To the left, set back from the road, is the **Bishop's Palace Gate**, thought to have been built *c*1436. This fine flint and stone gateway is unusual in having two arches, a large one for carriages and a smaller one for pedestrians. On the right is the Maid's Head Hotel, a 12th-century coaching inn.

You are now nearly back at the Erpingham Gate. (If you decided to miss the first part of the walk, this is where you join it.)

Church of St Martin at Palace

Magistrates' Court

River Wensum

Adam and Eve Pub

Cow Tower

BISHOPGATE

BISHOP BRIDGE ROAD

N

Bishop Bridge

Kett's Heights

RIVERSIDE WALK

Pull's Ferry

RIVERSIDE ROAD

Water Gate

Turn right at the mini-roundabout and proceed into Wensum Street. After fifty yards (50m) turn left into **Elm Hill**, one of the best-known historic streets in Britain.

At the corner of Elm Hill and Wensum Street is another redundant church, the **Church of St Simon and St Jude**, one of the oldest in the city. It contains a number of monuments to the Pettus family, who provided numerous mayors of Norwich. It was saved from demolition by the Norwich Society in the 1920s and is now used as an outdoor centre by the Scouts and Guides.

Opposite the church is Roaches Court. At the end of its alleyway is a small quay from where boats leave for river cruises and trips to the Broads.

Continue up the cobbled surface of Elm Hill, admiring the timber-framed houses, many with jettied walls and pastel washes over the plaster. Most of the buildings date from the 16th and 17th centuries, the earlier houses having been destroyed by fire. One building which survived was **Pettus House**, home of Sir John Pettus, knighted by Elizabeth I and mayor of the city in 1608. The upper storey windows have original leaded diamond glass. It is interesting to remember that in the 1920s Elm Hill was so run-down that it was on the point of demolition, being saved only by the efforts of the Norwich Society and the casting vote of the mayor.

A Church Museum and the Black Friars

At the top of Elm Hill is a small cobbled square. Fork left here and continue to Princes Street. Note on the corner the Briton's Arms coffee shop, which dates from the 14th century and was once a béguinage – a centre for a religious sisterhood whose members were not bound by strict vows and could return to the world if they chose.

Opposite the coffee shop is another redundant church, the **Church of St Peter Hungate**. Its Perpendicular windows reach almost to the roof, and there is a quaint stair-turret between the tower and the porch. Inside is a sensational hammerbeam roof with gilded ends. St Peter Hungate is now a museum and brass-rubbing centre.

Coming out of the museum, turn right along Princes Street until on your right you come to an open space, St Andrews Plain. The feature here is the combined building of **St Andrew's and Blackfriars Halls**, originally the choir and nave of the Convent Church of the Blackfriars. The Dominicans

Elm Hill

– the Black Friars – arrived in Norwich in 1226 and built their first church here between 1326 and 1413.

Looking at the building (largely constructed by Sir Thomas Erpingham) from here on Princes Street, St Andrew's Hall is the one on the left. It has an arcade of six windows in Decorated style with a handsome clerestory above; between each pair of windows is the Erpingham arms. The superb hammerbeam roof was a gift from the Paston family, whose coat-of-arms is seen in the 15th-century doorway.

The former choir, Blackfriars Hall, was once the chapel of the local guilds and later became the church of the Dutch population. Today both halls are used as meeting places for the citizens of Norwich and provide facilities for exhibitions, banqueting, conferences, concerts and speech days.

To the north of the halls are the remains of the friars' cloisters, dormitory, refectory and crypt. The first three are now used by Norwich School of Art, while the crypt has become a popular coffee bar.

Church and State

Cross St Andrews Street, noting on the left **St Andrew's Church**. Still open for worship, St Andrew's is the second largest church in Norwich (after St Peter Mancroft – see below). The windows are in Perpendicular style and are topped by a clerestory containing close-set windows. The sturdy flint tower has diagonal buttresses. The small graveyard obviously suffered when St Andrews Street was widened for trams at the start of the 20th century. The church is usually open and well worth a visit. Although the fittings are mainly Victorian, it has some of the most interesting church monuments in the city, particularly those to the Suckling family.

Step now into **Bridewell Alley**, a narrow pedestrian thoroughfare full of specialist shops. On the left is the **Bridewell Museum**, which is larger than it appears as its buildings occupy all four sides of a courtyard. Built c1325, it was originally a merchant's house. It was lived in by William Appleyard, first Mayor of Norwich. In 1583, it was bought by the city and turned into a 'bridewell' – a prison for petty criminals. In the 1800s it was successively a tobacco factory, a leather warehouse and a shoe factory. Today, it houses an exhibition of the typical industries of Norwich.

Also in Bridewell Alley is **The Mustard Shop**. Apart from selling a wide range of mustard, this contains a small museum tracing the history of Colman's Mustard. Such is the prosperity of the shop that there are plans to move to larger premises.

At the end of Bridewell Alley, turn right into Bedford Street, and cross Exchange Street into the short Lobster Lane. On the right is the **Church of St John Maddermarket**, once hemmed in – as its name suggests – by the houses of dyers.

This is one of the most fascinating churches in Norwich. The windows at both arcade and clerestory level are clearly Perpendicular. But it is the ground plan that causes controversy: this is a short, squat church, and a Decorated window at the east end has led to the theory that a now demolished chancel might once have been there.

As it is, inside the church one feels hemmed in by the surrounding screens and gallery constructed of dark wood. Look for the small, but delightful, chapel on the north side and for the monuments to former mayors of Norwich in the south aisle. No longer open for worship, St John Maddermarket is preserved with all its furnishings intact by the Redundant Churches Fund.

Leave the church and turn down St John's Alley, under the tower, noting on the left the Maddermarket Theatre, operating in what was once a Roman Catholic chapel. At the end turn left into Charing Cross. Some twenty yards (20m) along on the left is **Strangers' Hall**. Originally a merchant's house dating from *c*1320, with 15th-, 16th-, 17th- and 18th-century additions, this almost certainly got its name from the Dutch refugees who lived here during the 1500s. The home of at least three mayors and sheriffs of the city, it now functions as a museum of Norwich domestic life. There is a paved courtyard and some twenty rooms, many panelled; the rooms are furnished in the styles of different historical periods, and there are displays of shop signs, toys, costumes, domestic utensils and vehicles (including the lord mayor's coach, still used on civic occasions).

Leaving Strangers' Hall, turn left along Charing Cross, past the Hog pub, to **St Gregory's Church**, described as a humbler version of St Andrew's. Take the alley beside the church and walk into the small grass square to the south which gives you the best view of the church's architecture. Note the curious two-storied porch with a clock and pinnacled niche over the door. Behind this is a sturdy flint tower, while stretching away to the right are an arcade and clerestory in Decorated style.

Inside, the best features are the impressive Perpendicular window at the east end and the octagonal font with its panelled stem. Of the many monuments, the finest, dating from 1659, is that to Francis Bacon (1561–1626) in the southeast corner of the nave. St Gregory's is now the Pottergate centre for music and the arts.

Market Square, and a Church That's Not a Cathedral

Cross the small green and go over Pottergate. This area, as its name suggests, was the centre of the pottery industry in Saxo-Norman times.

Move now into Lower Goat Lane, at the end of which is Market Square. Immediately to the left is the **Guildhall**, an impressive building of knapped flint and stone built 1414–35 and claimed as the largest medieval city hall outside London. It is particularly attractive from the lower east side, where the area beneath the clock has a chequerboard pattern of lozenges and triangles made of contrasting freestone and flint. Apart from its civic functions, which were carried out here for over 500 years, the Guildhall contained a prison in its undercroft and also functioned as a courthouse. Today it houses the city regalia and is the home of the Tourist Information Centre.

Proceed along the west side of Market Square. From the steps of the **City Hall** you get a fine view across the market, located here since early medieval times, and over to the castle. The city hall was built 1932–8 of brick and has a classical entrance with six tall pillars. Its clock tower is a notable local landmark.

On the south side of Market Square is the **Church of St Peter Mancroft**, the largest church in Norwich; not surprisingly, many people mistake it for the cathedral. St Peter's was built between 1430–55 and is almost entirely in the Perpendicular style. Externally, the massive tower dominates, but the arcade and the close windows of the clerestory are perfectly proportioned. One's first impression inside is of the light, streaming in through the clerestory. The tall and remarkably slender pillars support a heavy hammerbeam roof.

There is much to see at St Peter's, but undoubtedly the finest feature is the superb east window. The original glass was blown out by an explosion during the Civil War, but enough was collected to fill the 42 panels. One of the chapels, the St Nicholas Chapel in the north transept, houses the Mancroft Heritage Exhibition. Many of the furnishings are Victorian, but don't miss the brass commemorating Sir Peter Rede which dates from 1568.

Turn down from St Peter Mancroft into Market Square, past the attractive old Sir Garnet Wolseley pub, which dates back to the 14th century although the name, referring to the military leader Viscount Garnet Wolseley (1833–1913), is obviously much more recent. The south side of the market area, Gentlemen's Walk, was in the 19th century a fashionable area for promenading.

Turn into **Royal Arcade**, a delightful Victorian shopping thoroughfare designed by the Norwich architect George Skipper in 1899. With its glass roof, hanging lanterns, soft green tiles and delightful friezes Royal Arcade is a delight.

At its end is a lane called Back of the Inns. Here you have another choice of routes. To the right is the glass-topped **Castle Mall**, a pedestrian shopping precinct controversially built into the side of the Castle mound. Alternatively, if time is short, you can turn left and proceed back towards the cathedral.

Norwich Castle and Tombland

Most people, however, prefer to cross Castle Meadow and climb the steps to **Norwich Castle**.

The Normans built the original wooden castle on an artificial mound at the time of the conquest in 1067. This was replaced by the present stone structure probably in 1120–30. It was constructed of flint and mortar-faced stone – the same Caen stone shipped by sea from Normandy that was used in the cathedral. Norwich Castle was a 'Royal Castle' – it was held for the king by the Constable in Residence. This situation was maintained until 1806, when George III gave the castle to the county of Norfolk. It housed a garrison and its keep was the city's gaol.

In 1887 the castle was converted into a museum, opened in 1894 by the Duke and Duchess of York. There are sections on local history, geology and archaeology, plus an gallery specializing in works by the Norwich School of painters, particularly John Crome (1768–1821) and John Sell Cotman (1782–1842). Other local painters represented are Sir Alfred Munnings (1878–1959) and Edward Seago (1910–1974).

Retrace your steps from the castle back towards Royal Arcade, turn right into Castle Arcade, and walk along this until you reach London Street, one of the city's main pedestrianized shopping streets. At its top turn left at Bank Plain and then immediately right into Queen Street, at the bottom of which is the area known as **Tombland**; the name means 'empty land'. This was the site of the old Saxon marketplace. After the Norman cathedral was built the market continued, and there were numerous disputes between the cathedral and the citizens about who should claim the market tolls. This led to the infamous riot of 1272.

Tombland today is lively and full of interest. Look for Augustine Steward's House, occupied by Kett's rebels in 1549, and the 17th-century house with the figures of Samson and Hercules guarding the door. Pubs, restaurants and even nightclubs abound in this active part of the city.

Use either Erpingham Gate or St Ethelbert's Gate to return to the Cathedral Close, where the walk ends.

Peterborough

Access: The A1 runs just to the west of the city and the A47 passes through it. National Express coaches run to Peterborough twice daily from Victoria. InterCity trains operate hourly from Kings Cross.

The Bronze Age site at nearby Flag Fen shows that people have lived in the Peterborough area for at least 3000 years, and the Romans had a settlement just upstream from the present city centre. According to the Venerable Bede (c673–735), a Mercian nobleman, Saxulf, founded the first abbey at the site in 655. Modern scholars believe it was Peada, the Christian King of Southern Mercia (reigned 655–6), who founded the abbey, probably in 654, with Saxulf as first abbot. The Abbey of Medeshamstede, as it was then called, was consecrated by Deusdedit, then Archbishop of Canterbury. Unfortunately, this first abbey was destroyed and its monks slaughtered by marauding Danes in 870.

A second abbey was built on the site in the 10th century by King Edgar (or Eadgar), and this was later fortified by earthworks. This abbey church too was fated, burning down in 1116. Traces of the Saxon buildings have been discovered under the present south transept. The only Saxon remains above ground are the Hedda Stone in the New Building and another stone set into the wall of the south transept.

The first Norman abbot, Turoldus, imposed by William the Conqueror, had been able to claim his abbey only after a pitched battle with Hereward the Wake. The abbot at the time of the fire was John de Sais, and it was he who in 1118 began the construction of the present building, beginning with the apse at the east end. It was to be a long time before the work was finished.

The stone came from quarries owned by the abbey at Barnack, to the northwest of Peterborough, being brought by barge here to the site along the River Nene. (This cream-coloured limestone, which had also supplied the material for the first two abbeys, can be seen in other East Anglian cathedrals.) By 1140, all the building to the east of the crossing had been completed. The transepts and the crossing were done by 1160. The nave, the work of Abbot Benedict (in office 1177–93), was, thankfully, executed in the earlier Norman/Romanesque style, so that much of the interior has architectural purity. However, the western transepts, constructed c1200, have a small element of Early English design; this is the only part of the building with high stone vaulting (the aisles have simple low vaulting – some of the earliest in England). The high roof of the nave (built c1220) and the presbytery (15th century) are both of wood.

Two western towers were intended. The north one was completed c1270, but the south tower was never built. Instead, a unique west front was built in Early English style dominated by three huge arches. The central, narrower arch after a while began to tilt outwards, and so c1380 a porch was added (in the Perpendicular style) to prevent further movement. Also in the 14th century a series of small spires was added.

The completed building (minus the porch) was consecrated by Robert Grosseteste (c1175–1253), Bishop of Lincoln, in 1238. Further 13th-century developments included the addition of tracery in the Norman windows of the nave and the construction of a Lady Chapel to the east of the north transept.

The final major addition to the cathedral was the New Building, completed in 1508, to the east of the apse. It contains some delicate fan vaulting and is thought to be the work of John Wastell, who also designed King's College Chapel at Cambridge. The abbot at the time was Robert Kirkton and his rebus, consisting of the initials 'AR' followed by a kirk and a tun, may be seen in a number of places.

At the time of the Dissolution, Peterborough was fortunate in having John Chambers as its abbot. Anticipating the Dissolution, he spent a considerable amount of time with Henry VIII's commissioners to ensure that, when the abbey was dissolved in 1539, it became reestablished as a cathedral. When this came about, three years later, he was made the first bishop. His diocese was taken largely from that of Lincoln and included the soke (jurisdictional area) of Peterborough, Northamptonshire and Rutland. Henry's benevolence may have been prompted by the fact that his first wife, Catherine of Aragon, was buried in the cathedral. Fifty years later another queen, Mary, Queen of Scots, was buried at Peterborough; later her son, James VI & I, had her body removed to Westminster Abbey.

During the Civil War a detachment of Cromwell's soldiers caused considerable damage to the cathedral in 1643, destroying the stained glass, statues, choir stalls and high altar – the cloisters and Lady Chapel were so badly damaged they were later demolished. As a result the nave, lacking in stained glass and monuments, today has a certain pristine quality which emphasizes the purity of the Romanesque architecture.

During the 18th century the cathedral slipped into a certain amount of decay, so it was left to the Victorians to mount a comprehensive renovation programme. This included the provision of replacement stained glass, the best of which can be seen in the south transept. Much of the renovation work was completed by J.L. Pearson. One problem he had to deal with was the large crack that appeared in the central tower in 1883. His solution was to dismantle the tower completely and rebuild it using the same stones. He planned also to rebuild the east and west crossing arches in their original Romanesque style, but this proposal was unfortunately rejected. Pearson's other work included the Cosmati floor of the presbytery and the ciborium over the high altar; he designed the choir stalls, the *cathedra* and the pulpit; he removed the stone screen east of the crossing, thus giving us an uninterrupted view along the length of the cathedral; and with G.F. Bodley, around the turn of the century, he partially restored the west front. The work was very sympathetically carried out, and the results are much less objectionable than at many of the other cathedrals the Victorians 'improved'.

The cathedral survived major damage during the two world wars. A notable and spectacular recent (1975) addition has been the hanging nave rood, done in aluminium and gilt. New figures, carved by Alan Durst, have been placed on the west front. In 1988 there was a major appeal to mark the building's 750th anniversary, while ongoing repair work continues with the help of the Friends of Peterborough Cathedral.

Peterborough's first great expansion came when the railways brought new industry to the city in the 19th century, adding engineering, railway repairs and textiles to the traditional agricultural industries. The growth of local brickmaking also dates from these times, being a response to the demand for new houses for the factory workers.

The 20th century saw Peterborough's second great expansion, when in 1967 it was designated a New Town. The population grew from 80,000 in 1967 to 114,000 at the time of the 1981 census. As a New Town, Peterborough attracted workers from all over the country, so new estates and industrial parks quickly appeared. High-technology firms are rapidly replacing the old, heavier industries.

Peterborough has had a chequered administrative history. Originally it was the main centre of the soke of Peterborough under the jurisdiction of Northamptonshire. Later it was part of Huntingdonshire, which was itself swallowed up by Cambridgeshire, in which county Peterborough remains today. From Victorian times it has been a municipal borough. It is now a thriving city, pleasantly combining old and new, and an important regional shopping and entertainment centre, with a wide range of leisure activities. Its cathedral has become the focal point of a new tourist industry.

TOUR OF THE CATHEDRAL

Start and finish: The west front.

The **west front** (1) is best viewed from the Cathedral Green, although photographers may find they have difficulty in retreating far enough for a good shot.

The west end was originally planned to have two transepts and two towers, to complete the Romanesque style of the building. Two transepts and one tower were completed by about 1270, but then the initial idea was scrapped and a new design followed. The result, in the prevailing Gothic style, is one of the most dramatic examples of cathedral architecture in England (although not without its critics). The dominant features are the three huge, recessed arches, some 85ft (26m) in height; the central arch is narrower than the others. The arches are flanked by square towers and topped by triangular gables with attractive rosettes. Both the main arches and the blind arcading on the front of the towers are pointed in the Early English style. The numerous small spires were added in the 14th century.

Two features detract from the overall symmetry. First, the west tower, left over from the original design, peers unhappily over the front – even had the second tower been built the overall effect would have been far from pleasing. Second, the Perpendicular porch, added in 1380 to fill the base of the central arch (which was showing a tendency to lean outwards), though in itself not unattractive, looks out-of-place in the overall scheme.

Nevertheless, the west front is a magnificent sight. Although the architectural features dominate, look carefully at the 13th-century sculptures in the corners of the arches (binoculars may come in handy for this); those portrayed include Peter, Paul and Andrew, to whom the cathedral is dedicated, plus an assortment of Apostles and kings. Some of the figures are modern, done by Alan Durst – such as the one of Elizabeth II.

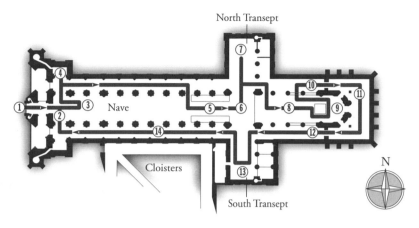

North Transept

Nave

Cloisters

South Transept

N

Key

1. West Front
2. West End
3. Nave
4. North Aisle

5. Choir
6. Crossing
7. North Transept
8. Sanctuary
9. Apse
10. Tomb of Catherine of Aragon

11. New Building
12. South Presbytery Aisle
13. South Transept
14. South Nave Aisle

Gravedigger by Royal Appointment

Enter through the porch – a plaque shows where the present queen has distributed Maundy Money. Once inside, look back at the **west end** (2) of the nave.

On either side of the door are portraits of Robert Scarlett, the Elizabethan gravedigger who during a long career buried both Mary, Queen of Scots and Catherine of Aragon, plus countless Peterborough denizens. The painting to the right of the door is poorly preserved, but the one on the left clearly shows a bearded man carrying a shovel with, in his other hand, a bunch of keys. A dog whip hangs from his belt – Scarlett was also the caretaker of St John's Parish Church in the town square. A simple stone on the floor indicates his grave. It is marked 'R.S.' and dated 1594.

Nave and Choir

Move on into the main body of the **nave** (3), passing a desk where you can get a small guide to the cathedral and where you will certainly be encouraged to make a donation to the upkeep of the building.

The vista along the length of the cathedral from this point is impressive: the architecture is largely Romanesque from end to end and your view is uninterrupted by a screen. The lack of monuments and stained glass adds to the effect. Although the building of the cathedral was carried out by a series of abbots, the purity of the Romanesque was maintained and Barnack stone was used throughout the long period of building. The arcade, tribune and clerestory levels harmonize pleasingly. Some of the principal arches have billet moulding, while at the tribune level chevron patterns may be seen. Between each bay an engaged shaft stretches from floor to ceiling, which to a certain extent counterbalances the long, narrow nave.

The roof of the nave is wood, and was painted *c*1220. The design consists of a series of ornamental diamond or lozenge shapes containing pictures with topics such as the Lamb of God and the Apostles. There's a mirror so that you can look at the ceiling without getting a crick in your neck; there's also a slot machine you can stick a coin in to light the ceiling up so that you can see it better.

The hanging rood overhead is worth attention as well; it takes the form of a wooden cross, painted red, and a gilded aluminium figure of Christ. The motto is *Stat crux dum volvitur orbis* ('The Cross stands while the earth revolves'), reminding us of the permanence of the cathedral amidst the turbulence of the history that surrounds it.

Move back now to the northwest corner of the **north aisle** (4), where you can look at a 19th-century lithograph of the painted nave ceiling. Nearby is the 13th-century **font**, made of Alwalton marble. It was retrieved from a canon's garden in Victorian times, from which period the supports date. Here you can also see one of many iron Gurney stoves, installed by the Victorians to keep the cathedral warm; originally these were coal-burning, but they have now been converted to gas.

Rejoining the north aisle, walk up the cathedral to the **choir** (5). The stalls were designed by Pearson and carved in the 1890s by Thompsons of Peterborough. Note the 15th-century brass-eagle lectern, made in Tournai in Belgium and donated by Abbot William Ramsey (in office 1471–96). The double-branched candlestick it originally had was vandalized by Cromwell's soldiers.

Lantern, Lady Chapel and Sanctuary

Walk through the choir into the **crossing** (6) and look up into the lantern of the central tower. The first tower was built largely in the time of Abbot William de Waterville (in office 1155–75), but by the 14th century the rubble core of the piers had settled and it became dangerous. It was therefore demolished, being replaced by a shorter tower that used the original stones (the crossing arches were in Decorated style). The whole tower was again rebuilt by Pearson during the Victorian restorations.

From here go into the **north transept** (7), which currently houses an exhibition, 'The Story of Peterborough Cathedral'. Both transepts show superb Romanesque work, with only some tracery added to the original Norman arches. The wooden ceilings are also partly original, and did not suffer from the Victorian renovations. The stained glass, however, is Victorian – and not particularly distinguished. Note the reassembled workings of the cathedral clocks, removed from the northwest bell tower in 1836.

On the east side of the north transept was an entrance to the Lady Chapel, which was demolished in the 17th century, the building materials being sold off to provide funds to repair the main building.

Behind a series of arches (corresponding with the chapels in the south transepts) is the new location of the treasury, formerly above the porch in the west front. A voluntary contribution at the entrance enables you to see a collection of ancient bibles, some of the original works of William Tyndale (*c*1494–1536), who translated the Bible into English, and the usual collections of silver and pewterware.

Leave the north transept for the **sanctuary** (8), or presbytery, noting en route the effigy of Abbot Benedict (in office 1177–1193), done in Alwalton marble; it is one of a fine series of Benedictine effigies originally in the old chapter house. The sanctuary was completed in 1140 and has similar architectural features to the nave.

The wooden ceiling, however, is from the 15th century, and imitates a stone vault. Its hundred-plus bosses can be better seen by illuminating the ceiling – there's another slot machine by the southwest pillar of the tower.

At ground level the sanctuary is more modern. Pearson designed the complicated Cosmati floor, made of Italian marble, and built the ciborium, which covers the high altar – most unusual in an English cathedral. The pillars of the ciborium are of Italian marble, while the elaborate stonework in the upper part is in alabaster from Derbyshire. Pearson was also responsible for the *cathedra* here.

The Tomb of a Queen

At the far end of the sanctuary you come to the **apse** (9), something of a rarity in English cathedrals though much more common on the European mainland. This was the first part of the cathedral to be built, being started by Abbot John de Sais in 1118. While the height of the apse is visually pleasing, the later insertion of Decorated windows is unfortunate.

A pair of 17th-century Flemish tapestries show Peter healing a lame beggar in the Temple and Peter being rescued from prison. The ceiling painting is by Sir George Gilbert Scott (1811–1878), and is based on a similar painting of medieval age which was destroyed by Cromwell's soldiers.

Retrace your steps a little way and then turn right to find yourself in the south presbytery aisle. Here you'll find the **Tomb of Catherine of Aragon** (10). Catherine, the daughter of Isobel and Ferdinand of Spain, was the first wife of Henry VIII. After she'd been married to Henry for over twenty years without producing a son, she was expelled from court while Henry arranged a divorce of dubious legality. She spent her last days at Kimbolton, 20 miles (32km) south of Peterborough, where she died in 1536. Henry, by now married to Anne Boleyn, could not afford to have her buried at Westminster Abbey, so she was buried here. Her tomb is a simple stone backed by a fine piece of wrought-iron. She was a well loved queen, and flowers are still frequently left on her tomb.

There are two banners over the tomb: the royal coat-of-arms of 16th-century England and the royal arms of Spain with, at the lower edge, Catherine's personal emblem (also the emblem of Granada), a pomegranate.

The New Building

Continue along the south presbytery aisle until you reach the **New Building** (11) (also called the **Eastern Building**, the **Lady Chapel** and the **retrochoir**, which can lead to confusion). It was built in 1496–1508 during the time of Abbot Robert Kirkton, whose rebus, involving the letters 'AR', a kirk and a tun, can be seen under the windows. The architectural style used throughout is Perpendicular, and the crowning glory is the magnificent fan vaulting.

Although there is no documentation, the New Building is clearly the work of John Wastell. There are two interesting modern sculptures here. In the northeast corner is a statue of St Peter, carved in wood by Simon Latham, Artist in Residence in 1991. In the southwest corner is a sculpture of Our Lady of Lamentations, carved in Beer stone by Polly Verity in 1992.

Of much greater antiquity is the Hedda (or Monks') Stone, thought to be a Saxon shrine dating from *c*780. It has twelve carved figures, seemingly Christ, the Virgin Mary and ten Apostles. The regularly spaced shallow holes in it are something of a mystery.

Benedictine Tombs

Walk along the **south presbytery aisle** (12), looking out for further Benedictine tombs. The first is the rather battered tomb of Abbot John Chambers, the last abbot (in office 1528–39) and first bishop (1541–56). Then follow the tombs of Alexander of Holderness, John de Sais and two unknowns.

The next feature of interest is the former burial place of Mary, Queen of Scots, directly opposite that of Catherine of Aragon. Mary's tragic and convoluted story is well known. After she was beheaded at Fotheringay, 10 miles (16km) west of Peterborough, on 8 February 1587, she was buried in Peterborough Cathedral. When Elizabeth I was succeeded in 1603 by James VI & I, Mary's son, he immediately had his mother's remains transferred to Westminster Abbey (see page 33).

Keep going until you can turn left into the **south transept** (13), which dates from *c*1150, like the north transept, and has similar architectural features. On the west wall is a Saxon sculpture showing two figures, possibly a bishop and a king, under a palm tree. It was found during the Victorian restorations and is believed to date from *c*800.

The east side of the transept has three chapels. The northernmost, **St Oswald's Chapel**, is dedicated to St Oswald, King of Mercia 634–42. Known for his generosity to the poor, he was killed in the Battle of Oswestry, but his right arm was miraculously preserved. It was brought to the abbey in 1060 and was its principal relic until the Reformation, when it disappeared. A rarity in this chapel is its watch tower, whence a duty monk kept an eye on the relic.

Next is the **Chapel of St Benedict**, dedicated to the founder of the monastic order; it has some well preserved blind arcading on the south wall. Third is the **Chapel of St Kyneburga, St Kyneswitha and St Tibba**; these were the three sisters of Peada, King of Southern Mercia, who founded the first monastery *c*654. The chapel has recently been restored by the women of the diocese. The screen along the entrance of the three chapels shows some evidence of medieval decorative painting.

Leave the transept and step into the **south nave aisle** (14). A small plaque on one of the pillars commemorates Nurse Edith Cavell (1865–1915), killed by Germans during World War I for helping French and British prisoners escape. Cavell, buried at Norwich Cathedral, was a pupil at Laurel Court School in the Peterborough Cathedral precincts. At the far end of the aisle is **St Sprite's Chapel**, restored thanks to money raised by former students of St Peter's, a teacher training college ¼ mile (400m) from the cathedral, in memory of a former principal. Note the regimental colours and the statue of the 12th-century Abbot Martin de Bec, in whose time the transepts were built.

Finally return to the west front.

WALKING TOUR FROM PETERBOROUGH CATHEDRAL

Peterborough is both an ancient city and a New Town. The figure-of-eight walk looks first at the cathedral's exterior and the remains of the old abbey and cloisters, then moves into the modern city, where elements of Georgian and Victorian architecture sit comfortably alongside 20th-century developments.

Start and finish: Minster Yard, at the west front of the cathedral.
Length: 2½ miles (4km).
Time: 1½ hours, but allow longer if you want to visit the museum.
Refreshments: Numerous fast-food outlets in the Queensgate Shopping Precinct. For more ambience, try some of the ancient pubs and former coaching inns, including the Tut and Shrive and the Wortley Almshouses (both in Westgate) and the Alderman (Cross Street). The Bull Hotel (Westgate), another possibility, offers accommodation.

The grassy area in front of the cathedral, Minster Yard, has three notable gateways around its perimeter. On the south side the **Bishop's Gateway**, known in monastery times as the Abbot's Gateway, leads to the bishop's palace. It was largely built in the early 13th century, although some of the windows may be older. Above the arch is the Knight's Chamber, built *c*1300. There are statues on both north and south sides; apparently original, these portray Edward I, an abbot, a prior and Peter, Paul and Andrew. The buildings to either side of the gate date back to medieval times although later alterations are obvious; they were once the abbot's offices.

On Minster Yard's west side, towards the city, is the **Cathedral Gate**, built *c*1180, in the time of Abbot Benedict. It is basically Norman (note the blind arcading, similar to that in the cathedral), but on the town side was faced in Perpendicular style in

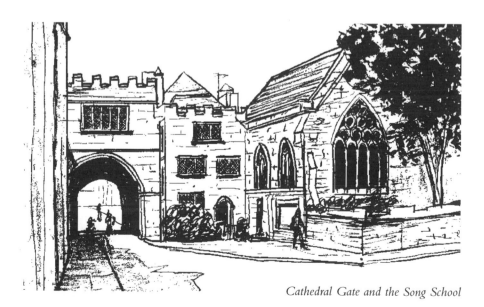

Cathedral Gate and the Song School

121

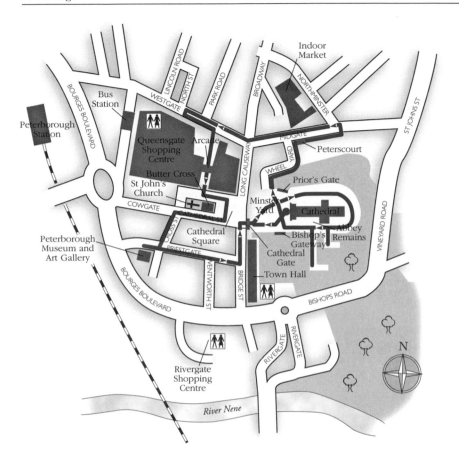

the 14th century. On the upper floor is the Norman Chapel of St Nicholas, while the arch itself was once fitted with a portcullis you can still see the grooves in the wall on either side. The building on the right was once the abbot's gaol. Further right is the present Song School, occupying the chancel of the Chapel of St Thomas the Martyr – the chapel's nave and aisles were demolished in the 15th century to provide building materials for the St John's Church (see page 124) in Cathedral Square.

On the northeast side of Minster Yard is the **Prior's Gate**, built *c*1510 by Abbot Robert Kirkton – look for his weathered rebus. The gate, believed to have once led to the abbot's private deer park, now directs you to the deanery and chapter house. Its other side is of little architectural merit, so walk instead along the north side of the cathedral, noting on your right the Layfolks' Cemetery and, past the transept, the site of the former Lady Chapel.

Remains of the Abbey

From the east end of the cathedral, in the region of the Monks' Cemetery, there are fine views of the exterior of the rounded apse, which makes an interesting contrast with the New Building. Approaching the south transept, you find yourself among the **abbey remains**. Take the path southwards towards a group of buildings that mark the site of the monks' infirmary, which opened into the small Chapel of St Lawrence. The main buildings here today are the archdeaconry and Norman Hall, both built into the old arcades of the infirmary.

Return to the south transept area and take a narrow alley, Monks' Walk, southwards. On the left is the site of the monks' dormitory, built by Abbot Ermulf *c*1110. A century later Abbot Robert Lindsey glazed some of the windows and divided the building into cubicles for privacy. Although no dormitory survives today, it is believed an upper storey was connected to the south transept by night stairs.

On the opposite side of the wall of Monks' Walk is the site of the refectory, built by Ermulf and extended by Abbot John de Sais. It was replaced in Early English style by Abbot Walter of Bury St Edmunds *c*1240.

Continue to the end of Monks' Walk to what has been called the Monks' Stables but was originally the almoner's hall. (The almoner was responsible for handing out alms to the poor of the town, keeping the abbey accounts and collecting rents from the townhouses owned by the monastery.) The almoner's hall until recently housed the Cathedral Visitor Centre, with displays showing the history of the abbey and cathedral, but this exhibition has now moved into the north transept and the building is used by the local college.

Return once more to the south transept, to the left of which you'll find the remains of the old abbey cloisters. There are in fact three historical stages, Norman, Early English and Perpendicular. The oldest, found in the west wall, dates from the end of the second abbey (*c*1100) and is therefore older than the cathedral. The second period, from *c*1245, is found in the east bays of the south wall, when the arches were still unglazed. Finally the cloisters were completely rebuilt in 1525 in Perpendicular style, complete with panelling, tracery and stained glass on all four sides. Look for the lavatorium, where the monks washed their hands on their way to meals.

On the east side of the cloisters is the site of the chapter house, which was not in the traditional English polygonal shape but rectangular. The original building was Norman, built by Ermulf, but it was modernized in Early English style by Lindsey. Its effigies of 12th- and 13th-century abbots are now in the presbytery aisles of the cathedral.

Both the cloisters and the chapter house were pulled down after the Dissolution, most of the building material being sold.

The City Centre

Walk from the cloisters along the path to the west front of the cathedral and cross Minster Yard to its northwest corner, where you leave *via* Wheelyard, a thoroughfare marking the focus of the city's former wheelwrights' industry. Keep going towards a modern stone archway. Noting a stone head of Henry VIII set into the wall, take the path to the right of the arch.

The road now swings leftward to join Midgate, near the corner of which is **Peterscourt**, probably the finest Victorian building in the city. Built in 1860 to the design of Sir George Gilbert Scott, it was a teacher training college (St Peter's); the modern block further along (now the offices of English Nature) marks the site of a small school for the students' teaching practice. A nearby curiosity is the milestone set in the wall showing the distances to London and Thorney.

Cross Midgate to the **indoor market**. Peterborough has had a market charter since 972, and for centuries the market was in Cathedral Square. It moved to its present position in 1979.

Turn and walk back along Midgate, noting on the right Hereward Cross, one of a number of indoor shopping complexes in the city. Go over Broadway and into **Westgate**, possibly once known as 'Webstergate' – the street of the weavers. Westgate today is a modern shopping street dominated by New Town buildings, but – remarkably – three old inns have survived. First, on your right, is the Bull Hotel, an old coaching inn; it probably dates from the late 17th century and may once have been the mansion house. Further along on your left is the Tut and Shrive, formerly the Royal Hotel. Once a Georgian residence, it is believed to have been built in 1730. The third inn is the Wortleys Almshouses, given to the city in 1744 by Edward Wortley Montagu, a local benefactor and MP. It is claimed Charles Dickens (1812–1870) based the workhouse in *Oliver Twist* on Wortley's Almshouses.

Walk back along Westgate until you're opposite the Bull again. Now enter the **arcade**, typical of those built in the 1920s. Full of specialist shops, it is now part of Queensgate, one of the largest covered shopping centres in the country, opened in 1982 by Queen Beatrix of the Netherlands.

Cathedral Square
Proceed straight through Queensgate to emerge along Cumbergate – an alley named after the combers who prepared wool for the weavers – to **Cathedral Square**. Although this has been much altered by the New Town developments, there are still a number of interesting buildings to give a flavour of the past.

Walk clockwise around the square. Immediately on your left, on the corner of Cumbergate, is the Miss Pears Almshouses, originally built in 1835 but much extended as a result of Miss Pears' will in 1903. It is now an Italian restaurant. On the east side of the square, the Cathedral Gate is flanked by the premises of two clearing banks, both imposing buildings.

On the square's south side is a curious building, designed in mock-Elizabethan style but built in 1911. You can see the cathedral arms in the gable; below are a number of brightly painted statues of men closely associated with the history of Peterborough, including King Peada, Henry VIII and Aethelwold (Bishop of Winchester, who refounded the second abbey *c*960). Unfortunately the overall effect is spoilt by the garish frontage of a fast-food chain. Further to the east, a small run of shops gives a good idea of what the square must have looked like in medieval times.

The centre of the square is dominated by two buildings. **St John's Church**, the parish church, was once sited east of the cathedral on marshy ground. After complaints by the townsfolk it was rebuilt in the early 15th century in its present position, using material from the original church as well as stone from the nave of the Chapel of St Thomas the Martyr, in Minster Yard. You can spot this latter material in the west door and in the arches supporting the tower. The nave has seven bays in Perpendicular style and the tower, too, is impressive, with large belfry windows, buttresses and parapets. The spire was removed during Victorian times, when many of the interior fittings were added.

The church is closed more often than not. If you wish to see the inside you may have to gatecrash a lunchtime concert.

The other building in the centre of the square is the **Butter Cross** (also known as the **Guild Hall** or **Market Cross**). Built in 1671 it basically comprises a large single-storey room supported by a number of arches. There is a clock in the gable on the east side, under which are the royal arms of Charles II. You can see four other coats-of-arms – those of Bishop Henslow, Dean Duport and two local families, the Montagues and the Ormes. A butter market was held here until 1926; the upper room has been used as a gaol, a magistrates' court and a schoolroom at various times in its history. Access is difficult except for pre-booked groups.

Priestgate and the Town Hall
Leave the Square *via* Cowgate (cattle for the local leather and boot and shoe industries were driven along here) and turn left into Cross Street, at the end of which is Priestgate.

Turn immediately right to see the **Peterborough Museum and Art Gallery** ahead of you. Originally built by Thomas 'Squire' Cooke in 1816, this was considerably enlarged in 1821. Later in the 19th century it was converted into a hospital. This, and a serious fire in 1884, mean there is little of the interior to remind us of gracious Victorian living.

The building has been a museum since 1931. Particularly impressive are the geology section – containing mammal bones and some from dinosaurs found in the local clay pits – and the social history section, showing domestic rooms from various decades of the 20th century. There is also an art gallery, whose exhibitions change regularly. Before you leave, look for the oil painting by Theodore Nathan Fielding in the entrance hall; this shows the marketplace in Cathedral Square as it was in 1795.

Leave the museum and proceed east along **Priestgate**, one of the oldest streets in Peterborough and an essential part of Abbot Martin de Bec's 12th-century town plan. Today it is an interesting mixture, with buildings varying from 16th-century to modern. The older buildings are on the south side; the one with a simple spire is all that's left of the demolished Trinity Chapel. Practically every property in Priestgate is now a solicitor's office – a remarkable example of functional clustering.

Your walk along Priestgate ends among modern office blocks that frame the **Town Hall** in the pedestrianized Bridge Street. The design of the Town Hall, built *c*1930, was by E. Berry Webber, who won a competition held for that purpose. The style is Neo-Georgian, and the entrance is through an imposing Corinthian portico. Step inside to see the wide Italian Renaissance-style staircase.

A few yards south along Bridge Street is the helpful Tourist Information Office.

Now go north along Bridge Street into Cathedral Square, then turn right through the Cathedral Gate to come back into Minster Yard.

Southwell

Access: Southwell is located on the A612, halfway between Nottingham and Newark. Pathfinder buses from Nottingham every twenty minutes, and some stop at Southwell en route to Newark. There are mainline stations at both Newark and Nottingham. The nearest airport is East Midlands Airport at Castle Donnington.

There is often confusion about the difference between a cathedral and a minster. A minster is best described as a subcathedral; in Southwell's instance the minster was in the diocese of York, along with Ripon and Beverley. It was administered by a college of prebendaries (or canons), who looked after local villages. All the canons had prebendal houses in Southwell. Unlike the case with many English cathedrals, there has never been an abbey on the Southwell site.

The minster has always been regarded as the mother church of Nottinghamshire. There has been a religious building on the site since Saxon times, and it is believed that Paulinus (d644) founded a church here c630. It was soon a place of pilgrimage, as the church contained the relics of St Edburga of Repton (fl 700). In 956, King Eadwig gave the manor of Southwell to the Archbishop of York, and succeeding archbishops remained the lords of the manor until the mid-19th century.

The present minster building was begun in 1108, and the Norman nave, transepts and towers remain today. The east end was rebuilt in the 13th century in Early English style, contrasting with the bulkier design of the west end. The octagonal chapter house, with its delightful carved stonework, was added in the late 13th century. The pulpitum, constructed of Mansfield stone, was built in 1290. The Perpendicular window in the west front was inserted towards the end of the 15th century.

Southwell survived the Reformation intact, largely because it was not an 'abbey church', but was not so fortunate during the Civil War. Cromwell's troops are believed to have stabled their horses in the nave and they inflicted considerable damage to the fabric, as well as wrecking the archbishop's palace. In 1711 a fire destroyed the roof, bells and organ. The spires on the western towers date from the 19th century, probably replacing earlier ones of similar design.

Southwell Minster became a cathedral with its own diocese in 1884; the imposing tomb of the first Bishop of Southwell, George Ridding, can be seen in the sanctuary. The centenary in 1984 was marked by the visit of Elizabeth II to distribute the Maundy Money.

TOUR OF THE MINSTER
Start: The west end.
Finish: The north porch.

To reach the **west end** (1) pass through the gate in Westgate, from where there is a superb view towards the west front along a path called The Broadwalk. This vista was not always free of obstructions; where today there is a grassy open space with some early-18th-century headstones, until the 1820s there were various buildings here including an alehouse, a limehouse, a shop and, remarkably, a pigsty!

The west end was completed *c*1140. The rather 'flat' Norman facade, with typical round arches, has twin towers capped with pyramidal spires. The original spires were removed *c*1800 and the towers strengthened before restoration in 1880, giving the west end a somewhat Germanic look. The central Perpendicular window was inserted in the 15th century.

Old Architecture and New Sculpture

Move now to the north side of the exterior and enter the building through the **north porch** (2), which consists of a series of round Norman arches with dogtooth and chevron decoration. A room over the porch (probably used by the Sacristan) has Norman windows and above it are two pinnacles, one of which serves as the room's chimney. The sides of the porch's interior contain a series of interlaced arches from the transitional Norman period. The door is equally impressive, its silver grey wood dating from the 14th century.

Walk into the **nave** (3), which is dominated by solid Norman architecture. The arcade level has round drum pillars, replicated above, but with square columns, in the triforium. Above this is the clerestory, which has a row of smaller arches. The pattern of the three levels may remind you of a Roman aqueduct. The stonework supports a wooden wagon roof of Victorian age.

If you turn to the west end you'll see that the Perpendicular window is filled with subtle modern glass. This, the **Angel Window** (4), was completed in 1996. (A brochure giving a detailed description is available in the bookshop.) If you look in the opposite direction you can see above the nave altar the hanging sculpture ***Christus Rex*** (5) by Peter Ball, made in wood, beaten copper and gold leaf and erected in 1987.

Move to the south aisle, where you'll find the **font** (6), which has a descending dove on its lid. Dating from 1661, the font was the work of a local school of font carvers. The stained glass in the south aisle is Victorian and of little distinction.

Continue along the aisle and into the south transept. Here the most fascinating features are the **bread pews** (7), ancient wooden seats where the needy of the parish waited for alms. Beneath the pews you can see small pieces of mosaic floor, possibly taken from a nearby Roman villa to form part of the floor of the original Saxon church. Also here are a modern wooden sculpture of the Madonna and Child by Alan Coleman and a small board showing the coat-of-arms of Charles II.

Turn now into the **crossing** (8), where sturdy Norman columns and arches support the central tower. These arches – like those in the transepts – have well defined rope mouldings.

Dominating the crossing is the chancel screen or **pulpitum** (9), which separates the Norman nave from the Early English chancel. Made like much of the rest of the minster of Mansfield stone, it is of Decorated style and probably dates from *c*1340. A slim central doorway is flanked by richly carved arches and canopies, with nearly 300 faces of men and animals. Unfortunately, the organ fills the space above the pulpitum completely, so there is no vista along the full length of the building.

Now walk into the south choir aisle and from here into the **quire** (10), where the architecture is firmly Early English period, with rib vaulting, shafting on the pillars and lancet windows. Among the rich woodwork of the stalls are six 14th-century misericords.

Note the brass 16th-century eagle **lectern** (11), which has an interesting history. It once belonged to Newstead Abbey, some 15 miles (24km) west of Southwell, and was thrown into the lake at the time of the Reformation. It was later recovered, cleaned and presented to the minster.

Walk along the quire towards the high altar and, once you're about halfway there, look to your right to see two chapels. The east transept is occupied by the **Southwell Saints' Chapel** or **Chapel of Christ** (12), with another modern sculpture by Peter Ball. Next to it, at the end of the south choir aisle, is the **Chapel of St Oswald** (13), which has an attractive reredos by Caröe. The altar front shows St Oswald's symbol of a raven, designed by John Piper (1903–1992). Oswald (d992), a Benedictine monk, was successively Bishop of Worcester and Archbishop of York.

The **sanctuary** (14), just beside the latter chapel, gives you an opportunity to look at the east window, with its tall Early English lancets. Although the upper panes have Victorian glass, the lower ones are filled with 16th-century Flemish glass brought from Paris and given to the minster in 1818. In front of the simple high altar, which has a pair of 16th-century brass standard candlesticks, is a wooden altar rail by the 20th-century Yorkshire wood carver, Robert Thompson; you can have fun looking for the carved mice on the lower rails.

To the south of the high altar is a beautiful five-seater **sedilia** (15), attributed to the same carvers as were responsible for the pulpitum.

Martyrs to War

Retreating from the high altar, turn right and go into the **Airmen's Chapel** (16). Its main interest is the wooden altar made from the wreckage of planes shot down over France during World War I. Note, too, the highly original triptych and the Katyn Memorial donated by the Anglo-Polish Society to commemorate the Poles killed in Russia during World War II.

Outside the Airmen's Chapel, on the left as you emerge, is the imposing **Ridding Memorial** (17), depicting Southwell's first bishop, who was also the 43rd headmaster of Winchester. The other small eastern transept is occupied by the **Chapel of St Thomas** (18), which is devoted to private prayer.

Now go along the north quire aisle and turn into a vestibule leading to the great delight of Southwell – the

Chapter House

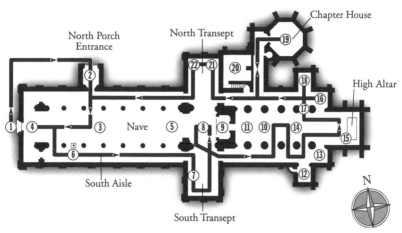

North Porch
Entrance

North Transept

Chapter House

High Altar

Nave

South Aisle

South Transept

N

Key

1. West End
2. North Porch
3. Nave
4. Angel Window
5. Christus Rex Sculpture
6. Font

7. Bread Pews
8. Crossing
9. Pulpitum
10. Quire
11. Lectern
12. Southwell Saints' Chapel
13. Chapel of St Oswald
14. Sanctuary

15. Sedilia
16. Airmen's Chapel
17. Ridding Memorial
18. Chapel of St Thomas
19. Chapter House
20. Pilgrims' Chapel
21. Tomb of Archbishop Sandys
22. Saxon Tympanum

chapter house (19). Built at the end of the 13th century at a time when the Decorated style was beginning to evolve, it is the only octagonal English chapter house not to have a central supporting column; the absence of a central pillar allowed the construction of a superb star-vault, which has a bulky central boss. Entry is through an elegant double-arched doorway with contrasting plain pillars of Mansfield stone and pilasters of Purbeck marble. On both capitals and arches there is exquisite carving – almost entirely of plant and tree leaves found in the local area at that time: oak, ivy, hawthorn, buttercup, hop and whitethorn can be readily identified.

Inside the chapter house you'll almost certainly be impressed by the tall geometrical Decorated windows, which let light flood into the building; they are mainly plain glass with occasional fragments of medieval stained glass. Beneath the windows the arcades have shallow recesses with thirty-six wooden seats, one for each canon of the parish. Above them stone canopies with trefoil arches show more leaves and also heads, some damaged by Cromwell's men. Within one carved set of hawthorn leaves is a green man. This entity, although entirely pagan, is a frequently found motif in church decoration. The chapter house's 'Leaves of Southwell' are a national treasure and will not disappoint you.

A Prolific Bishop

Return along the vestibule and turn into the north transept. On the east side is the **Pilgrims' Chapel** (20), which replaced an earlier semicircular apse. The chapel, which has had many uses during its history, is currently a place of prayer for all pilgrims who visit the minster. Although most of its accoutrements are modern, note the two *piscinas* (basins for the water used to wash the sacred vessels) and also the aumbries (wall cupboards where the communion plate was kept).

In the corner of the north transept is the striking alabaster **Tomb of Archbishop Sandys** (21). His statue is held up by four angels, while the side of the tomb shows his two wives and eight children praying for him. Sandys (d1588) was Bishop of Worcester and later Archbishop of York.

In the opposite corner is a small doorway above which is a richly carved **Saxon tympanum** (22), possibly from the old Saxon church. The carvings show David rescuing a sheep from a lion and St Michael fighting a dragon.

Leave the north transept and walk along the north nave aisle to the north porch.

WALKING TOUR FROM SOUTHWELL MINSTER

Southwell (often pronounced 'suth'll', but to most locals 'south well') is probably England's smallest cathedral city, and so this walk covers little more than a mile (1.6km). There are no museums or monuments; the tour concentrates on domestic architecture, particularly the prebendal houses.

Start: The north porch of the minster.
Finish: The Visitor Centre.
Length: 1¼ miles (2km).
Time: Half an hour.
Refreshments: The minster's refectory is popular. Other decent eating places are few and far between, but the Saracen's Head in Westgate has a good lunchtime menu and offers accommodation.

Standing at the **north porch** you have an opportunity to view some of the external features of the cathedral. Pass the octagonal chapter house and look out for the numerous carvings of heads, birds and foliage. Higher up you can see a variety of gargoyles and the flying buttresses supporting the nave. Note, too, the clerestory windows which, although arched on the interior, have a bull's-eye shape on the outside.

At the east end of the minster is a wide grassy area which once contained a well. This was blocked up in the 18th century after a clergyman fell down it and drowned.

Opposite the east end is the **Vicars' Court**, a series of fine Georgian houses on three sides of a garden. These were built towards the end of the 18th century to house the Vicars Choral. At the far end of the court is the most impressive building, The Residence, home of the Provost of Southwell.

Continue around the east end of the minster and along the south side. To the left are the ruins of the **archbishop's palace**. Rebuilt in the early 15th century, this was a favourite resting place of many of the archbishops of York. The building was largely destroyed by Cromwell's men during the Civil War and later local people pilfered much of the building materials. What remains is the remodelled great hall. Once a seminary for young ladies, it was reclaimed for the minster at the end of the 19th century. It is not open to the public.

Opposite the palace is the minster's **south door**, once used by the archbishop to reach the minster from his palace. The doorway is Norman in style with elaborate dogtooth carving, a pattern repeated in the window above it.

From the west end of the minster, take the diagonal path to a gap in the church-yard wall. Immediately to your left there is a view into the garden of **Bishop's Manor**, the residence of the Bishop of Southwell, framed by the ruins of the old palace. To your right is a single-storey building, the **Trebeck Memorial Hall**. Once the Choristers' Song School, it is now used by the general public for local functions.

Prebendal Houses

At the end of the path turn right into Bishop's Drive and then right again into Westgate. A little way along on the right, the minster's west gate acts as a frame for a good view of the west end. On the opposite side of the road you get your first glimpse of the prebendal houses, the residences of the secular canons – who often leased them out. Today most are in private hands. **Dunham Prebend** is largely hidden by trees, but there is a better view of the 17th-century **Rampton Prebend**, which has three gables and a pleasing symmetry. To its right is **Sacrista Prebend**, where the minster choristers live.

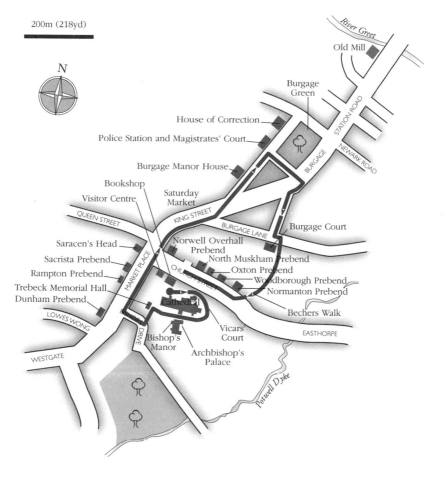

You now come to the **Saracen's Head**, an old coaching inn dating back to the late 14th century. The 'post and pan' half-timbered work on the front was revealed during repair work in 1978. The hotel has now taken over the assembly rooms next door, but their early-19th-century portico can be plainly seen. Further old coaching inns in this general area include the Crown, the Admiral Rodney, the Black Bull (now a shop) and the Wheatsheaf.

Walk north to the junction with Queen Street and King Street. Here a building has been demolished to reveal some fine half-timbered work.

Go rightwards into King Street, at whose top is an open space formed by the demolition of several houses. This is the site of the lively **Saturday market**.

Burgage Green
Ahead is the county library building. Pass to its left and the road will lead you to the attractive **Burgage Green**, full of shady lime and chestnut trees.

Immediately on your left is the elegant facade of **Burgage Manor House**. This building has had a varied and interesting history. Once the home of the mother of Lord Byron (1788–1824) – the poet often stayed here as a youth – it has also been a convalescent home, a girls' school and a youth hostel. Compare the beauty of the manor house with the ugly white Victorian residence opposite.

Set in the wall a few yards past the manor house is a Victorian letterbox. Also Victorian are the nearby **police station** and **magistrates' court** and, further on the left, the old **House of Correction**. The latter dates from the early 19th century and could house nearly 150 prisoners. Among its punishment equipment was a treadmill!

(If you'd like a longer walk, go to the lower part of the Green and take Station Road, which leads down to the River Greet, beside which is an old flour mill. The old railway track here is a nature trail. Then retrace your steps to rejoin the main walk.)

Back in Prebendary Country
Cross the green to its lower part, then go past the war memorial and along a lane towards the somewhat dilapidated Georgian **Burgage Court**, a once fine house in extensive grounds. Turn left along Burgage Lane and then immediately right down a pathway, Becher's Walk. After two hundred yards (180m) you reach Church Street.

(Here there is another option for the more energetic. Turn left and a few hundred yards until you see, on your left, a pub called the Bramley Apple. Four doors away, at 73 Church Street, is the small cottage where the first Bramley apples were grown. After you've covered this, return along Church Street to rejoin the main walk.)

You are now back in prebendary country. The first house on the right, set well back from the road, is the late-18th-century **Normanton Prebend**, which once had a tithe barn in its grounds. No. 31, now known as Ashleigh, was once the **Woodborough Prebend**; in the early years of the 20th century it was a girls' school. Next along is the **Oxton Prebend**, now called Cranfield House, a delightful Queen Anne building with pleasing symmetry. Now look for the **North Muskham Prebend**, formerly a boys' school and now occupied by solicitors' firms. Finally, to the west of the carpark entrance, is the **Norwell Overhall Prebend**, which is now a branch of the National Westminster Bank.

Just across the road is the Visitor Centre, which is where the walk ends.

Lincoln

Access: Road access is usually *via* the A1 and the A46 from Newark in the south (the Roman Fosse Way), the A57 from Retford in the north, or the A15 from London. Rail links with London are *via* Newark or Peterborough on the main east coast line; local services connect with Nottingham and Sheffield. The nearest international airport, East Midlands, is some 45 miles (72km) to the west.

Celts, Romans, Anglo-Saxons and Vikings all had settlements at Lincoln. Some built churches and in late Roman times there was even a bishop, but the history of Lincoln Cathedral effectively goes back only to the arrival of the Normans in 1066.

William the Conqueror appointed Remigius, a Benedictine monk and one of his staunch supporters, to be bishop of a huge diocese which stretched from the Humber to the Thames. The first cathedral was at Dorchester-on-Thames, but William soon realized the strategic importance of Lincoln, where he had already built a castle, so in 1072 he commanded Remigius to build a cathedral there. Remarkably, the new building was complete within twenty years, although Remigius himself died just before the cathedral was consecrated.

This first cathedral was much shorter than the present building, with transepts, a tower (in the present position) and, at the east end, a semicircular apse. The roofs were almost certainly of timber, and in 1141 a fire seriously damaged the building. The third bishop, known as Alexander the Magnificent, was responsible for a partial rebuilding. He had travelled widely on the European mainland and was clearly influenced by some of the architectural developments he saw there. It is believed he vaulted the entire building in stone and was responsible for the Romanesque frieze and doorways on the west front, making what was probably the finest cathedral in the country at that time.

Unfortunately, what seems to have been an earthquake destroyed the greater part of the cathedral in 1185, and, though the west front and its towers could be retained, a major reconstruction was required. This task fell to Hugh, Bishop of Lincoln 1186–1200. A Carthusian monk from Avalon, near Grenoble, Hugh built the new parts of the cathedral in Early English style, with pointed windows and arches. The windows were larger and the walls were supported by flying buttresses. In addition to the normal transepts, a smaller eastern pair was added, while the east end was extended with chapels and apses so that the building broke through the line of the old Roman city wall. It is said that Hugh was often seen carrying a hod to help complete the building, but unfortunately he died before the nave was complete. Hugh (*c*1140–1200) was canonized in 1220, and the choir was named St Hugh's Choir.

More disasters were in store. In 1237 the central tower collapsed, destroying part of the choir. Its repair and the completion of Hugh's cathedral were largely the work of Bishop Robert Grosseteste (*c*1175–1253). By the time of his death, the chapter house had been completed and the east end enlarged, mainly to accommodate the hordes of pilgrims who flocked to visit St Hugh's tomb. In the 14th and 15th centuries, all three towers were raised and had spires added. This, it is believed, made Lincoln Cathedral the tallest building in the world at that time.

In 1548 the central spire blew down in a storm (the western spires remained until 1807, when they were demolished for safety reasons). Another disaster occurred in 1609, when part of the library was destroyed by fire. Its replacement, designed by Christopher Wren (1632–1723), was completed in 1675.

As with many cathedrals, the period from the 14th to the 18th centuries was a time of decay and neglect. Much destruction of statuary, glass and shrines took place during the Reformation, while further damage was committed by both sides during the Civil War. Not until the mid-18th century was there some attempt at restoration; this process has continued ever since, particularly in Victorian times, when much of the stained glass was replaced. Today, the Fabric Fund is responsible for raising the enormous amounts of money required to keep the structure of the cathedral in good shape.

The 1990s were not happy for Lincoln Cathedral. Problems began when the cathedral's copy of the Magna Carta was taken on a tour of Europe to raise money – and instead, a huge loss was made. A new dean was brought in, and that saw the start of some very public infighting among the factions at the cathedral – which the media delighted in reporting. Eventually, to bang some heads together, the bishop boycotted his own cathedral. In 1997, rightly or wrongly, the dean resigned, and hopefully peace will return.

TOUR OF THE CATHEDRAL
Start and finish: The west front.

The late Alec Clifton-Taylor once described the **west front** (1) as an 'architectural hotchpotch'. Although there is a certain amount of truth in this, one cannot help but be impressed by the sheer size and uniqueness of the feature. Much of the early Norman fortress-like stonework remains along with the rounded arches, but the most imposing feature is the carved frieze over the doorways, dating from the time of Bishop Alexander. He is thought to have copied the idea from the cathedral at Modena, which he probably saw on his way to Rome. The frieze shows scenes from the Old Testament on the south side and from the New Testament on the north. As with many cathedral features, such as stained glass and murals, it was designed to tell a moral story to a congregation who were largely illiterate.

Above the frieze is a lofty set of tiers of arcades, culminating in a steep-angled gable and, at the ends, a pair of octagonal angle turrets, on the top of which are two small statues. That on the south is of St Hugh and the one on the north, blowing his horn, is the Swineherd of Stow, renowned for giving his life savings – sixteen silver pennies – to the cathedral.

Unfortunately for keen photographers, the west front is festooned with scaffolding and will remain so for the foreseeable future while the frieze and other stonework are restored.

A Feeling of Space

Enter the cathedral not through the richly carved central doorway but *via* the south-west door. In the **nave** (2) you'll find a welcoming desk manned by volunteers who will not demand an entrance fee but who will expect a donation.

The first impression of the nave is of height and narrowness. There are the usual three levels – arcade, triforium and clerestory – with the abundant trefoil decoration typical of the Early English period, topped by impressive tierceron vaulting with regular bosses along the ridge-rib. If there is a criticism of the overall design, it is about the proportions, both at the various levels and in terms of the vaulting, which seems to spring from too low a level. The stone used is cream-coloured local lime-stone with rich brown Purbeck marble, a combination used throughout the cathedral. Each of the main pillars, for example, is enriched by eight free-standing Purbeck marble shafts, linked to the pillars halfway up by annulets.

The nave is also mercifully free of memorials, which, with the absence of seating, adds to the feeling of space. Tomb slabs on the floor have all had their brass-work removed.

Cross over to the mid-12th-century **font** (3), by the south aisle. It is made of dark Tournai marble and is on a base, added in Victorian times, of Ashford limestone from Derbyshire. The carving on the font's sides shows lions, dragons and griffins in combat, no doubt representing the struggle between good and evil.

The Dean's Eye and the Bishop's Eye

Walk down the south aisle. The stone benches built into the wall provided seats for frail members of the congregation (hence the saying 'the weakest go to the wall').

Soon you reach the **great transept** (4). In almost every other English cathedral there are two transepts, north and south, but at Lincoln there are the great transept and two smaller eastern transepts (northeast and southeast).

Stand under the **crossing** (5) and look up at the lantern, with its stone vaulting. Above this is the tower, containing the main cathedral bell, Great Tom, put in position in 1835. The north and south walls of the great transept each have a fine rose window above lancet windows, dating from the 1220s. The rose window to the north, the **Dean's Eye** (6), has plate tracery and a considerable amount of the original glass, which has the theme of the Last Judgement. The five lancet windows below have *grisaille* glass. The rose window on the south side, the **Bishop's Eye** (7), replaced an earlier window *c*1330. It has bar tracery in the form of two immense leaves filled with fragments of glass of various ages and origins reassembled from other parts of the cathedral, giving a quite beautiful effect unique in English cathedrals. The four lancet windows below have medallions of 13th-century glass, again drawn from other parts of the cathedral.

On the east side of the crossing is the 14th-century stone **pulpitum** (8), marking the west end of St Hugh's Choir. It has a profusion of carving – saints, animals, monsters and flowers – plus a series of ornate double-curved arches. Traces of red, blue and gold here and there on the stonework hint at the colourful scene that confronted medieval worshippers.

Walk into the **south side of the great transept** (9) – what would normally be called the south transept. Here there are a couple of memorials of interest. On the

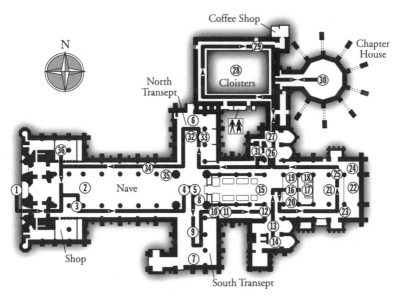

Coffee Shop

Chapter House

N

North Transept

Cloisters

Nave

Shop

South Transept

Key

12. Trondheim Pier
13. Southeast Transept
1. West Front
14. Bishop Grosseteste's Tomb
2. Nave
15. St Hugh's Choir
3. Font
16. Sanctuary
4. Great Transept
17. High Altar
5. Crossing
18. Easter Sepulchre
6. Dean's Eye
19. Tomb of Remigius
7. Bishop's Eye
20. Chantry of Katherine Swyford
8. Pulpitum
21. Angel Choir
9. South Side of Great Transept
22. Great East Window
10. South Choir Aisle
23. Eleanor of Castile's
11. Shrine of Little Hugh
    Visceral Tomb

24. Head Shrine of St Hugh
25. The Lincoln Imp
26. Damini Wall Paintings
27. Touch Exhibition
28. Cloisters
29. Wren Library
30. Chapter House
31. Treasury
32. North Side of Great Transept
33. Services' Chapel
34. North Nave Aisle
35. Tournai Marble Tomb Slab
36. Morning Chapel

west wall are the remains of the **Shrine of John Dalderby**. Dalderby was Bishop of Lincoln in the early years of the 14th century. His relics, kept in a silver reliquary, attracted pilgrims, but were destroyed during the Reformation. At the far end of the transept is a striking bronze statue of Bishop Edward King, who was tried (and acquitted) by the court at Canterbury for his High Church practices. The statue, which rests on a plinth of Dent marble, was originally meant to be outside in the cathedral grounds.

A Murdered Boy and Nineteen Murdered Jews

Leave the great transept and enter the **south choir aisle** (10) through a wonderfully carved 13th-century door. Purbeck shafts and vertical bands of roses and dogtooth decoration lead at about eye level to capitals showing angels and birds. The arch has a broad band of openwork foliage, reminiscent of the stonework in Ely's Lady Chapel (see page 96).

Immediately to your left is the ruined **Shrine of Little Hugh** (11). In 1255 a young boy called Hugh was discovered dead in a Lincoln well, and the Jewish community was promptly charged with his ritual murder. After anti-Semitic riots, nineteen Jews were executed for this supposed crime and others were imprisoned. In an early example of ecumenism, the Benedictines intervened for the release of these innocents, who were nevertheless heavily fined. Later a small shrine was placed in the cathedral. The original canopy over it was destroyed during the Civil War. The legend of Little St Hugh is encountered in 'The Prioress's Tale' in Chaucer's *Canterbury Tales*.

Further along on the left are some late 15th-century wood carvings thought to be from Bavaria. On the right of the aisle is a stone screen, believed to be of the same age as the pulpitum.

At the end of the aisle, again on your right, is the **Trondheim Pier** (12), one of a pair of unusual pillars (the other is in the north aisle). It consists of three strongly carved limestone shafts and, on the outside, complementary shafts of Purbeck marble, all rising to boldly carved leaf capitals. The only other known examples of this distinctive design are found in Trondheim Cathedral, Norway, which suggests that 13th-century stonemasons were more peripatetic than is generally realized.

Now you come to the **southeast transept** (13) and **Bishop Grosseteste's Tomb** (14), which is in front of the Chapel of St Peter and St Paul. Grosseteste, Bishop of Lincoln 1235–53, was a distinguished academic, scientist and theologian, and first Chancellor of Oxford University. Known as a strict disciplinarian, he was highly thought of in his diocese. It is a surprise that he has never been canonized. His original chest tomb was destroyed during the Civil War; the modern slab replacement was rededicated in 1953.

St Hugh's Choir and the Sanctuary

Now cross the aisle into **St Hugh's Choir** (15). The architecture here is clearly Early English, with pointed arches, lancet windows and the by now familiar combination of local limestone and Purbeck marble. The vaulting is tierceron in style (this was probably one of the first examples of the kind in Europe) and highly irregular, particularly along the ridge, so that this is commonly described as the 'crazy vault'.

It is the wooden choir stalls, however, that give St Hugh's Choir its unique atmosphere. They are luxuriant with pinnacles, canopies and outstanding carving; the numerous misericords have been dated at *c*1370. Name plates mark the seats of the canons of the cathedral, each allocated the first line of a psalm. The stalls were extended eastward in 1778 to accommodate the bishop's throne.

Other items of interest here include the Victorian pulpit, designed by Sir George Gilbert Scott (1811–1878), and the much older brass eagle lectern, which dates from 1667.

Now walk into the **sanctuary** (16). Nominally part of the Angel Choir (see below), this is boxed off from it by a stone screen, most of which dates from a Gothic-style restoration done in 1769.

Dominating the area is the **high altar** (17). Once a simple table, this has a stone reredos to match the surrounding screen. The tracery was once filled with artwork, later removed to give a better view of the east window. The northern screen features an **Easter sepulchre** (18) – more accurately, Christ's tomb, guarded at floor level by three seated soldiers.

The next three bays to the left contain what is believed to be the **Tomb of Remigius** (19), the founder of the original cathedral at Lincoln. On the south side of the sanctuary is the narrow **Chantry of Katherine Swyford** (20); she was mistress and later wife of John of Gaunt (1340–1399), an influential figure in Plantagenet times.

Burial in Parts

Walk back into the south aisle and round to the **Angel Choir** (21), at the east end. Built primarily to cater for the pilgrims visiting the Shrine of St Hugh, it is one of the great successes of English Gothic, continuing the geometrical Decorated style of St Hugh's Choir, using local cream limestone and darker Purbeck marble. It gained its name from the profusion of angels carved in the stonework at triforium and clerestory levels.

Dominating the Angel Choir is the **great east window** (22), with eight lights and 60ft (18m) high – a great technical achievement for its time, when bar tracery was in its early days of development. The Victorian glass is perhaps unworthy of the window.

There are four chantry chapels in the Angel Choir: going anticlockwise, the Russell Chantry, the Cantilupe Chantry, the Burghersh Chantry and the Fleming Chantry. All are worth a brief look.

Of more interest is **Eleanor of Castile's Visceral Tomb** (23). Eleanor was queen and wife of Edward I – the marriage lasted thirty-five years and produced thirteen children. She died nearby at Harby, and Edward took her body in procession to London for burial, the twelve stops along the way being marked by the famous Eleanor Crosses. She was buried in Westminster Abbey, but her heart went to Blackfriars Church in London and her internal organs were returned to Lincoln. Her tomb here was destroyed in the Civil War; the present monument is a copy made in 1890.

We now come to the *raison d'être* of the whole Angel Choir – the **Head Shrine of St Hugh** (24). The body of St Hugh was exhumed and transferred to a prepared shrine in 1280. Unfortunately, the head came off, and for a while two shrines existed. The Body Shrine has since vanished, but the Head Shrine is said to have been the third most popular place of pilgrimage in England. It was stripped of its jewels and other decorations by Henry VIII and later, during the Civil War, the head and its reliquary disappeared. What remains is probably just the base of a portable shrine (which could have been used in processions). In 1986, to celebrate the 800th anniversary of St Hugh's arrival in Lincoln, a bronze canopy was attached. Opinions differ widely as to its suitability – make up your own mind!

You can't leave the Angel Choir without looking at a feature which charms old and young alike – the **Lincoln Imp** (25). The small carved figure above the pier nearest to the Head Shrine, sitting with his legs crossed, has horns, claws and a seemingly feathered body. The tale is that he was once alive, but behaved so badly the angels turned him to stone. The image has today become a good-luck symbol and is closely associated with the city.

Cloisters and Chapter House

Leave the Angel Choir, walk down the north choir aisle and turn into the northeast transept, marked on the west side by the second Trondheim Pillar. Immediately to your left are the **Damini Wall Paintings** (26) – four 12th-century bishops of Lincoln painted by the 18th-century Venetian artist Vincenzo Damini. They are probably restorations, as medieval paintwork has been discovered underneath. Further along on the left is the **Touch Exhibition** (27), offering a tactile experience of building materials and other items for the benefit of the blind.

Now go through a vaulted passage, The Slype, to the **cloisters** (28). They might be considered something of an extravagance, as Lincoln did not have a monastic foundation, but no doubt the canons, choristers and priests made as much use of them as monks would have done, with similar enjoyment. The vaulting in the cloisters is of wood, as are the delightfully carved bosses, many of which have been made with considerable wit.

The north cloister is obviously an odd one out among the other three; the original was pulled down in the 15th century to accommodate the dean's horses, so what you now see today is a 17th-century replacement designed by Sir Christopher Wren at the behest of Dean Honywood, who was donating his valuable collection of books to the cathedral and wanted them to have a proper home. This is now called the **Wren Library** (29) and incorporates at its eastern end the 100 or so manuscripts from the Medieval Library, which was destroyed by fire.

Leave the cloisters from the east side and enter the **chapter house** (30). Built in the mid-13th century and measuring nearly 22 yards (20m) across, Lincoln's was the first cathedral chapter house to be polygonal – it has ten sides. The elegantly slender central pier supports a number of ribs which fan out into a tierceron vault, supported outside by flying buttresses and pinnacles.

The oak seat on the far side of the entrance was probably provided for Edward I when he called a parliament here in 1301 to declare his son (the future Edward II) the first Prince of Wales. Later, in 1536, the leaders of the Lincolnshire Rising who resisted the Reformation met here to hear Henry VIII's response to their demands. The stained glass chronicles other events in the building's history.

Servicemen Remembered

Return *via* The Slype and the northeast transept to the north choir aisle. Turn right. Immediately on your right is the **treasury** (31), formerly the Medicine Chapel, which contains a collection of silver plate belonging to the cathedral and other churches in the diocese.

Further along the aisle, turn right into the **north side of the great transept** (32). On its east side you find the **Services' Chapels** (33) – successively the Soldier's, Seamen's and Airmen's. A quick look in all three reveals some fine modern stained glass.

Walk back along the nave *via* the **north aisle** (34), where there are two monuments of interest. The first is a Romanesque **Tournai marble tomb slab** (35), once thought to be the tomb of Remigius but now believed to be that of Bishop

Alexander. Nearer the west end is a more modern memorial to Bishop Kaye (1827–1853).

Just by this latter monument, turn right into the **Morning Chapel** (36). Once used as a parish church, it is now the venue for Matins and, at other times, for private prayer. The obvious feature of architectural interest is the slender central pier of Purbeck marble.

Finally, leave the Morning Chapel and return to the west front.

WALKING TOUR FROM LINCOLN CATHEDRAL

The tour is in two parts. The first looks at that part of the city known as 'uphill', which is close to the Cathedral and has a number of historic buildings in a largely residential area. The second part looks at the 'downhill' section of the city, which is more commercial in character. The return walk to the 'uphill' area involves a steep climb; you might want to opt for a taxi.

Start and finish: The west front of the cathedral.
Length: 3 miles (4.8km).
Time: 2½ hours (because of the steep slopes). Allow more time if you want to visit museums, etc.
Refreshments: Excellent cathedral refectory. Plenty of choice in the city to suit all tastes and pockets. Old inns of character offering good pub lunches include: the Magna Carta (Exchequer Gate), the Lion and Snake (Bailgate), the Wig and Mitre (Steep Hill) and the White Hart (Bailgate). Waterside pubs include the Royal William (Brayford Wharf) and the Witch and Wardrobe (Waterside).

From the west front, cross the cathedral close and leave it *via* the **Exchequer Gate**; this fine stone gateway dates 1320. About fifty yards (50m) beyond the gate is a crossroads, with, on the corner, a fine, half-timbered house with jettied walls that is now the city's **Tourist Information Office**. The helpful staff here can provide you with much useful material.

Turn right into Bailgate, a street full of old coaching inns and good domestic architecture from various historical periods. The brick and stone circles you see in the roadway are believed to be the bases of Roman columns.

At the end of Bailgate is the stone-built **Newport Arch**, a 3rd-century gateway into the Roman city, claimed to be the oldest Roman archway in Britain under which traffic still passes. The Romans came to the area in 48 and built a magnificent walled settlement on this site. A number of Roman sites can be visited in the upper part of the city, including sections of the city wall, an interval tower and an aqueduct.

An Elegant Mental Hospital

Just before the arch, turn left along Chapel Lane. When this runs into Westgate, go right for about a hundred yards (100m) until you reach a road junction. Turn left (south) into Union Road. A little way along on the right is a complex of buildings, the **Lawn Visitor Centre**.

The main building here is a stately-looking mansion with an imposing Classical portico. First impressions, however, can be deceptive, because the Lawn was built in

1820 as a lunatic asylum. The complex was reopened in 1990 as a tourist attraction. Its features include a 5000 sq ft (465m^2) tropical conservatory, with a comprehensive collection of plants. There is also an archaeological interpretative centre, a fudge factory, an RAF museum and another rather gruesome interpretative centre depicting the history of treating mental illness, including some of the more barbaric methods used in Victorian times.

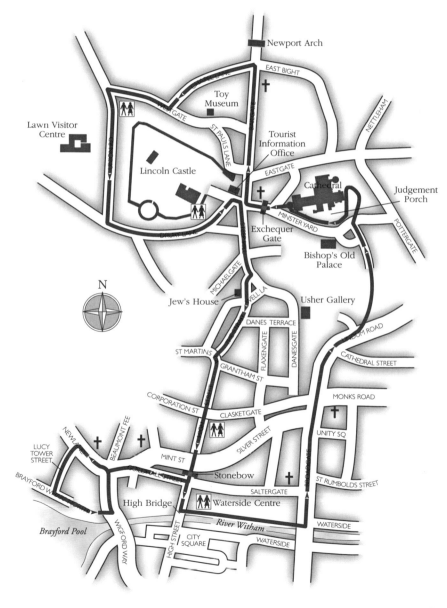

Lincoln Castle

Opposite the Lawn is the west entrance to **Lincoln Castle**. If you want to look at the castle from inside the walls, enter here. If you decide to give the castle a miss, continue south along Union Road and turn left into Drury Lane, which swings back round to the Tourist Information Office.

Built from 1072 on the instructions of William the Conqueror, the castle was constructed on the site of the original Roman castle and used some of its building materials. You can stroll along the ramparts to the **Observatory Tower**; the climb to its 19th-century turret is rewarded by stunning views over the cathedral, the city and the surrounding countryside.

Also don't miss the **Cobb Hall**, the section of the castle which acted as a prison until 1878 and where public executions were watched by enthusiastic crowds. You can also visit the rather depressing Victorian prison chapel, which has models of both chaplain and prisoners in their individual, coffin-like pews.

Leave by the east entrance (you will then find yourself back by the Tourist Information Office).

'Downhill'

Now head towards the 'downhill' part of the city by way of **Steep Hill**, the usual route for pilgrims as they plodded uphill to the Shrine of St Hugh at the cathedral. Today, Steep Hill is cobbled and pedestrianized, and has a range of pubs, historic houses and specialist shops.

The road continues into The Strait where, on the right, you can see one of Lincoln's most famous buildings: the **Jew's House**, dating from *c*1170 and almost certainly the city's oldest domestic building. The ornate entrance arch also served the adjacent Jew's Court, believed to have been the site of a synagogue. Once powerful in the community, the Jews were expelled in the latter part of the 13th century, after much anti-Semitic feeling. The two buildings were restored during the 20th century, and today the House is a restaurant and the Court a specialist bookshop.

The Strait leads on into High Street. Ahead of you is the imposing stone arch known as the **Stonebow**, located at the southern entrance to the old town. The present arch was built in the 15th century, replacing predecessors from Roman and medieval times.

Above it are the city's council chambers and the mayor's office, while to one side is the **Guildhall**, where, in a small museum, Lincoln's civic insignia are displayed. The Mayoralty of Lincoln was established in 1206 and is one of the oldest in the country. The insignia and other items include the city charter, dating from 1141, and the swords of both Richard II and Henry VII.

Brayford Pool and High Bridge

Pass through the Stonebow and turn right. Take the first left to reach **Brayford Pool**, located at the point where the River Witham makes a right-angled turn as it cuts through the Lincoln Edge. Here, too, the Fossdyke Canal leads off to join the River Trent to the west.

There has been a settlement at this place since Celtic times, and it was a busy port under the Romans, Vikings and Normans. The stone for the cathedral was unloaded here, while grain and wool were exported. The most important period for Brayford Pool was during the 18th and 19th centuries, when, despite being over forty miles (64km) from the sea, it was the fourth busiest port in England, with warehouses and industry lining the poolside. Today, pubs, prestigious hotels and the new university take pride of place. Sightseeing cruises leave the jetty near Wigford Way Bridge during the summer months.

Retrace your steps to the High Street and look to the right, towards a remarkable structure, **High Bridge**. The bridge is constructed of stone with a vaulted roof and dates from Norman times. Above it is a two-storeyed half-timbered building with gabled rooms in its tiled roof. High Bridge is thought to be the oldest bridge in the country still to bear buildings. Certainly it is the city's most photogenic spot!

Go down the steps at the nearer side of High Bridge and walk along **Waterside**. On the left of this redeveloped area is the new indoor Waterside Shopping Centre, home to more than forty retail outlets. Continue along past the **Central Market**, housed in a Grade II listed building. The square outside the market is a favourite spot for buskers.

You now arrive at Broadgate. Turn left. Here the hard walk back up the hill to the cathedral begins, and you might prefer to hail a taxi or jump on one of the open-topped buses which, between Easter and the end of October, ply this route back to the cathedral.

Assuming you're made of sterner stuff and want to walk back, follow Broadgate, which eventually becomes Lindum Road. Shortly after a rightward bend, take the fork left up a set of well used steps, the Greestone Stairs. These lead you to the south side of the cathedral close, Minster Yard.

Here you have an excellent opportunity to view the external features of the cathedral. Walk past the east end to the **chapter house**, where you can appreciate the full beauty of this building, with its conical roof and massive flying buttresses. The **east end**, by contrast, is rather disappointing from outside. The upper window seems too large and balances precariously on the tip of the window below, while the excess of crocketing on the numerous pinnacles gives an over-fussy impression.

So move hastily on to look instead at the exceptional southeast porch, or **Judgement Porch**, which demonstrates some of the cathedral's best carving, with some fine gargoyles. It was built in the mid-13th century, largely to offer an impressive entrance to the increasing numbers of pilgrims bound for the Shrine of St Hugh.

Finally, cross to the south side of Minster Yard and the **Bishop's Old Palace**, in the shadow of the cathedral. Although largely derelict, it has the remains of the banqueting hall, offices and the luxurious accommodation which housed many a visiting monarch. On the south-facing slopes of the palace is a vineyard, claimed as England's most northerly, the vines having been donated by Lincoln's twin town, Neustadt an der Weinstrasse in Germany. The ruins of the palace are administered by English Heritage, who, during the summer months, arrange medieval music recitals and other displays.

Leaving the palace, return by way of Minster Yard to the cathedral's west front.

York

Access: By road from the south *via* the M1 and A1(M); major road links in other directions using the A19 and A64. National Express coaches from London and other large cities, arriving at and departing from Roujier Street. Rail journey time from London is under two hours; there are also direct services from Edinburgh, Liverpool, Manchester and Birmingham. Two international airports – Leeds/Bradford and Manchester – are within easy reach. North Sea ferries arrive at nearby Humberside from Belgium and Holland.

The first building on the site of York Cathedral was not a religious institution but the northern headquarters of the Roman army. Constantine the Great, who later declared Christianity a permitted religion of the Empire, was proclaimed Emperor at York in 306. There was not much Christianity in the area, however, when Paulinus (d644) came to York in 625 with Princess (later St) Ethelburga (d647) in order to marry her to Edwin, the pagan King of Northumbria. Two years later Edwin was baptized by Paulinus in a small wooden church built specially for the ceremony.

That wooden building is usually regarded as the first York Minster. It was replaced *c*640 by a stone building dedicated to St Peter. This Anglo-Saxon cathedral was rebuilt and renovated several times before being almost completely destroyed by William the Conqueror's soldiers during the 'harrowing of the North'.

The first Norman cathedral was started by Archbishop Thomas of Bayeux *c*1080 and completed by the turn of the century. (Some of the stonework of this building can still be seen in the Foundations Exhibition below the present minster.) From 1200 onwards, the first Norman cathedral was gradually replaced by a Gothic-style building. Under Archbishop Walter de Gray, the transepts were rebuilt in Early English style. The south transept was not entirely successful, but the builders learned from their mistakes and the north transept is much more pleasing. The chapter house and its vestibule were added between 1260 and 1290.

The builders then moved on to the nave, which must have looked uninspiring compared with that by William of Sens at Canterbury. The replacement, one of the glories of English cathedral architecture, is in Decorated Gothic style; at the time of its completion it was one of the largest building spaces in Europe. This in itself caused problems: the planned stone vaulting was never put in place – the roof has always been wooden.

Attention was then turned to the east end of the minster. As this area was in constant use, the new work had to be completed around and over the existing structure. The style here is Perpendicular Gothic, but remains in keeping with the nave. The work began in 1361 with the Lady Chapel and proceeded westwards towards the choir. While this was going on, part of the central tower collapsed. The plan was to replace it with a new tower surmounted by a lantern and spire, but it soon

Plate 29: Lincoln Cathedral, showing its magnificent west front and lofty towers. The cathedral is located on a commanding hill-top site. Steep streets link it with the newer part of the city (see page 133).

Plate 30: Lincoln. The cathedral is surrounded by narrow streets, coaching inns and historic houses, such as this half-timbered house, which now acts as the city's Tourist Information Office (see page 140).

Plate 31: York. View of York Minster from Lendal Bridge. Nearby is a stretch of the city walls, with a number of gateways, many of which had barbicans or fortified entrances (see page 151).

became evident that the existing masonry would not support the weight, so this notion was abandoned.

By 1472, the minster was complete apart from the western towers, and the building was consecrated.

No new building works have been carried out since the 15th century. The minster escaped serious damage during the Reformation and the Civil War. There have been other difficulties, though, mainly as the result of fire: there were two serious conflagrations during the 19th century, one destroying the roof of the choir and the other the roof of the nave. A major problem was discovered in 1967, when it was found that the foundations were unstable; a large-scale civil-engineering operation strengthened the foundations with enormous concrete collars reinforced with steel rods, and as a by-product gave us improved archaeological knowledge of the Roman, Saxon and Norman building processes. In 1984 yet another fire, probably caused by lightning, destroyed the roof of the south transept, though fortunately the 16th-century rose window survived. A sum of £2½ million was quickly raised for the restoration, and the roof was replaced within four years using the traditional structure and materials of medieval craftsmen.

Today, some 2¼ million people visit York Minster annually. Few of them leave without being impressed by this magnificent building.

TOUR OF THE MINSTER
Start and finish: The west end.

Enter the cathedral through the door on the south side (wheelchair users should take the door on the north side). There is no entrance fee, but a donation is recommended. (There are entrance fees to visit the chapter house, the crypt, the foundations and the tower.)

Walk to the centre of the nave and look back at the **great west window** (1). The tracery is in the 'flamboyant' Decorated Gothic style and contains a heart-shaped central feature – the window is often known as the 'Heart of Yorkshire'. It was glazed in 1338 by Master Robert Ketelbarn. The lower line of pictures shows eight of the cathedral's archbishops with, above them, the Apostles.

A Superb Nave
Move to the centre of the **nave** (2), which is uncluttered with memorials so your eye is not distracted from the simplicity and elegance of the architecture. The lack of memorials may be because until 1862 the nave was not used for services, but instead for secular activities – even today it is often the venue for civic functions and degree ceremonies.

The nave provides one of the best examples of Decorated Gothic in the country. Architectural purists criticize the proportions – rather too broad for its height – undersized capitals, variable thickness of shafts, rather boring tracery in windows and lack of a stone vaulting. All this may be true, but the fact remains that this is an extraordinary nave, and its sheer majesty, elegance and spaciousness are almost awe-inspiring.

The roof is an exact Victorian copy of the original, destroyed by fire in 1840. The roof bosses, each about a yard (1m) across, show the life of Christ. One used to show Mary breast-feeding Jesus, but here the Victorians abandoned their fidelity to the original and depicted the Virgin instead bottle-feeding the babe!

The minster retains much of its original medieval glass. Two windows are of particular note. On the third bay to your right is the **Jesse Window** (3), dating from *c*1310, which takes the form of a family tree with Jesse at the base of the trunk, the prophets sitting on the branches and the Virgin Mary and Jesus in the canopy.

On the sixth bay to your left is the **Bell Founder's Window** (4), donated by Richard Tunnoc, a local Member of Parliament, in 1390. He owned the local bell foundry, and the window has bells everywhere – like a gigantic medieval advertising hoarding!

Before you leave the nave, look for the **Dragon's Head** (5), which protrudes from the triforium. It is often claimed this was a hoist to lift the lid of the font but, as there are no records of a font ever having been in this position, the theory is dubious. It may be no coincidence that there is a small carving of St George on the opposite side of the nave at the same level.

The Five Sisters Window and the Chapter House

Walk along the north nave aisle into the north transept, built 1240–65. Note the Purbeck marble shafts on the columns – a typical feature of the Early English style. Dominating the transept is the **Five Sisters Window** (6), named for the five lancets filled with green–grey *grisaille* glass. It is said to contain over 100,000 pieces of glass arranged in geometrical patterns. This was cheaper than a pictorial display, and it was probably thought that a benefactor would fund a replacement, but no such benefactor ever appeared.

Note the small patch of blue glass at the lower end of the central lancet. This is believed to be glass which survived from the original Norman cathedral.

One of the two chapels in the transept, St Nicholas's Chapel, contains the only surviving medieval brass in the cathedral. The transept's two clocks are of mild interest, though neither is of any great antiquity.

Turn along the vestibule that leads to the **chapter house** (7). Built in the late 13th century in the Decorated Gothic style, the chapter house is octagonal and owes its feeling of spaciousness largely to the lack of a central column. The roof is wooden, although it looks like stone from below.

The tracery in the windows is strictly geometrical. Much of the glass, here as in the vestibule, dates from the 13th century. The overhanging canopies of the forty-four stalls have some fine free-flowing carvings featuring animals, heads and foliage. A Victorian restoration programme removed the remains of the medieval gilding and painting and installed the Minton floor.

The Choir, Sanctuary and Great East Window

Leave the chapter house *via* the vestibule and walk through the north transept into the crossing. Look up into the **central tower** (8), built in the mid-15th century to replace one that collapsed in 1407. It rises to over 200ft (60m) and was in fact

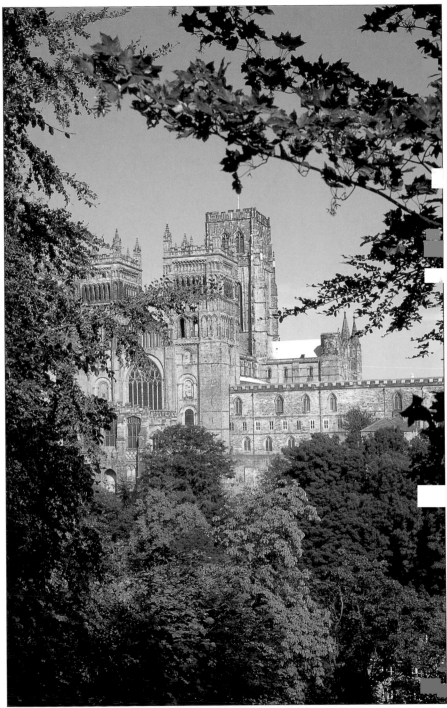

Plate 35: *Durham Cathedral. Arguably the most impressive Romanesque building in Europe, the cathedral is located in the core of an incised meander of the River Wear (see page 156).*

Plate 32: York. The 'Red' Devil' – a figure on a shop front in the pedestrianized Stonegate. It is believed to be a printer's devil (or errand boy) (see page 155).

Plate 33: York. The Shambles is York's most famous street. This narrow thoroughfare was once lined with butchers' shops and retains much of its medieval atmosphere (see page 152).

Plate 34: Durham. The Town Hall and the Tourist Information Centre in the Market Place. With its attractive buildings, the Market Place is the social and economic hub of the city. There has been a market here since 1180 (see page 165).

planned to go even higher until it was realized that the foundations would not stand any more weight. The wooden lantern is notable for its fine collection of gilded bosses (binoculars are useful here); the central boss, showing St Peter and St Paul, is at 4ft (1.5m) wide the largest in the minster.

Back at ground level, the **pulpitum** (9) dates from 1461. The central band shows the figures of the kings of England from William I to Henry VI. Note the particularly miserable expression on the face of William II.

Pass through the central doorway of the pulpitum, which has the only fan vaulting in the cathedral, and move into the **choir** (10), where the style is now Perpendicular. The stalls are Georgian – a pyromaniac had destroyed the originals. Note the brass plaques under the stall canopies; these represent the parishes in the diocese, but apparently their real purpose was to hide the marks on the woodwork made by the Victorian canons' hair oil!

The archbishop's *cathedra* on the south side is balanced on the north side by the equally large wooden pulpit.

Move forward to the **sanctuary** (11), which has a 20th-century high altar. From here you get a good view of the windows of St William (to your left) and St Cuthbert (to your right). Both date from the 15th century, but their styles contrast considerably. Also, this is the best place to view the great east window (see below).

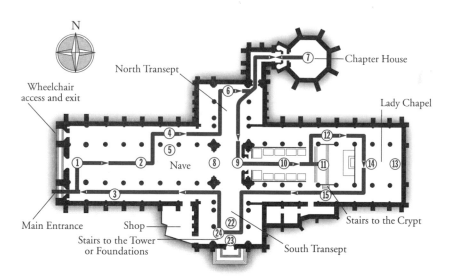

Key

1. Great West Window
2. Nave
3. Jesse Window
4. Bell Founder's Window
5. Dragon's Head
6. Five Sisters Window
7. Chapter House
8. Central Tower
9. Pulpitum
10. Choir
11. Sanctuary
12. North Choir Aisle
13. Great East Window
14. Lady Chapel
15. Stairs to Crypt
16-21. See plan of Crypt
22. South Transept
23. Rose Window
24. Stairs to the Tower or Foundations, see Foundations plan

Leave the sanctuary for the **north choir aisle** (12), which is cluttered with a plethora of tombs and memorial tablets, the most imposing being the tombs of Archbishop Thomas Savage and Prince William of Hatfield (brother of the Black Prince and son of Edward III). The latter is the only royal tomb in the cathedral.

Walk along the north choir aisle to the east end, which is dominated by the Perpendicular **great east window** (13). Dating from 1405–8 and the world's largest area of medieval stained glass, it tells the story of the Creation and the destruction. It is said that the glazier, John Thornton of Coventry, received a £10 bonus for finishing the work on time. Because of the internal stone screen which supports the glass, you get a better view of the window from the sanctuary than from here.

The east end is taken up with three chapels. Occupying the whole of the central space is the **Lady Chapel** (14). The tombs in it include that of Archbishop Richard le Scrope (*c*1350–1405), who was beheaded for becoming involved in the failed rebellion against Henry VI. The screen rails are modern, the work of 'Mousey' Thompson of Kilburn, North Yorkshire – look for his trademark carved mice.

The other two chapels in the east end are St Stephen's, with a large Victorian reredos, and All Saints'.

The Crypt and Foundations

Leave the east end *via* the south choir aisle and go down some stairs to the right into the **crypt** (15). In the Norman cathedral this was the space below a platform built to raise the high altar. It is divided into the eastern crypt and the western crypt (filled in during the 14th century and excavated after the 1829 fire).

From the entrance, turn right and into the eastern crypt. Here on your right you will see the **Doomstone** (16), a 12th-century carved slab which probably came from the west front of the old Norman cathedral. On the east wall is the **York Virgin** (17), a headless figure on a plaque, discovered after the 1829 fire; this Romanesque work had, remarkably, been used as rubble filling in the 14th-century east wall of the cathedral!

Close by is a **Roman column base** (18), dating from the 4th century. It appears to

Crypt

Crypt

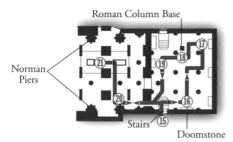

Roman Column Base

Norman Piers

Stairs

Doomstone

Foundations

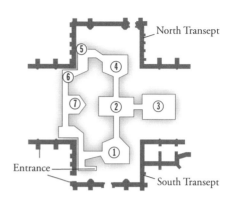

North Transept

Entrance

South Transept

Key

15. Stairs from South Choir Aisle
16. Doomstone
17. York Virgin
18. Roman Column Base
19. Font
20. Norman Piers
21. Shrine of St William of York

Key

1-7. Chambers 1-7

be in its original position as part of the colonnade of the house of the commanding officer of the Roman legion here. Alongside it are red stud marks on the floor; these approximate to the eastern apse of the 11th-century Norman cathedral.

Against the south wall is the **font** (19), the only one in the minster. It dates from the mid-15th century, but also has a modern cover which was designed by Sir Ninian Cooper.

Now walk through into the western crypt, which is dominated by some massive **Norman piers** (20) carved with dogtooth and spiral patterns in the manner of those in Durham Cathedral (see page 158). The most important part of this area of the crypt is the **Shrine of St William of York** (21). William (d1154) was Archbishop of York in the 12th century. After a period in exile he returned to the city to be greeted by thousands of people on the bridge over the River Ouse. Such was their weight that the bridge collapsed. Although the river was in flood, it is said that St William's prayers ensured not a single person drowned. His bones are contained in a Roman coffin with a medieval lid. Nearby are modern mosaics telling his story.

Also in the western crypt is the treasury, which has some impressive silver, but is otherwise of mild interest.

Go back up the steps to the south choir aisle, turn right and go left into the **south transept** (22), the first part of the Gothic cathedral to be built and not generally considered an architectural success. It is dominated by the 13th-century **rose window** (23), which was probably originally glazed with *grisaille* glass. The tomb of Archbishop Walter Gray, in whose time the south transept was built, can be seen close to the aisle.

The south transept was the scene of the disastrous 1984 fire, which was probably caused by a lightning strike. As part of the restoration programme, a new series of bosses was made – including six designed by children through television's *Blue Peter* programme.

From the corner of the transept, steps lead up to the tower (entrance charge). If you are claustrophobic or have no head for heights, miss out the tower and take the steps to the right which lead to the **foundations** (24). This is basically space excavated in something of a hurry between 1967 and 1972 when the central tower seemed in danger of collapse. The foundations present a cross-section of the early history of the city and the cathedral, and are definitely not to be missed. The Roman, Anglo-Saxon and Norman remains discovered during the excavation can be seen in a series of chambers separated by the massive reinforced concrete walls that now support the tower.

Chamber One was at the ground level of the Roman basilica. The base of one of the pillars can be seen in its original position.

Chamber Two shows part of the foundations of the Norman cathedral. Some steps lead up to the treasury, which was probably visited from the western crypt.

Chamber Three has some large models demonstrating the relative positions of the various buildings.

Chambers Four and Five take us outside the boundary of the Norman cathedral.

Chamber Six returns to the Roman area, revealing a culvert that ran from north of the minster to the River Ouse. Also on view here is an interesting Roman military wall painting.

The route through *Chamber Seven* reenters the basilica. It was roughly at this spot that Constantine was proclaimed Caesar on the death of his father in 306.

Finally, leave the foundations by returning up the steps to the south transept. Walk back along the south nave aisle to the west door.

WALKING TOUR FROM YORK MINSTER

The route includes sections of the city walls, a stretch of the Ouse riverside and parts of the pedestrianized streets of the medieval core. Note that many of the placenames have Viking origins. Gates in the walls, for instance, are known as 'bars' (they barred entry as well as letting people through), while many of the streets include the word 'gate', which derives from the Norse 'gata' for street. The walk does not cover all the historic sites of the city (this would be impossible in such a short time), but detours are suggested.

Start and finish: The west front of the minster.
Length: 3 miles (4.8km).
Time: 2½ hours. Allow extra time depending on how many museums, churches and other attractions you want to visit.
Refreshments: A number of ancient inns on or close to the route provide pub lunches and bar meals, notably the Punchbowl and Ye Olde Starre Inn (both in Stonegate), the Hole in the Wall (High Petergate; it has a resident ghost), the Three Tuns (Coppergate) and the Golden Fleece (Pavement).

From the west front of the minster head to the right along High Petergate, named after the minster's patron saint; it follows the route of the Roman Via Principalis.

After about 150 yards (135m) you reach **Bootham Bar**, one of four original gates in the city walls (the others are Micklegate, Monk and Walmgate). All once had barbicans (fortified entrances); only that at Walmgate Bar survives. The gates also had portcullises, and you can see the one under the arch at Bootham Bar. The original Roman gateway, the Porta Principalis Dextra, lies beneath the present bar.

Immediately on your left through Bootham Bar you'll find toilets and the helpful Tourist Information Office. Across the road opposite Bootham Bar is a complex of buildings around the Museum Gardens which would make a profitable detour for any visitor with an extra half day to spend in the city. Immediately opposite the bar is the City Art Gallery. To its left is the King's Manor, a Stuart building with Charles I's coat-of-arms over the door. It is now part of the university. Nearby is the Yorkshire Museum, which concentrates on archaeological treasures. Alongside the museum are the ruins of St Mary's Abbey, which was dissolved in 1536.

A Walk on the Walls

Otherwise, climb the steps at the side of the toilets and go through the upper part of Bootham Bar onto a section of the **city walls**. Built of the same magnesian limestone from Tadcaster as the minster, the walls date from the 13th and 14th centuries and rest on Roman foundations. They stretch for three miles (5km) and almost completely encircled the medieval city, which had four times as many inhabitants as does the same area today – though also rather more filth and squalor.

Walk leftwards along the wall. On your right you can see the Dean's Park and, above the shrubs and trees, good views of the minster and of the minster's library, a building which was once a chapel of the medieval archbishop's palace.

At the clearly signed Robin Hood Tower, the walls swing around to the southeast, and finally you come to **Monk Bar**. This was the most heavily fortified of the gateways. The portcullis still works, but the barbican was removed in Victorian times. The upper floor used to be a prison in the 17th century, and it is reputed that heads would be hung from the gate after executions.

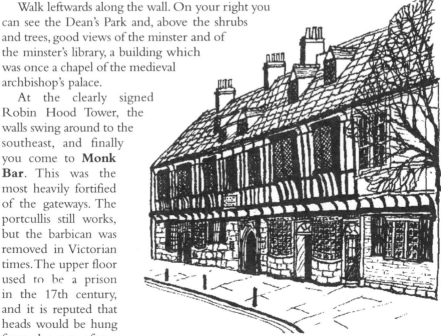

St William's College

An Ancient Church and a Roman Column

Descend the stairs into Goodramgate; about fifty yards (50m) along this street fork left. After a further hundred yards or so (100m) turn right through an iron gateway into the graveyard of **Holy Trinity Church**. This remarkable little building, undoubtedly the best of the many parish churches in York, is claimed to be the oldest church in England, and certainly records go back to 1080. It has a rare saddle-back roof, some 17th-century box pews, a 15th-century font, Jacobean altar rails and much, much more. A little gem – don't miss it!

Head back along Goodramgate to the fork and cross over the road into College Street. On your right is the half-timbered **St William's College**, built in 1467 and named after the Norman archbishop. Formerly the royal mint for Charles I and college for the minster's priests, it is now an information and conference centre with an excellent restaurant and bistro. At the top right of the main entrance door you can spot one of 'Mousey' Thompson's little rodents. From the college, there is an excellent view of the minster's great east window in all its Perpendicular glory, while to the right is the chapter house with its external buttresses.

Walk now past the south side of the cathedral along Deangate and Minster Yard. On your left you'll see a **Roman column** which in the 4th century stood in the great hall of the 6th Legion. It was found in 1969 during the excavation of the minster's south transept, lying where it had collapsed. It was erected on this site by the York Civic Trust in 1971 to mark the 1900th anniversary of the founding of the city by the Romans.

This is a good spot to look at the architecture of the south side of the minster, notably the rather unfortunate south transept, with its strange relationships, lack of sculpture and three irritatingly steep gables over its door.

Minster Yard leads towards the west front of the minster. On your left is the simple little early-16th-century **Church of St Michael le Belfry**, said to be the only church in York to be built during a single architectural period. The interior has a plain, Presbyterian feel to it. There is some stained glass dating from the 1330s, but the church's main claim to fame is that Guy Fawkes (1570–1606) was baptized here; his birthplace, now Young's Hotel, is just across the road.

From the Shambles to a Viking Centre

Leaving the church, turn left into Low Petergate and go along it to King's Square, reputedly named after the Viking kings who lived hereabouts in the 7th to 10th centuries. From the right-hand corner of the square, enter York's most famous street, the **Shambles**.

Until the early 1930s, almost every building here was a butcher's shop; the street got its name from the 'fleshammels', ledges beneath the windows used to display the meat. Many of these ledges can still be seen, although the shops are now much more varied. Narrow and with overhanging walls and roofs, the Shambles remains full of medieval atmosphere.

At its end, turn right briefly into Pavement, the first street in York to be paved and the site of political executions; it once had stocks and pillories. Turn almost immediately left into Piccadilly where, on the banks of the River Foss (a tributary

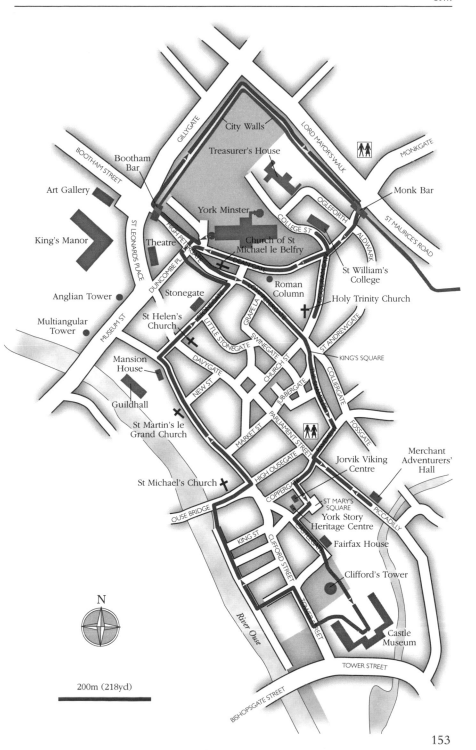

City Walls
Treasurer's House
Bootham Bar
BOOTHAM STREET
GILLYGATE
LORD MAYOR'S WALK
MONKGATE
Art Gallery
Monk Bar
ST MAURICE'S ROAD
ST LEONARDS PLACE
York Minster
OGLEFORTH
King's Manor
HIGH PETERGATE
College St
Theatre
DUNCOMBE PL
Church of St Michael le Belfry
ALDWARK
St William's College
Anglian Tower
Roman Column
Holy Trinity Church
Stonegate
Multiangular Tower
MUSEUM ST
St Helen's Church
GRAPE LA
LITTLE STONEGATE
SWINEGATE
ST ANDREWGATE
CHURCH ST
KING'S SQUARE
Mansion House
DAVYGATE
COLLIERGATE
Guildhall
NEW ST
UBBERGATE
St Martin's le Grand Church
PARLIAMENT STREET
MARKET ST
FOSSGATE
Merchant Adventurers' Hall
HIGH OUSEGATE
Jorvik Viking Centre
St Michael's Church
COPPERGATE
PICCADILLY
OUSE BRIDGE
ST MARY'S SQUARE
York Story Heritage Centre
KING ST
CLIFFORD STREET
Fairfax House
Clifford's Tower
N
River Ouse
Castle Museum
TOWER STREET
BISHOPSGATE STREET
200m (218yd)

153

of the Ouse) to your left, you see the **Merchant Adventurers' Hall**. This half-timbered building was the Guildhall of the Merchant Adventurers Company of the City of York, founded 1357. For 500 years these were the most powerful people in the area. Their ships went as far afield as Russia and the Middle East, dealing in such commodities as wool, lead, timber, sugar, dyes and silks. Inside the building is a magnificent timbered great hall, festooned with the emblems of the various guilds. Below, in the undercroft, is delightful little chapel, today a popular venue for local weddings.

Retrace your steps along Piccadilly to Pavement and turn left into Coppergate – nothing to do with copper: coopers (barrelmakers) worked here. On your right is All Saints Church, with its prominent lantern tower. Turn left into Coppergate Walk. On your right is the **Jorvik Viking Centre**.

When the foundations of a nearby modern shopping centre were being dug, remains of a Viking settlement were found along with a tremendous number of artefacts. This museum, built on the site, has won many awards. Visitors travel backwards on a 'time car' and then forwards through a reconstructed Viking settlement complete with sounds and smells. Be assured that this will be a highlight of your visit to York!

The Story of York

Walk through the modern St Mary's Square shopping complex, leaving it on the right-hand side. A little way along on your right is the **York Story Heritage Centre**, based in a redundant church. The exhibitions within trace York's development over the ages using models and audiovisual displays.

On leaving, turn left along Castlegate to reach **Fairfax House**, claimed, with justification, to be one of the finest Georgian townhouses anywhere in Britain. It was built in 1762 for the 3rd Baron Fairfax (1612–1671), victor over Charles I at the Battle of Naseby (1645). Although a staunch parliamentarian at this time, Fairfax later refused to march on the Scots, supporters of the Old Pretender (later Charles II), and retired from his military posts. Later he headed the commission sent to The Hague to organize the Old Pretender's accession to the throne. The house, restored in 1982–4 by the York Civic Trust, contains a fine collection of furniture, clocks and art.

At the end of Castlegate is **Clifford's Tower**, an artificial mound topped by a stone building. This was the keep for the castle built by Henry III. The mound was there before, however: William the Conqueror built a wooden tower on its top during his 'harrowing of the North'. This was burned down during anti-Semitic riots in 1190. The extant tower is named after Roger Clifford, one of its hereditary constables. Another name associated with the tower is that of Robert Aske, who was hung here in chains in 1537 for leading the Pilgrimage of Grace – the protest against the Dissolution of the Monasteries.

Walk across the green to the **Castle Museum**, housed in some old prison buildings in which the highwayman Dick Turpin (1705–1739) spent his last night before being hanged. The museum has a high reputation, and includes some authentic reconstructions of Victorian and Edwardian street scenes and shops – although you may find the innumerable school parties an irritation.

A Stroll by the Water and Two Fine Churches

Leave the Castle Green and, with Clifford's Tower on your right and St George's Field on your left, head towards the bank of the **River Ouse**. Turn right on reaching the river and walk along South Esplanade and King's Staith towards Ouse Bridge. This is a good place to pick up a river cruise; the floodlit ones in the evening are particularly recommended. Most trips last about an hour.

The east side of the river along here is mainly residential, with Edwardian and Victorian houses, but you'll see across the water that the west side, which once consisted largely of warehouses and riverside industry, is being redeveloped with expensive apartments, restaurants and hotels.

Leave the riverside at Ouse Bridge and turn right, into Ousegate. On your left is **St Michael's Church**, one of York's many redundant parish churches. The interior is mainly 12th-century; the tower was added three centuries later. The church has some notable 15th-century stained glass. In Victorian times, some 7ft (2m) of the south wall was removed in order to improve access to Ouse Bridge. St Michael's was refurbished in 1989 to serve as a Christian Centre.

Turn left into Spurriergate, which soon becomes the modern Coney Street. A fair way along on your left you'll come to **St Martin's le Grand Church**. Built in the 15th century, this was largely destroyed in an air raid in 1942, but the remains have a modern extension that imaginatively blends old with new. The most remarkable feature is a large painted clock jutting out over the street; on top of the clock is the figure of an 18th-century sailor, usually known as the **Little Admiral**, using a cross-staff sextant.

Old Public Buildings and an Old Public House

At the end of Coney Street, St Helen's Square was the site of the main Roman entrance to the city. On the square's southwest side are two important public buildings. The **Mansion House** was completed in 1730 and is still occupied by the Lord Mayor during his year in office. Next door is the stone **Guildhall**, best seen from the other side of the Ouse. Constructed in 1446 as a headquarters for the local craft guilds, it was damaged by bombs during World War II but has been sympathetically restored and is now occupied by York City Council.

Tucked into the corner of the north side of the square is **St Helen's Church**, which has a small lantern tower and some 15th-century glass.

Leave St Helen's Square to the left of the church and walk along **Stonegate**, one of York's fascinating pedestrianized streets. Full of speciality shops and old inns, Stonegate has some interesting architectural features. Note the Tudor building to the left whose jettied walls are covered in Minton tiles. Kilvington's shop to the right has a figurehead taken from one of the many ships abandoned at York when the Ouse gradually silted up. Further along is **Ye Olde Starre Inn**, licensed in 1644 and believed to be the city's oldest inn. Don't miss the Red Devil, sitting on top of a window on the right-hand side; it is believed to represent a printer's devil (or errand boy) – there were certainly print shops in Stonegate at one time.

Turn left at the top of Stonegate and walk along High Petergate until the west front of the cathedral is to your right.

Durham

Access: The A1, the usual route from the south, is of motorway classification for much of its length. The cross-Pennine A66 provides a scenic link with the Lake District to the west. There are luxury coach services from London and other centres. InterCity trains from London; journey time under three hours. The nearest international airports are at Newcastle and Teesside. Ferries run from Tyneside to Bergen, Stavanger, Amsterdam, Gothenburg and Hamburg. Within Durham, a City Courier minibus runs a shuttle service from the Market Square to the Palace Green outside the cathedral.

The historic core of Durham lies within an incised meander of the River Wear, an area known locally as the Peninsula. At the south end is the cathedral; protecting it at the north end is the castle, the seat of the prince–bishops who controlled the region from the Scottish border to the River Tees.

The cathedral owes its location to the story of St Cuthbert (*c*634–687), appointed Bishop of Lindisfarne in 685. On his death, not long afterwards, he was buried in the church on the island. Ten years later his coffin was opened and his body was found to be without signs of decay. This was hailed as a miracle, and his body was placed in a shrine.

Two centuries later, frequent Danish raids made it impossible for the monks to stay on Lindisfarne. The shrine was dismantled and St Cuthbert's body and other relics, such as the head of St Oswald and manuscripts including the Lindisfarne Gospels, were taken by the monks in their search for a new home. In fact, they wandered around northern England for over a century before finally settling at Durham, where initially they made a wooden shelter for the saint's body. This was followed by the stone-built White Church, which was to remain until Norman times.

In 1071 William the Conqueror built the castle at Durham in an effort to introduce some law and order into the area, and shortly thereafter he established the first of the prince–bishops, who were expected to be both religious leaders and military commanders. Meanwhile, the first Norman bishop, Walcher of Lorraine, had evicted the Congregation of St Cuthbert and introduced Benedictine monks.

His successor, William of Calais, demolished the White Church and the shrine so that a new cathedral could be built. This was begun in 1092 and by 1133 the choir, transepts and nave had been completed, all with stone vaulted roofs – unique at that time in northwest Europe. The stone used for the construction was quarried locally. (The Coal Measures have a number of sandstone strata and a particularly thick layer was used, which inevitably became known as the Cathedral Sandstone.) By this time a new shrine had been constructed for St Cuthbert behind the high altar. The chapter house was finished in 1140 and in the same year an attempt was made to construct a Lady Chapel at the east end; this was abandoned because of unstable ground, so it was built at the western end and known as the Galilee Chapel. The main entrance to the cathedral was now moved to the north side.

By the 13th century improved building techniques meant that some additions could be made to the east end. The Chapel of the Nine Altars was constructed to provide better facilities for the Benedictine monks to celebrate mass. At the Dissolution the monastery was dissolved, but in 1541 it was reconstituted as a cathedral. The last prior, Hugh Whitehead, became the first dean, and twelve canons were appointed to replace the monks. Fortunately, the monastic buildings survived almost intact – indeed they are the most complete of any English cathedral. A good deal of damage was done to the cathedral during the Reformation – the Shrine of St Cuthbert was broken up, among other things – and further damage was wrought during the Civil War: after the Battle of Dunbar, Cromwell housed some 4000 Scottish prisoners in the cathedral, and they tore up woodwork to make fires to keep themselves warm.

By the 18th century the fabric of the cathedral was in a bad state, so the usual Victorian renovation was much needed. Sir George Gilbert Scott (1811–1878) designed a new pulpit and choir screen. The great doors of the west end were opened up, but then blocked up again. Some of the windows in the nave were altered and filled with mediocre stained glass. There was some restoration of the tower as well, with the replacement of a number of statues, while parts of the former monks' quarters were renovated.

Today the cathedral looks in good shape, but it is a constant battle to raise the funds to maintain the building. In 1987 Durham Cathedral and Castle were designated a World Heritage site of architectural and historical interest.

TOUR OF THE CATHEDRAL
Start and finish: The north door.

Just before you enter through the **north door** (1), take a look at the Sanctuary Knocker, which was provided for any fugitive who might happen to come seeking sanctuary inside. There were chambers above the door so that the monks could watch for such fugitives, who were granted thirty-seven days' refuge. During the 16th century more than three hundred people sought the sanctuary of St Cuthbert.

The inside of the door is much as it was when it was built in the 12th century, but the outer porch and chambers have been demolished. The present Sanctuary Knocker is not the original (which can be seen in the treasury) but the 20th-century bronze replica looks authentic enough.

Step inside the cathedral and, ignoring the nave for the time being, walk to the right into the **Galilee Chapel** (2). If you're familiar with southern Spain the regularly spaced pillars of Purbeck marble and rounded dogtooth arches will immediately remind you of the Mesquita in Cordoba. Note the 12th-century wall paintings behind the altar; these are reputed to be of St Cuthbert and St Oswald but, as only their lower halves are represented, you need a bit of imagination.

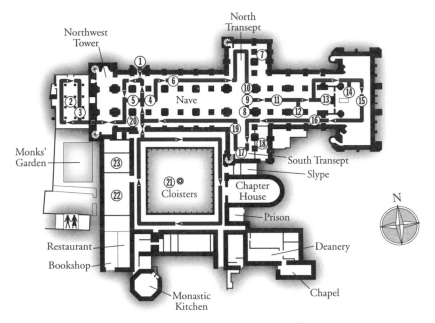

Key

1. North Door
2. Galilee Chapel
3. Tomb of the Venerable Bede
4. Nave
5. Font
6. North Nave Aisle
7. Gregory Chapel

8. Pulpit
9. Choir Screen
10. Lectern
11. Choir
12. Bishop's Throne
13. Neville Screen
14. Tomb of St Cuthbert
15. Chapel of the
    Nine Altars

16. Millennium Window
17. Prior Castell's Clock
18. Chapel of the Durham Light
    Infantry
19. Statue of Shute Barrington
20. Miners' Memorial
21. Cloisters
22. Treasury
23. Monks' Dormitory

Venerable Bones

On the south side of the Galilee Chapel is the **Tomb of the Venerable Bede** (3). Bede (*c*673–735) was a notable scholar and wrote the first history of England, *Historia Ecclesiastica Gentis Anglorum* ('The Ecclesiastical History of the English People'). His bones were brought to Durham in 1022 and placed in the chapel in a magnificent shrine in 1370. Sadly, the shrine was destroyed in the Reformation, but the bones remain, marked by a simple black tombstone carved with a Latin inscription that can be loosely translated as: 'In this tomb are the bones of the Venerable Bede.'

Return now to the massive and awesome **nave** (4), undoubtedly the most impressive piece of Romanesque architecture in Britain. The proportions are satisfying, with the arcade 2½ times the triforium. Both clerestory and triforium have galleries. It is, however, the pillars which dominate. They are nearly 22ft (6.6m) in both circumference and height, and alternate between plain and composite design. The round pillars are ornamented with diamonds, chevrons and vertical fluting (spiral designs appear only in the transepts and choir).

The arches have a strong dogtooth ornamentation, a pattern continued at triforium level. Above is the earliest British example of stone vaulting, and the dogtooth ornamentation is again prominent. The overall effect may not be elegant but it certainly has an austere strength.

At the west end of the nave is the **font** (5), placed there by Bishop John Cosin (1594–1672) towards the end of the 17th century. By contrast with the simplicity of the font, its cover is one of the most ornate to be found in any English cathedral. Richly carved in dark wood, it stands on eight prodigiously tall pillars. Just in front of the font is a long, thin slab of black Frosterley marble, said to mark, in monastic days, the limit to which women were allowed to go.

Modern Aspects

Turn now to the **north nave aisle** (6), where the main item of interest is a modern stained glass window, *Daily Bread*, designed by Mark Angus. It represents a vertical view of the Last Supper, and was donated by the staff of the local Marks & Spencer to commemorate the firm's centenary. Some find it inspiring; others, more conservative, compare it to a Marks & Spencer fruit and vegetable counter, and wonder whether it has a place in a Romanesque cathedral. It is certainly difficult to be neutral.

Walk to the north transept, where the architectural pattern of the nave is repeated, this time with spirally ornamented pillars prominent. On its east side is the **Gregory Chapel** (7), which is reserved for private prayer. This chapel was restored in Victorian times and furnished by the Mothers' Union in 1992. Look for the aumbry – a small cupboard set in the wall by the altar; here items of the Sacrament were kept.

Move into the crossing. The black-and-white marble floor, dating from the 17th century, was brought here from the choir as part of the Victorian alterations. Also Victorian is the ornate marble **pulpit** (8), designed by Sir George Gilbert Scott in a (failed) attempt to replicate the design of the nave. The marble and alabaster **choir screen** (9) is also Scott's work. The aim was to remove the organ screen and replace it with something to allow a continuous view towards the east end. Another failed attempt! The **lectern** (10), again Victorian, shows, rather than the more customary eagle, a pelican feeding its young from its own breast.

The Choir and the Bishop's Throne

Pass through the screen into the **choir** (11). The richly carved stalls here date from 1662, when they replaced medieval originals; the identity of the designer and carver are not known for certain. The misericords are certainly worth a look. At the end of the choir stalls is the **bishop's throne** (12), undoubtedly the tallest in the country. Richly gilded and coloured, it was built for Thomas Hatfield, Bishop of Durham 1345–81, and includes his tomb in a chantry underneath the throne.

Continuing eastward, you come to the high altar, behind which is the superb **Neville Screen** (13), donated by Lord Neville in 1380. Made of Caen stone, it was carved in London, shipped to Newcastle and finally brought by wagon to Durham. Its niches are now empty, an estimated 107 statues having been removed during the Reformation.

Just by the altar steps is a brass to the memory of Bishop Beaumont which must be one of the largest brasses in England. Unfortunately it is usually covered by a carpet.

St Cuthbert's Tomb

Turn into the north choir aisle and immediately climb the steps behind the altar screen to the **Tomb of St Cuthbert** (14). His body used to lie here in an elaborate and bejewelled shrine; you can still see the grooves worn in the floor as the untold pilgrims who came here throughout the Middle Ages shuffled past. After the demolition of the shrine, St Cuthbert's coffin was buried at the site. A statue near the tomb shows Cuthbert holding the head of St Oswald (d642), King of Northumbria, which was buried with him.

In case you were wondering, the line of lead on the floor marks the original line of the apsidal east end of the cathedral.

Go back down the steps and into the extreme east end of the cathedral, the **Chapel of the Nine Altars** (15). Under each of the nine lancet windows here there used to be an altar, separated from its neighbour(s) by a screen. Started in 1242 but not finished until 1280, the chapel shows the evolution of architectural styles during this period.

The rose window is much later, having been redesigned in the late 18th century. Note the thin shafts of black Frosterley marble with prominent sections of white fossil coral.

The Millennium Window and Prior Castell's Clock

Leave the chapel by the south choir aisle, where the main item of interest is the **Millennium Window** (16). The glass was installed in 1995 to celebrate the 1000th anniversary of the building; donated by the Binks family of Thornley, County Durham, it was designed by Joseph Nuttgens of High Wycombe. The window shows the stages in the life of the cathedral and the surrounding area, beginning with St Cuthbert on Lindisfarne and ending with more modern features such as the Tyne Bridge, Stephenson's *Locomotion* and local coalmining – all delightfully enhanced when the sun streams in from the south.

Walk on into the south transept, which is dominated by **Prior Castell's Clock** (17). Dating from c1500, this probably survived the Cromwell's Scottish prisoners because a thistle features prominently among the decoration. The Victorians (predictably) moved it about, but in 1938 the Friends of the Cathedral restored the clock and returned it to its original position.

On the east side of the transept is the **Chapel of the Durham Light Infantry** (18), which replaced a medieval chapel after World War I. Colours from the various campaigns hang from the walls and a Book of Remembrance holds the names of those killed in battle.

At the exit to the transept is the **Statue of Shute Barrington** (19). Barrington (1734–1826), Bishop of Durham from 1791 until his death, is arguably the most highly regarded bishop in the cathedral's history. In addition to his religious duties he was a patron of the arts and contributed much to agricultural development in the area.

Stroll down the south aisle, past the site of the Neville Chantry, until you reach the **Miners' Memorial** (20). Erected in 1947 and appropriately made of black wood, thought to be 17th-century Spanish, this remembers Durham miners who lost their lives in the pits. The last coalmine in Durham closed in 1994, but the Durham Miners' Gala continues to take place annually.

Associated Buildings

Go through the door into the **cloisters** (21). These were restored in 1827–8. The roof, however, is original and there are some fine bosses with 15th-century coats-of-arms.

Turn left and stroll round the cloisters in a clockwise direction. Many of the buildings you pass – including the chapter house, prison and monastic kitchen – are unfortunately not open to visitors.

On the opposite corner from where you entered is the prior's hall undercroft, in which is the Audiovisual Display Area. The restaurant and the bookshop are at the next corner you reach, and alongside them is the **treasury** (22), which contains the relics of St Cuthbert, including his coffin, cross and vestments. (At the time of writing the treasury was being renovated with a grant from the Heritage Lottery Fund.)

Past the treasury, go up some steps to the former **monks' dormitory** (23). This could accommodate up to forty monks, each with a private cubicle. A blocked-up doorway at its cathedral end once led to the 'night stairs', the route the monks used to go into the cathedral for prayers at night. Today, the dormitory's most impressive feature is its beamed roof, around 600 years old and said to have required the wood from over twenty oak trees. Now used as a library and study centre for students, the dormitory also contains a collection of over seventy Anglo-Saxon stones – some originals, others moulds – mainly in the form of crosses.

Leave the cloisters and return through the nave of the cathedral to the north door, where the tour began.

WALKING TOUR FROM DURHAM CATHEDRAL

This walk circumnavigates the Peninsula and includes stretches of the Riverside Walk, the castle and parts of the university, plus the older section of the city. The whole site encompassing the cathedral, castle, Palace Green and the surrounding buildings has deservedly been recognized by UNESCO as a World Heritage Site.

Start and finish: Palace Green, just outside the north door of the cathedral.
Length: 2 miles (3.2km).
Time: 1½ hours, but allow longer if the castle is open.
Refreshments: The spacious cathedral restaurant is recommended. Surprisingly few pubs and inns of character, but you could try the Market Tavern (Market Place) or the Swan and Three Cygnets (next to Elvet Bridge). The Three Tuns (New Elvet) and the County Hotel (Old Elvet) provide more expensive food as well as accommodation.

Between the cathedral and the castle is a large grassy open space, **Palace Green**. Once called 'The Place', it was covered with houses until the 12th century, when these were pulled down as a health hazard. It is surrounded by buildings once closely connected to the cathedral but now largely used by the university.

On the east side are: Bishop Cosin's Hall, a late-17th-century mansion that is now a university hall of residence; the Bishop's Hospital, now the Students' Union building; the more modern infill of the Pemberton Building, used as a debating chamber; and the Queen Anne-style Abbey House, now occupied by the Department of Theology. Between the latter and the cathedral is the cobbled Dun Cow Lane, named after the animal which, legend tells us, decided the ultimate resting place of St Cuthbert's coffin. Note the carving nearby on the northeast transept of the cathedral showing a dun cow and a milkmaid.

The west side of the Green has: the 15th-century exchequer and chancery, once the mint and bishops' court; Bishop Cosin's Library (note his coat-of-arms over the door); the old University Library, built in the mid-19th century; the Diocesan Registry, now part of the library; and the Grammar School, built in the 1660s, once a private residence and now the University Music School.

Durham Castle

Looming over the northern end of the Green is the imposing **Durham Castle**. The building was started *c*1072 and is on the typical Norman 'motte and bailey' plan. Shortly after completion it was given to Bishop Walcher, and it was to remain in cathedral hands for 750 years, with the prince–bishops maintaining a combined religious and military rule. The castle successfully carried out its defensive role – despite frequent skirmishes with the Scots, there is no record of the building ever being taken.

As times became more peaceful and the castle no longer needed to be a fortress, the prince–bishops gradually converted it into a residence where they could entertain lavishly, and over the centuries the original Norman architecture became mixed with other styles. In the 1930s, Bishop van Mildert established the University of Durham, and the castle became University College. Shortly afterwards the Norman keep, by now little more than a ruin, was restored; sympathetic renovation of the building continues to this day.

If you take a tour of the castle you'll see much of the original Norman architecture, particularly in the gatehouse, interior doorways, gallery and chapel (which dates from 1080). Also of interest are the great hall, the bishop's dining room, the state rooms and Tunstal's Chapel.

St Cuthbert's Well and a Riverside Stroll

Leave Palace Green *via* a small alleyway (or vennel), Windy Gap, between the University Music School and the old registry. The vennel leads to the Upper Riverside Walk. Turn left on this and after about fifty yards (50m) you'll see a sign pointing down through the trees to **St Cuthbert's Well**. This has some stonework around it with a 17th-century inscription, now difficult to read. These days only a trickle of water emerges from the well, and it often dries up completely in the summer.

Continue down the path through the woodland, which is carpeted with pungent wild garlic in the spring, until you reach the Lower Riverside Walk. Turn left and, with the water close by on your right, follow this path to the old fulling mill (fulling is the scouring and thickening of fabric), now the **University Museum of Archaeology**. The displays inside chart the archaeological history of Durham and its surrounding area.

162

Walk further along the path to **Prebends' Bridge**, built in 1778 after an earlier footbridge had been swept away in a flood. There are superb views northwards along the wooded gorge toward Framwellgate Bridge, with the tips of the cathedral towers peeping above the trees. This vista inspired Sir Walter Scott

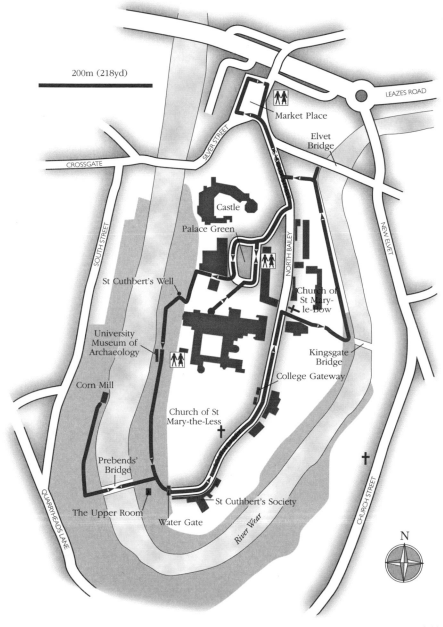

(1771–1832), and lines from his *Harold the Dauntless* are inscribed in a tablet on the wall of the bridge:

> *Grey towers of Durham,*
> *Yet well I love thy mixed and massive piles.*
> *Half church of God, half castle 'gainst the Scot.*
> *And long to roam these venerable aisles*
> *With records stored of deeds long forgot.*

Cross the bridge and turn right along the path to a **corn mill**, on the other end of the weir from the fulling mill. The two mills were originally the Prior's Mills, and the profits from them paid for work in the cathedral. You can't go into the corn mill, but the terrace with picnic tables on its north side, with a view across the river and the weir and up the slopes to the cathedral, provides great photo-opportunities!

Return to Prebends' Bridge, cross the river again, and make a short detour to the right to a group of dead elm trunks carved to represent the Last Supper. Called the **Upper Room**, this is the work of Colin Wilbourn, the first Artist in Residence at Durham Cathedral (1986–7). Twelve trunks denote both the twelve Apostles and the arches of the room, while the thirteenth tree has an integral seat representing Christ's place, and here you can sit – an extraordinary experience.

A City of History

Go back once more to Prebends' Bridge, turn right and walk up the hill to the **Water Gate**. Also known as **Bailey Gate**, this was constructed in 1778, shortly after Prebends' Bridge, and made a gap in the city's walls through which carriages could travel to the south.

Pass through the gate into **South Bailey**, a road which runs along the east side of the cathedral and merges eventually into North Bailey. The street was named after the area between the inner and outer walls of the castle, the Baileys. This has always been a fashionable area of the city, and provides some wonderful examples of domestic architecture. On the right, for example, is the **Home of St Cuthbert's Society**, which dates from the early 18th century and has a stunning moulded doorway with a shell-hood above.

Next, on the left, is the **Church of St Mary-the-Less**, built in the 12th century but heavily restored in early Victorian times. This charming little building, once the parish church of South Bailey but now the chapel for St John's College, retains its Norman windows and a dogtooth arch over the main door.

Further up the hill, again on your left, is the **College Gateway**, the old monastery gatehouse, dating back to the 16th century. The gateway is vaulted and has some interesting bosses, one of which has the arms of Prior Castell, responsible for the gate's construction. If you peer through the gateway you'll see College Green (also known as the Cathedral Close), surrounded by monastery buildings which were handed over to the cathedral at the time of the Reformation. In the centre of the Green is an octagonal well house, built (it is believed) *c*1750.

Continue past the gateway. The road now becomes North Bailey. On the left is a fine view of the east end of the cathedral. Almost opposite, on your right, is

St Mary-le-Bow Church, which probably occupies the site of the original wooden church where St Cuthbert's body was sheltered when first brought to Durham. The church was named after the arch or 'bow' which crossed the bailey. The arch and attached tower collapsed in 1637, demolishing much of the nave of the church, but it was speedily rebuilt using local taxes. The church finally closed in 1967, and ten years later it was converted into a Heritage Centre and Museum offering audiovisual displays and opportunities for brass rubbing.

Go down Bow Lane, by the side of the church, until you get to **Kingsgate Bridge**. This footbridge was provided as a link for students between the colleges and the administration blocks on the east side of the river. It was designed by the Danish architect Ove Arup, who produced the original design for Sydney Opera House. Walk onto the bridge for views north along the gorge towards Elvet Bridge and south to see the tower of St Oswald's Church rising above the trees on the far side of the river.

Return to Bow Lane and take the steps down the right-hand side of the bridge to the level of the River Wear. Turn left along the path, Fearon Walk, and walk along the riverside to **Elvet Bridge**. The original bridge, built c1160, was badly damaged in a serious flood in 1771. It was extensively rebuilt in 1805, doubling its width with dry arches and massive buttresses on the upstream side. There are shops over the dry arch on the east side; on the city side, one of the first buildings you see was once a prison. Since the building of the New Elvet Bridge to the north in 1975 to relieve traffic in the city centre, the old bridge has been reserved for pedestrians.

Market Place and Saddler Street
Turn left at the bridge, climb up the steps and fork right into **Market Place**. Always busy with shoppers, tourists and students, Market Place is the social and economic hub of the city. The market first received its charter in 1180, but most of the buildings around the square date from Victorian times, with some impressive bank fronts.

The Church of St Nicholas on the north side (to your right as you enter the square) dates from 1888 and is Victorian Gothic in style. Alongside is the Town Hall complex, with Guildhall and Art Gallery. Behind these are the indoor markets.

Dominating Market Place are two statues. Next to the church is the equestrian statue of the 3rd Marquess of Londonderry, a leading political figure in Victorian times. On the south side of Market Place is a more modest statue of Neptune which once stood over a wellhead in the square. This latter statue was given to the city in 1729 by George Bowes MP to represent the scheme to link Durham to the sea by improved navigation along the River Wear. After spending half a century exiled to a local park, Neptune was renovated and returned to Market Place in 1991.

Leave Market Place the way you entered it, *via* what was once called Fleshergate, the butchers' quarter. Mustard was ground at a mill behind No. 73 until c1900, though nothing remains to be seen today. Go past the steps down to Elvet Bridge and fork right into **Saddler Street**, named after Sir Richard Saddler, whose 16th-century house is probably the oldest residence in a street whose delightful domestic architecture may cause you to pause and browse for a while. During the 18th century this was also Durham's theatreland. At the head of Saddler Street is the site of the North Gate, demolished in 1820.

Here fork right into Owengate, a cobbled street that leads back to Palace Green.

Further Information

Visitors to English cathedrals are welcome to attend public services, but should bear in mind that access to parts of the buildings may be restricted at such times. They should also be aware that the naves of cathedrals are frequently used for events such as concerts and ceremonies. At such times the buildings may be closed to visitors.

The information below gives contact details for each cathedral. Also listed are opening hours, access details and an indication of any entrance charge required for each cathedral and any nearby places of interest.

LONDON: ST PAUL'S
St Paul's Cathedral
Open daily 08:00–1730, except Sun 08:30–1600. For pre-recorded information messages, tel 020 82364128. Wheelchair access throughout the ground floor. Toilets in southwest corner of crypt. No cathedral refectory, but plenty of food outlets in surrounding streets.

Dr Johnson's House
Open daily May–Sept 10:00–17:00 and Oct–May 11:00–17:00. *Entrance fee.*

LONDON: WESTMINSTER
Westminster Abbey
Open: the nave and the cloisters (which are free) are open daily 09:00–16:45. The rest of the Abbey (which has an *entrance fee*) is open Mon–Fri 09:00–16:45 and Sat 09:45–14:45, 15:45–17:45. There is an additional *entrance fee* to be paid to visit the Chapter House and Pyx Chamber (run by English Heritage), which are open daily 10:30–16:00. For information, contact the Chapter Office, tel 020 72225152. Wheelchair access over most of abbey, although large visitor numbers can make things difficult. Bookshop outside west door. You will search in vain for toilets.

Houses of Parliament
Open to visitors: 16:30 Mon–Thurs and 10:00 Fri. To attend Prime Minister's Question Time a special ticket is needed; tel 020 72194272.
Guards Museum
Open daily 10:00–16:00. *Entrance fee.*

LONDON: SOUTHWARK
Southward Cathedral
Open 09:00–18:00 throughout the year. For information, contact the Vergers Office, Southwark Cathedral, London Bridge, London SE1 9DA, tel 020 74072939. The Friends of Southwark Cathedral may be reached via the Secretary, tel 020 74073708. Wheelchair access throughout cathedral. Toilets in chapter house, which also houses a commercially run restaurant.

HMS *Belfast*
Open daily 10:00–18:00 summer, 10:00–17:00 winter. *Entrance fee.*
Tel 020 74076434. Disabled access difficult.

London Dungeon
Open daily 10:00–18:30. *Entrance fee.*
Old Operating Theatre Museum
Open daily (not Mon) 10:00–16:00; closed 15 Dec–5 Jan. *Entrance fee.*
Golden Hinde **Replica**
Open daily 10:00–17:00. *Tickets* can be bought at the office opposite the ship.
The `Clink Prison'
Open daily 10:00–18:00. *Entrance fee.*
New Globe Theatre
Open daily 10:00–17:00. *Entrance fee.*
Bankside Gallery
Open during exhibitions 10:00–17:00. *Entrance fee.* Bookshop.

CANTERBURY
Canterbury Cathedral
Open 08:45–19:00 Easter– Sep, 08:45–17:00 Oct–Easter. For information, contact The
Cathedral Office, The Precincts, Canterbury, Kent, tel 01227 762862. For information about
the Friends of Canterbury Cathedral, tel 01227 471000. No cathedral refectory. Pay toilets,
with facilities for disabled, on south side of precincts. Bookshop in southwest transept. Larger
gift shop close to Christ Church Gate. Permit needed for photography within cathedral.

Westgate
Open Mon–Sat 11:00–12:30 and 13:30–15:30. *Entrance fee.* No toilets or wheelchair access.
Eastbridge Hospital of St Thomas the Martyr
Open Mon–Sat 10:00–17:00. *Entrance fee.* No disabled access.
Royal Museum and Art Gallery
Open Mon–Sat 09:00–17:30. *No entrance fee.* Disabled access to ground floor only.
Canterbury Tales
Open: opening and closing times depend on day and time of year. High *entrance fee.* Shop
and restaurant. Tel 01227 454888.
St Mildred's Church
Open Apr–Oct. No entrance fee.
Roman Museum
Open Mon–Sat 10:00–17:00, Sun during Jun–Oct 13:30–17:00. Small *entrance charge.*
Disabled access. Tel 01227 785575.

ROCHESTER
Rochester Cathedral
Open daily 07:00–18:00. For information, contact the Cathedral Office, tel 01634 843366.
The Friends of Rochester Cathedral, tel 01634 832142. Cathedral refectory and toilets in
deanery. Wheelchair access to cathedral *via* north door.

Guildhall
Open daily 10:00–17:30. No entrance fee.
Draper's Museum of Bygones
Open daily 10:00–17:00. *Entrance fee.*
Rochester Castle
Open daily 10:00–18:00 Apr–Sep, 10:00–16:30 Oct–Mar. *Entrance fee* for the keep.
Eastgate House/Charles Dickens Centre
Open 10:00–17:30; last admission 1645. *Entrance fee.*

ST ALBANS
St Albans Cathedral
Open daily 08:00–17:45 winter, 08:00–18:45 summer. No entrance charge, but donation expected. For information, contact The Administrators Office, Cathedral and Abbey Church of St.Albans, Sumpter Yard, St Albans, Herts. AL1 1BY. The Friends of the Cathedral are located at the same address. Full facilities for the disabled, who should enter by east end door. Excellent refectory, open 10:30–16:30.

Hypocaust
Open Mon–Sat 10:00–17:30, Sun 14:00–17:00. No entrance fee.
Glebe House Nature Reserve
Open Mon–Fri 10:00–16:00 summer, Sun 12:00–16:30.
St Michael's Church
Open 14:00–17:00 Easter–Oct.
Roman Theatre
Open daily 10:00 to 17:00 (dusk in winter). *Entrance fee* (reduced for children).
Verulamium Museum
Open Mon–Sat 10:00–17:30, Sun 14:00–17:00. *Entrance fee* (reduced for students and OAPs).
Kingsbury Water Mill
Open Mon–Sat 11:00–18:00, Sun 11:00–17:00. *Entrance fee.*
Clock Tower
Open weekends Easter–Sep, also bank holidays, 10:30–17:30.

BURY ST EDMUNDS
Bury St Edmunds Cathedral
Open 09:00–17:00. For information, contact The Cathedral Office, Abbey House, Angel Hill, Bury St Edmunds, Suffolk, tel 01284 754933. The Friends of the Cathedral may be reached at the same address. Coffee shop in Cathedral Centre. Toilets near Abbey Gateway and in Cathedral Centre. Shop near entrance porch. Wheelchair access throughout cathedral.

St Mary's Church
Open: times posted on west door; at time of writing they are: Sun/Mon 14:00–16:00, Wed 09:00–14:00, Fri 10:00–12:00, Sat 11:00–14:00; closed Tue and Thu.
Manor House Museum
Open Mon–Sat 10:00–17:00, Sun 14:00–17:00. *Entrance fee.* Tearoom attached.
Abbey Visitor Centre
Open daily from 10:00; closing time depends on season. *Entrance fee.*
Moyse's Hall
Open Mon–Sat 10:00–17:00, Sun 14:00–17:00. No entrance fee.

ELY
Ely Cathedral
Open Mon–Sat 07:00–19:00 and Sun 07:30–17:00 summer, Mon–Sat 07:30–18:00 and Sun 07:30–17:00 winter. The Stained Glass Museum (located in the south triforium and approached via the west tower) is open daily 11:00–16:30. For information, contact The Chapter Office, Ely Cathedral, Ely, CB7 4DN, tel 01353 667735. The same telephone number will also reach The Friends of Ely Cathedral. Small refectory at west end of north nave aisle; cathedral also runs Almonry Restaurant in High Street. Limited toilet facilities in

refectory; main toilets on Palace Green and near sacrist's gate (facilities at latter for disabled). Ground floor of cathedral has ramps for wheelchairs. Shop next to refectory.

Oliver Cromwell's House
Open 10:00–18:00 summer, 10:00–1715 winter. *Entrance fee.* Oliver Cromwell Exhibition. Tel 01353 662062.

Ely Museum
Open Tue–Sun 10:30–13:00 and 14:15–17:00 summer, Tue–Sun 11:30–15:30 winter; also open Bank Holiday Mondays. *Entrance fee.* Unsuitable for the disabled (the museum is largely on the first floor and there is no lift).

PETERBOROUGH
Peterborough Cathedral
Open Mon–Fri 08:30–17:15, Sat 08:30–17:45 and Sun 12:00–17:45 May–Sep; Mon–Fri 08:30–17:15, Sat 08:30–17:15 and Sun 12:00–17:15 Oct–Apr. For information, contact The Chapter Office, Peterborough Cathedral, Laurel Court, The Minster Precincts, Peterborough, PE1 1XS. The Association of the Friends of Peterborough Cathedral may be contacted at the same address. Refectory and bookshop in Cathedral Close. Toilets at rear of refectory. Wheelchair ramps throughout cathedral.

Peterborough Museum and Art Gallery
Open Tue–Sat 10:00–17:00. *Entrance fee.*
Tourist Information Office
Open Mon–Fri 09:00–17:00, Sat and bank holidays 10:00–16:00.

NORWICH
Norwich Cathedral
Open daily 07:30–18:00 mid-Sep–mid-May, 07:30–19:00 mid-May–mid-Sep. For information, contact the Visitors Office, Norwich Cathedral, Norwich, NR1 4EH. The Friends of Norwich Cathedral may be reached at 12 The Close, Norwich, NR 1 4EH. Refectory up steps outside shop and over cloisters. Toilets under steps leading to refectory. Good wheelchair access to cathedral; use south transept door.

Cathedral Shop
Open Mon–Sat 09:15–17:00.
St Peter Hungate Museum
Open Mon–Sat 100:00–17:00. No entrance fee.
Bridewell Museum
Open Mon–Sat 10:00–17:00. *Entrance fee.* Ticket affords reduced charge for other museums.
The Mustard Shop
Open during shop hours. No entrance fee.
Church of St John Maddermarket
Open daily 10:00–16:00. No entrance fee.
Strangers' Hall
Open Mon–Sat 10:00–17:00. *Entrance fee.*
Guildhall
Open 09:30–18:00. No entrance fee.
Norwich Castle
Open Mon–Sat 10:00–17:00, Sun 14:00–17:00. *Entrance fee.* Tours of battlements and dungeons at weekends and bank holidays. Coffee bar and shop.

SOUTHWELL
Southwell Minster
Open daily 08:00–18:00. Information may be obtained from the Minster Office, Trebeck Hall, Bishops Drive, Southwell, Notts. NG 25 0JP, which will also supply details of The Friends of Southwell Cathedral, tel 01636 812649. Modern complex on southwest of cathedral houses spacious refectory, toilets and shop. Visitor Centre, with small audiovisual room, is next door in a former bank.

LINCOLN
Lincoln Cathedral
Open Mon–Sat 07:15–18:00 and Sun 07:15–17:00 winter, Mon–Sat 07:15–20:00 and Sun 07:15–18:00 summer. For information, contact the Communications Office, Lincoln Cathedral, Lincoln, LN 2 1PZ, tel 01522 544544. Details of the Association of Friends of Lincoln Cathedral may be obtained from 4 Priory Gate, Lincoln, LN2 1PZ. Coffee shop on northeast side of cloisters. Toilets on south side of cloisters. Shop in southwest corner of nave. Wheelchair access throughout cathedral.

Lawn Visitor Centre
Open 10:00–17:00 Easter–Sep, Oct–Easter 10:00–16:00. No entrance fee. Pub. Restaurant. Grounds ideal for picnics.
Lincoln Castle
Open Mon–Sat 09:30–17:30 and Sun 11:00–17:30 summer, Mon–Sat 09:30–16:00 and Sun 11:00–16:00 winter. *Entrance fee.*
Sightseeing Cruises from Wigford Way Bridge
Summer months only. Contact Cathedral City Cruises, tel 01522 546853.
Bishop's Old Palace
Open Thu–Mon 10:00–18:00 (summer only). *Entrance fee* with concessions. Tel 01522 527468.

YORK
York Minster
Open 07:00–20:30 summer, 07:00–17:00 winter. For information, contact the Visitors' Department, St. Williams College, 4–5 College Street, York, YO1 2JF, tel 01904 557216. Details of the Friends of York Minster can be obtained from the same address. No toilets or restaurant in cathedral itself, but plenty of facilities nearby. Ramps for wheelchair users in most parts of cathedral – enter through north door of west front. Shop next to south transept.

Merchant Adventurers' Hall
Open Mon–Sat 08:30–17:00 Mar–Nov, 08:30–15:30 Dec–Feb. *Entrance fee.*
Jorvik Viking Centre
Open 09:00–17:30 Apr–Oct, 09:00–15:30 Nov–Mar. *Entrance fee* with concessions.
York Story Heritage Centre
Open Mon–Sat 10:00–17:00, Sun 13:00–17:00. *Entrance fee.* A combined ticket may be obtained for this museum and the Castle Museum.
Fairfax House
Open Mon–Thu 11:00–17:00, Sat 11:00–17:00, Sun 13:30–17:00. *Entrance fee.*
Castle Museum
Open Mon–Sat 09:30–17:30, Sun 10:00–17:30 Apr–Oct, Mon–Sat 09:30–16:00, Sun 10:00–16:00 Nov–Mar. *Entrance fee.*

Guildhall
Open Mon–Fri 09:00–17:00. No entrance fee.
St Helen's Church
Open daily 10:00 to dusk. No entrance fee.

DURHAM
Durham Cathedral
Open daily 09:00–17:30. For information, contact The Chapter Office, The College, Durham, DH1 3EH, tel 0191 384 5266. For details of The Friends of Durham Cathedral, contact the Secretary at the same address. Restaurant in undercroft in southwest corner of cloisters. Toilets nearby, with facilities for disabled. Shop near restaurant.

Durham Castle
Open daily 10:00–12:30 and 14:00–16:00, 22 Mar–30 Sep. *Entrance fee.* Tel 0191–374 3800.
University Museum of Archaeology
Open daily 11:00–16:00; reduced hours at weekends and in winter. Small *entrance fee.*
Heritage Centre and Museum
Open Sat–Sun 14:00–16:30 Apr–May, daily 14:00–16:30 Jun and Sept, daily 11:00–16:30 Jul–Aug. Small *entrance fee.*

Bibliography

Most cathedrals have official guidebooks, usually approved by the dean and chapter, which can be obtained in cathedral shops.

Clifton-Taylor, Alec *The Cathedrals of England*, London, Thames & Hudson, 1967
The late Alec Clifton-Taylor's very personal account of the architecture of English cathedrals. A classic and very readable.

Ditchfield, R.H. *An Illustrated Guide to the Cathedrals of Great Britain*, London, J.M. Dent, 1902
There have been countless new editions and reprints. Now out of print, so scour the second-hand bookshops.

Howarth, Eva *Crash Course in Architecture*, Brockhampton Press, 1994

Morris, R. *Cathedrals and Abbeys of England and Wales*, J.M. Dent, 1979

Morris, Richard and Curbishley, Mike *Churches, Cathedrals and Chapels*, London, English Heritage, 1996
Designed for teachers, but equally useful for younger readers.

Pitkin Guide *Cathedral Architecture*, Pitkin, 1992
Brief pictorial account of the architecture of English cathedrals.

Pitkin Guide *Dissolution of the Monasteries*, Pitkin, 1995

Tatton-Brown, T. *Great Cathedrals of Britain*, BBC Books, 1989

Wilson, C. *The Gothic Cathedral*, Thames and Hudson, 1990

Index

Abbey Gate, Bury 84, 89
Abbey Gateway, St Albans 75, 78, 80
Abbey House, Durham 162
Abbey Mill Lane, St Albans 75, 80
Abbey Mills, St Albans 80
Abbeygate Hill, Bury 89
Abbeygate Street, Bury 90
Adam, Robert 162
Adam and Eve pub, Norwich 107, 109
Admiral Rodney pub, Southwell 132
Admiralty, London 37
Admiralty Arch, London 38
Alderman pub, Peterborough 121
All Saints Church, York 154
All Saints Court, Canterbury 62
All Saints Lane, Canterbury 62
Alleyn, Edward 49
Almoner's Yard, Canterbury 62
Amen Court, London 25
Anchor Brewery, Southwark 49
Anchor Inn, Southwark 45, 50
Angel Hill, Bury 84, 89, 90
Angel Lane, Bury 90
Angus, Mark 159
Anne, Queen 19
Apothecaries Hall, London 28
Applebye, Dorothy 44
Archbishop's Palace, Southwell 130
architectural styles 14–15
Arup, Ove 165
Aske, Robert 154
the Athenaeum, Bury 84, 89–90
Auden, W. H. 34
Augustine Steward's House, Norwich 113
Austin, Joyce 42

Babylon marina, Ely 101
Back of Inns lane, Norwich 113
Bacon, Sir Francis 80, 112
Bailgate, Lincoln 140
Baker's Walk, Rochester 72
Ball, Peter 127
Bank Plain, Norwich 113
Bankside, Southwark 45, 50
Bankside Gallery, Southwark 50
Bankside Power Station, Southwark 50
Barrow Boy and Banker pub, Southwark 48
Barry, Sir Charles 36
Bayeux Tapestry 29
Bean, Ellen 59
Becher's Walk, Southwell 132
à Becket, Thomas 25, 51, 52, 54, 55, 56, 60, 61
Venerable Bede 158
Bedford House, Ely 100
Bedford Street, Norwich 111
Beer Cart Lane, Canterbury 57
HMS *Belfast* 45
bell (Goldsmith's) tower, Ely 97
Big Ben, London 36, 37
Bird, Francis 19, 20
Birdcage Walk, London 39
Bishop's Bridge, Norwich 108
Bishop's Drive, Southwell 131
Bishop's Gateway, Peterborough 121
Bishop's Hospital, Durham 162
bishop's house, Ely 99
Bishop's Manor, Southwell 131
Bishop's Old Palace, Lincoln 143
Bishop's Palace, Ely 99

Bishop's Palace, Norwich 107
Bishop's Palace, Peterborough 121
Bishop's Palace Gate, Norwich 109
Black Bull pub, Southwell 132
Black Hostelry, Ely 98–9
Black Lion pub, St Albans 79, 82
Blackfriar pub, London 25, 28
Blackfriars, London 28
Blackfriars Bridge, London 28
Blackfriars Lane, London 28
Blackfriars Playhouse, London 28
Blake, William 24
Blisse, Richard 42
de Blois, Henry 40, 48
Blow, John 31
Blue Anchor pub, St Albans 79
Bluehouse Hill, St Albans 81
Bodley, G. F. 42, 115
Bootham Bar, York 151
The Borough, Canterbury 61
Borough High Street, Southwark 40, 45, 47, 48, 49
Bossanyi, Ervin 57
Boswell, James 27
Boudicca, Queen of the Iceni 81–2
Bow Lane, Durham 165
Bower, Stephen Dykes 22, 84–5, 86
Bowes, George 165
Boys, Sir John 61, 62
Sir John Boys's House, Canterbury 61
Bramley Apple pub, Southwell 132
Branch Road, St Albans 82
Brayford Pool, Lincoln 142–3
Breakspear, Nicholas (Pope Adrian IV) 77
Bride Lane, London 28
Bridewell Abbey, London 28
Bridewell Alley, Norwich 111
Bridewell museum, Norwich 111
Bridge Street, Peterborough 125
Britten, Benjamin 31
Broad Street, Ely 101
Broadgate, Lincoln 143
The Broadwalk, Southwell 126–7
Broadway, Peterborough 124
Browning, Robert 34
Buck, Sir Peter 73
Duke of Buckingham, 39
Buckingham Palace, London 38, 39
Bull Hotel, Peterborough 121, 124
Bunch of Grapes pub, Southwark 47
Burgage Court, Southwell 132
Burgage Manor House, Southwell 132
Burgate, Canterbury 64
Bury St Edmunds Cathedral 83–7
Cathedral Centre 87
choir 86
cloisters 85, 87
crossing 86
font 85–7
gates 86
high altar 86
kneelers 86
Lady Chapel 86
nave 86
northwest porch 85
organ 86
plan 85
Reynolds memorials 86

St Edmund's Chapel 86–7
sedilia 86
tower 84–5
treasury 87
war memorial 85
west end 85, 86
windows 86
Bury St Edmunds Cathedral walk 87–90
Butchery Lane, Canterbury 57, 64
Butter Cross, Peterborough 125
Buttermarket, Canterbury 60, 64
Byron, Lord 34, 132

Cakehouse Restaurant, London 35, 38
Cannon Street, London 25
the canonry, Ely 98
Canterbury Castle 64
Canterbury Cathedral 51–7
archbishop's palace 60
Bell Harry Tower 55, 58
Bible Windows 56
Black Prince's Chantry 55
Black Prince's tomb 57
bosses 52, 60
cemetery gate 58
chapter house 60
Chichele tomb 56
Christ Church Gateway 53, 60
choir 56
choir screen 56
Corona 57
crypt 54–5
Dark Entry 59
deanery 60
font 54
Great Cloister 60
Green Court 59, 60
Hales Family Monument 54
Henry IV and Joan of Navarre tomb 56
Infirmary Chapel 59
Jesus Chapel 55
Lady Chapel 54
Martyrdom Chapel 54
miracle windows 57
John Morton's tomb 55
nave 53
necessarium 60
Opus Alexandrinum 56
Our Lady of the Undercroft Chapel 54
plans 53, 55
precincts 58
pulpit 54
Queningate 59
Rose Window 56
Royal East Kent Regiment memorials 55
Royal Window 54
St Andrew's Chapel 56
St Anselm Tower 58
St Augustine's Chair 56
St Gabriel's Chapel 55
St Michael's Chapel 55
treasury 59
Trinity Chapel 56
war memorial 59
water tower 59
west end 53, 54
windows 54, 56, 57
Canterbury Cathedral walk 57–64
Canterbury city walls 64
Cardinal's Cap Alley, Southwark 50
Cardinal's Cap Inn, Southwark 50
Cardinal's Wharf, Southwark 50

Carnary Chapel, Norwich 107
Carter Lane, London 28
Castle Arcade, Norwich 113
Castle Gardens, Canterbury 64
Castle Green, York 154, 155
Castle Mall, Norwich 113
Castle Meadow, Norwich 113
Castle Museum, York 154
Castle Street, Canterbury 64
Castlegate, York 154
cathedra 8
Cathedral Close, Norwich 107, 108
Cathedral Gate, Peterborough 121–2, 124
Cathedral Gate Hotel, Canterbury 57
Cathedral Green, Peterborough 116
Cathedral Square, Peterborough 124–5
Catherine of Aragon 115, 117, 119, 120
Cavell, Edith 103, 107, 120
Caxton, William 28, 35
Cenotaph, London 37
Central Criminal Court, London 26
Central Market, Lincoln 143
Chambers, John 115
Chapel Lane, Lincoln 140
Charing Cross, Norwich 112
charnel house, Bury 89
Chaucer, Geoffrey 34, 41, 42, 63
Cherry Hill, Ely 99
Chertsey's Gate, Rochester 69–70
Chichele, Henry 56
Christ Church Gateway, Canterbury 53
Christ Church Priory, Canterbury 51, 52, 57
church services 11–12
Church Street, Southwell 132
Churchgate Street, Bury 90
Churchill, Sir Winston 31, 37
City Arms pub, Canterbury 57
City Hall, Norwich 112
Clarence House, London 38
Clarke, Sir Francis 73
Classical style 11, 18, 96
Claughton, Thomas Legh 78
Clifford's Tower, York 154, 155
'Clink Prison' Southwark 49, 50
Clink Street, Southwark 48
Clock Tower, Canterbury 64
Clock Tower, St Albans 82
Cobb Hill, Lincoln Castle 140
Cockpit Steps, London 39
Coleman, Alan 127
College Gateway, Durham 164
College Green, Durham 164
College Green, London 37
College Green, Rochester 73
College Street, York 152
Collingwood, Lord 23
Collins, Alan 48
Collins, Wilkie 74
Comper, Sir Ninian 44, 149
Coney Street, York 155
Conquest House, Canterbury 61
Cook, Nell 59
Cooke, Thomas 'Squire' 125
Cooper, Sidney 63
Cooper's Arms pub, Rochester 73
Coppergate, York 154
Corn Exchange, Bury 90
Bishop Cosin's Hall, Durham 162
Bishop Cosin's Library 162

Cosmati family 31, 32
Cotman, John Sell 109, 113
Cotman House, Norwich 109
Cottingham, L. N. 69
County Hotel, Durham 161
Cow Tower, Norwich 108-9
Cowgate, Peterborough 125
Prior Crauden's Chapel, Ely 99
Cromwell, Oliver 38, 52, 54, 80, 92, 100, 115
Oliver Cromwell's House, Ely 92, 100
Crome, John 113
Cross Green, Ely 97
Cross Street, Peterborough 125
Crow Lane, Rochester 73
Cubitt, Sir William 46
Cumbergate, Peterborough 124
Cupola House, Bury 90
Cutter Inn, Ely 99, 101

Daily Express building, London 26
Daily Telegraph building, London 26
Damini, Vincenzo 139
Dane John Gardens, Canterbury 64
Dane John Mound, Canterbury 64
Dartmouth Street, London 35, 39
Davis, Roger 56
de la Mare, Thomas 75, 78, 80
Deanery Gate, Rochester 74
Deangate, York 152
Dean's Park, York 151
Decorated style 10, 65, 68, 69, 77, 87, 94, 99, 100, 111, 112, 118, 119, 129, 138
Defence Ministry, London 37
Dickens, Charles 34, 41, 60, 68, 73-4, 124
Charles Dickens Centre, Rochester 73-4
Disraeli, Benjamin 37
Docklands, London 26
Dominican Monastery, Canterbury 62
Donne, John 18, 22, 26
Doubleday, John 58
Downing, George 38
Downing Street, London 38
Drake, Sir Francis 48
Draper's Museum of Bygones, Rochester 70-71
Drury Lane, Lincoln 142
Duke Street Hill, Southwark 47
Dun Cow Lane, Durham 162
Durham Castle 156, 157, 162
Durham Cathedral 156-61
    Anglo-Saxon stones 161
    Angus window 159
    aumbry 159
    Shute Barrington statue 160
    Venerable Bede tomb 158
    bishop's throne 159
    bosses 161
    Prior Castell's clock 160
    chapter house 156
    choir 159
    choir screen 157, 159
    cloisters 161
    crossing 159
    Durham Light Infantry Chapel 160
    east end 157
    floor 159
    font 158
    Galilee Chapel 157, 158
    Gregory Chapel 159
    Thomas Hatfield tomb 159
    high altar 156, 157
    Lady Chapel 156-7

lectern 159
library 161
Millennium Window 160
Miner's Memorial 160-61
monk's dormitory 161
nave 158-9
Neville Screen 159
Nine Altars Chapel 157, 160
north door 157
north nave aisle 158
north transept 159
pillars 157, 158, 159
plan 158
pulpit 157, 159
restaurant 161
roof 156, 161
Rose Window 160
St Cuthbert shrine 157, 160
St Cuthbert tomb 160
Sanctuary Knocker 157
south choir aisle 160
south transept 160
stone vaulting 156, 158-9
tower 157
treasury 161
wall paintings 157
west end 157
windows 159, 160
Durham Cathedral walk 161-5
Durham University 161-2
Durham University Museum of Archaeology 162
Durst, Alan 115, 116

Eagle Tavern, Rochester 69
Early English style 10, 31, 40, 43, 44, 52, 56, 65, 67, 68, 77, 95, 100, 114, 116, 123, 126, 127-8, 133, 135, 137, 144
Earp, Thomas 69
Eastbridge Hospital of St Thomas the Martyr, Canterbury 63
Eastgate House, Rochester 73
Easton, Hugh 32
Elgar, Sir Edward 31
Elizabeth I, Queen 18
Elm Hill, Norwich 110
Elvet Bridge, Durham 165
Ely Cathedral 91-7
    Bishop Allcocks Chantry 92, 95-6
    Almonry 97
    bells 97
    chapter house 99
    choir 94
    east end 91, 92, 95
    Galilee Porch 91-2, 93
    Lady Chapel 92, 96-7, 98
    nave 91, 93
    north aisle 91
    north choir aisle 96
    north transept 91
    northwest transept 91
    Octagon and Lantern Tower 92, 94
    organ 96
    Ovin's Stone 94
    plan 96
    presbytery 94-5
    prior's door 94
    refectory 97
    St Catherine's Chapel 93
    St Dunstan and St Ethelwold Chapel 94
    St Edmund Chapel 96
    St Ethelreda Chapel 95
    St George Chapel 96
    south aisle 93
    south choir aisle 95
    south transept 91, 94
    southwest transept 91, 93
    Stained Glass Museum 93, 97
    towers 91, 93

war memorials 96
west end 93
Bishop West's Chantry 92, 95
windows 94, 96
Ely Cathedral walks 97-101
Ely Museum 100
Erpingham, Sir Thomas 107, 111
Erpingham Gate, Norwich 107, 109, 113
Esplanade, Rochester 72
Essex, James 92., 94
Exchange Street, Norwich 111
Exchequer Gate, Lincoln 140
Eversden, Hugh 78
Express Dairy, St Albans 82

Fairfax House 154
Fawkes, Guy 18, 152
Fearon Walk, Durham 165
Feibusch, Hans 94
Fielding, Theodore Nathan 125
Fighting Cocks Inn, St Albans 79, 80
Firmary Lane, Ely 98
Fisher, John 67, 73
Fishpool Street, St Albans 82
Flaxman, John 20
Fleet Prison, London 26
Fleet stream 26
Fleet Street, London 25, 26, 27, 28
Fleur-de-Lys Inn, St Albans 82
Foreign Office, London 37
Fossdyke canal 142
Founders Arms, Southwark 45
Fox (Foxe), Richard 41, 42, 44
Framwellgate Bridge, Durham 163
French Row, St Albans 82
The Friars, Canterbury 62
Frink, Elizabeth 89

Gadshill, Rochester 74
The Gallery, Ely 99, 101
Gardiner, Stephen 41, 44
Gentleman's Walk, Norwich 113
The George pub, Southwark 45, 48
George Street, St Albans 82
Gibbons, Grinling 19, 21, 23, 26
Gibbons, Orlando 31
Giffard, William 40
Gilbert, Sir Alfred 77
Gilbert, Sir Giles 50
Gladstone, William 31
Glaziers' Hall, Southwark 48
Glebe House, St Albans 80
Globe Theatre, Southwark 28, 41, 44, 49, 50
Golden Fleece pub, York 150
Golden Hinde 48
Goodramgate, York 152
Gothic style 9, 10-11, 18, 29, 34, 52, 56, 65, 76, 105, 116, 137, 138, 144, 145, 146, 149
Gough Square, London 27
Gower, John 42
Great Churchyard, Bury 88-9
Great Fire of London 11, 18, 22, 26, 28
green man 129
Greenstone Stairs, Lincoln 143
Grimthorpe, Edmund Beckett 75, 76, 78
Guards Chapel, London 39
Guards Museum, London 39
Guildhall, Bury 84, 90
Guildhall, Lincoln 142
Guildhall, Norwich 112
Guildhall, Rochester 70
Guildhall, York 155
Guildhall Street, Bury 90
Gundulf's Tower, Rochester 74

Guy, Thomas 47
Guy's Hospital, Southwark 47

Haig, Earl 37
Haldane, Lord 39
Hales, Sir James 54
Hampstead Heath, London 26
Handel, George Friedrich 34
Messiah 34
Harvard, John 42
Hawksmoor, Nicholas 30
Hay's Dock, Southwark 46
Hay's Galleria, Southwark 46
Hay's Wharf, Southwark 45
Henslowe, Philip 49, 50
Hervey, Elizabeth 88
High Bridge, Lincoln 143
High Petergate, York 150-51, 155
High Street, Canterbury 62, 63
High Street, Ely 100
High Street, Lincoln 142
High Street, Rochester 69, 70, 73
Hog pub, Norwich 112
Hogarth, Catherine 74
Hogarth, George 74
Hole in the Wall pub, York 150
Holland, Lady Margaret 55
Holliday, Henry 42
Holy Trinity Church, York 152
Honey Hill, Bury 84, 88
Hop and Malt Exchange, Southwark 49
Hope Theatre, Southwark 50
Hopton Street, Southwark 50
Horniman, Thomas 46
Horniman pub, Southwark 45, 46
Horse Guards building, London 38
Horse Guards Parade, London 38
Horse Guards Road, London 38
House of Correction, Southwell 132
Howard, F. E. 85
Howard, John 23
Howe, Earl 23
Hunt, Holman 23
Hurley, William 94

Ireland, William 28
Ireland Yard, London 28

Jew's Court, Lincoln 142
Jew's House, Lincoln 142
John XXIII, Pope 52
Johnson, Samuel 26, 27, 34, 50
Dr Johnson's House, London 27
Johnson's Square, London 27
Jonson, Ben 34
Jorvik Viking Centre, York 154

Kemp, David 46
Kempster, William 23
Kent, William 38
Ketelbarn, Robert 145
Kett, Robert 108, 109, 113
Kett's Heights, Norwich 108
King Street, Canterbury 61, 62
King Street, Southwell 132
King's Bench prison, Southwark 49
Kings Head Hotel, Rochester 69
Kings Manor, York 151
Kings School, Canterbury 59, 60, 62
King's School, York 99
King's School, Rochester 73
King's Square, York 152
King's Staith, York 155
Kingsbury Water Mill, St Albans 82
Kingsgate Bridge, Durham 165
Kirkton, Robert 115, 119, 122
Kitchener, Lord 19

La Providence, Rochester 74
Lamb Hotel, Ely 99, 100
Lambeth Palace, London 51
de Langham, Simon 30
Latham, Simon 119-20
Lawn Visitor Centre, Lincoln 140-41
Layfolks' Cemetery, Peterborough 122
Leaning House, Canterbury 61
Lincoln, Abraham 37
Lincoln Castle 142
Lincoln Cathedral 133-40
  Angel Choir 137, 138
  arcades 134
  bells 135
  Bishop's Eye Window 135
  Chantry of Katherine Swyford 138
  chapter house 134, 139, 143
  cloisters 139
  crossing 135
  John Dalderby shrine 136
  Damini Wall Paintings 139
  Dean's Eye Window 135
  east end 133, 134, 143
  east window 138
  Easter sepulchre 138
  eastern transepts 133
  Eleanor of Castile's Visceral tomb 138
  font 135
  Great Tom (bell) 135
  great transept 135-6, 139
  Bishop Grosseteste's tomb 137
  high altar 137-8
  St Hugh Head shrine 138
  Judgement Porch 143
  Bishop Kaye memorial 140
  Bishop Edward King statue 136
  lantern 135
  lectern 137
  Lincoln Imp 138
  Little Hugh shrine 136-7
  Magna Carta 134
  Medicine Chapel 139
  Medieval Library 134, 139
  Morning Chapel 140
  nave 135, 139
  north aisle 137, 139
  north choir aisle 139
  northeast transept 139
  pillars 135, 137, 139
  plan 136
  pulpit 137
  pulpitum 135
  refectory 140
  Remigius tomb 138
  roof 133
  St Hugh's Choir 137
  St Hugh's tomb 134
  St Peter and St Paul Chapel 137
  sanctuary 137
  Services' Chapels 139
  The Slype 139
  south aisle 134
  south choir aisle 136-7
  southeast transept 137
  spires 134
  Touch Exhibition 139
  Tournai marble tomb slab 139-40
  towers 133, 134, 135
  treasury 139
  Trondheim Piers 137, 139
  west front 133
  windows 133, 134, 135, 138, 139, 143
  Wren Library 139
Lincoln Cathedral walk 140-45
Lindum Road, Lincoln 143

Lion and Snake pub, Lincoln 140
the Little Admiral, York 155
Lobster Lane, Norwich 111
Lockyer, Lionel 42
London Bridge 40, 45, 46, 48
London Dungeon, Southwark 46
London Street, Norwich 113
Londonderry, Marquess of 165
Louis Marchesi pub, Norwich 107
Low Petergate, York 152
Lower Goat Lane, Norwich 112
Lower Red Lion pub, St Albans 82
Ludgate Circus, London 26
Ludgate Hill, London 25
Lutyens, Sir Edwin 26, 37

Macaulay, Lord 27
McFaul, David 58
Macro, Thomas 90
Maddermarket Theatre, Norwich 112
Magdalen Street, Norwich 102
Magna Carta 78, 84, 86, 134
Magna Carta pub, Lincoln 140
Maid's Head Hotel, Norwich 107, 109
Maine, Jonathan 19
The Mall, London 38
Maltings, Ely 101
Manor House Museum, Bury 84, 88
Mansion House, York 155
Market Cross, Bury 90
Market Place, Durham 165
Market Square, Bury 84, 90
Market Square, Ely 100
Market Square, Norwich 112, 113
Market Taverne, Durham 161
Marlowe, Christopher 62, 49
Marlowe Theatre, Canterbury 57, 62
Marshalsea Prison, London 49, 74
Mary, Queen of Scots 115, 117, 120
Mary Tudor 32, 44, 84, 88
Mathew, Hugh 85
Mercery Lane, Canterbury 60
Merchant Adventurers' Hall, York 154
de Merton, Walter 67
Methodist Central Hall, London 39
Midgate, Peterborough 123-4
Millais, Sir John 24
Milton, John 35
Minerva House, Southwark 48
Minor Canon Row, Rochester 73
Minster Yard, Lincoln 143
Minster Yard, Peterborough 121, 124, 125
Minster Yard, York 52
Mint Yard Gate, Canterbury 60, 61
Monastic Barn, Ely 99
Monk Bar, York 151
Monk's Walk, Peterborough 123
Montagu, Edward Wortley 124
Montague Close, Southwark 48
Montgomery, Field Marshal Bernard 24, 27
Moore, Henry 22
Morton, John 55
Moyse's Hall, Bury 90
Mudlark pub, Southwark 48
Munnings, Sir Alfred 113
Museum Gardens, York 151
The Mustard Shop, Norwich 111

Nash, John 38, 39
Nelson, Lord 23, 24, 35, 107

Neptune statue, Durham 165
New Bridge Street, London 28
New Dover Road, Canterbury 64
New Foundation 8
New Globe Theatre, Southwark 50
New Globe Walk, Southwark 50
Newgate Prison, London 26
Newport Arch, Lincoln 140
Norman Conquest pub, Rochester 69
Norman style 9-10, 72, 76, 78, 91, 93, 96, 100, 104-5, 121, 122, 123, 126, 127, 130, 134, 144, 162, 164; *see also* Romanesque style
North Bailey, Durham 164-5
Norwich Castle 102, 113
Norwich Cathedral 102-7
  ambulatory 106
  bosses 105, 106, 107
  Cauchon Chapel 106
  cathedra 105
  Edith Cavell's grave 107
  choir 105
  cloisters 107
  crossing 105
  Despenser Reredos 106
  Erpingham Window 106
  font 106
  Jesus Chapel 106
  Lady Chapel 103, 106
  lectern 105
  nave 104-5
  north transept 105
  pillars 104-5
  plan 104
  presbytery 103, 105
  priors door 107
  pulpitum 105
  refectory 107
  reliquary arch and treasury 106
  Royal Norfolk Regiment Chapel 106
  roof 102-3, 105
  St Andrew's Chapel 105
  St Luke's Chapel 106, 107
  St Saviour's Chapel 106, 107
  south transept 106
  spire 109
  Taylor Ramsden Window 106
  tower 102-3, 104, 109
  vaulting 105, 107
  wall paintings 106
  west end 104
  windows 104, 105, 106
Norwich Cathedral walk 107-13
Nutshell pub, Bury 90
Nuttgens, Joseph 160

Observatory Tower, Lincoln Castle 141
Old Bailey, London 26
Old Bishop's Palace, Rochester 73
Old Corn Exchange, Rochester 70
Old Fire Engine House restaurant, Ely 100
Old Foundation 8
Old Operating Theatre Museum, Southwark 47
Old Queen Street, London 39
Old Synagogue, Bury 90
Old Thameside Inn, Southwark 48
Oriel House, Rochester 73
Ouse Bridge, York 155
Ousegate, York 155

Painted Chamber, Ely 98
Palace Green, Durham 161-2
Palace Green, Ely 93, 99
Palace Street, Canterbury 61

Palace Street, Norwich 109
Palace of Westminster, London 36
Palmerston, Lord 39
the Park, Ely 101
Park Street, Southwark 49
Parliament Square, London 37
Parliament Street, London 36
Parry, Thomas Gambier 93
Paternoster Square, London 25
Pavement, York 152, 154
Pearce, David 76
Pearson, J. L. 115, 118, 119
Peel, Sir Robert 31
the Peninsula, Durham 156
Perpendicular style 11, 30, 32, 35, 52, 53, 58, 60, 65, 66, 69, 76, 96, 105, 110, 111, 112, 114, 116, 121-2, 123, 125, 127, 147
Peterborough Abbey 114, 122-3
Peterborough Cathedral 114-20
  apse 115, 119
  Benedictine tombs 120
  bosses 119
  cathedra 115, 119
  Catherine of Aragon tomb 119, 120
  Edith Cavell plaque 120
  choir 115, 118
  cloisters 115
  clocks 118
  Cosmati floor 115, 119
  crossing 114, 115, 118
  Durst figures 115, 116
  effigies 119
  font 118
  Hedda stone 120
  high altar 115, 119
  Lady Chapel 115, 122
  lectern 118
  Mary, Queen of Scots tomb 120
  medieval painting 120
  nave 114, 115, 116, 117-18
  nave rood 115, 118
  New Building 115, 119-20
  north aisle 118
  north transept 118
  plan 117
  porch 114, 116, 117
  presbytery 114, 123
  roof 114, 118, 119
  St Benedict's Chapel 120
  St Kyneburga, St Kyneswith and St Tibba Chapel 120
  St Sprite's Chapel 120
  sanctuary 118-19
  Scarlett portraits 117
  south nave aisle 120
  south presbytery aisle 119, 120
  south transept 120
  spires 114
  tapestries 119
  towers and lanterns 114, 115, 116, 117, 118
  treasury 118
  vaulting 114, 115
  west front 114, 115, 116
  windows 115, 118
Peterborough Cathedral walk 120-25
Peterborough market 124
Peterborough Museum and Art Gallery 125
Peterborough Town Hall 125
Peterscourt, Peterborough 123-4
Pettus House, Norwich 110
Piccadilly, York 152, 154
Pickford's Wharf, Southwark 48
Pilgrims' Hotel, Canterbury 57
Piper, John 35, 128
Pitt, William (the Elder) 31